THE ART & HISTORY OF BOOKS

THE ART & HISTORY OF BOOKS

by Norma Levarie

WITH A FOREWORD
BY NICOLAS BARKER

OAK KNOLL PRESS &
THE BRITISH LIBRARY

Published in 1995 by
OAK KNOLL PRESS
414 Delaware Street, New Castle, DE 19720, USA

Published in the UK by
THE BRITISH LIBRARY
Great Russell Street, London WC1B 3DG, UK

First published by James H. Heineman, Inc. 1968
Reissued by Da Capo Press 1982

This edition has been published by arrangement with James H. Heineman, Inc.

ISBN 1-884718-02-7 (Oak Knoll Press Hardback)
ISBN 1-884718-03-5 (Oak Knoll Press Paperback)
ISBN 0-7123-0394-4 (The British Library Paperback)

Distributed in the USA by Lyons & Burford, Publishers
31 West 21 Street, New York, NY 10010

Library of Congress Cataloging-in-Publication Data
Levarie, Norma.
    The art & history of books / Norma Levarie.
        p.   cm.
    Previously published: New York : Da Capo Press, 1982.
    Includes bibliographical references and index.
    ISBN 1-884718-02-7 — ISBN 1-884718-03-5 (pbk.)
    1. Books—History.   2. Printing—History.   3. Illustration of
books—History.   I. Title.   II. Title: Art and history of books.
    Z4.L58   1994
    002'.09—dc20   94-14734
                                                CIP

Printed in the United States of America

Reprinted 1995

CONTENTS

Acknowledgements

At the completion of a book one's mind turns gratefully to the institutions and persons who contributed to one's work and to one's pleasure in it.

The Pierpont Morgan Library, of New York, figured largely in all stages of this book; much of my research was done among its splendid collection. Many libraries graciously photographed manuscripts and books according to my specifications. The Yale Beinecke Rare Book Library and the Harvard Houghton Library were especially generous in permitting our printers to make plates directly from their books. Our printers, the Meriden Gravure Company, have in this and in other respects shown a skill and concern more typical of an earlier than of our age of printing.

Arabel Porter, a dear friend now editor at Houghton Mifflin, read the manuscript of this book and made detailed suggestions at a moment when the lonely burden of writing made them particularly welcome. Janet Levarie companionably weighed matters of grammar and syntax, to which she is far closer than I. Siegmund Levarie, my husband, provided the special service of being on hand at odd hours to answer scholarly questions. Edward Hamilton kindly held luncheon conversations with me on the subject of this book at an early stage; and Gabriel Austin, Librarian of the Grolier Club, read the first draft with an austere eye. To all of these I am grateful.

My publisher, James H. Heineman, deserves and is offered my heartfelt thanks for his vision, confidence, and sangfroid which—first and last—made this book possible.

New York, 1968

FOREWORD TO 1995 EDITION

by Nicolas Barker

The Art & History of Books is a unique book. It is not a history of book-production, nor of book-illustration, but of a subject more elusive but no less vital – the book as a work of art. It is, in the best sense of the word, an amateur book; there can be no professionalism that could cover so many specialist fields, in time or subject-matter. Only a fresh eye, unbiased by individual interest, can give it the unity to be found here.

It is interesting, in this respect, to compare it with another great American work of historic synthesis, Daniel Berkeley Updike's *Printing Types. Their history, forms and use*, originally published in 1922. Updike knew printing type, both historically and as a practical printer, as few others have ever known and understood it. He had collected and studied examples of its use, and viewed them externally but with the insight that came from handling type and planning its composition himself. He reviewed the work of his predecessors, letter-designers, the engravers of punches for type, compositors and printers, with an inward understanding, but also critically, measuring it against what he would have preferred or done himself, had he undertaken the same task. The result is inevitably biased, notably in his treatment of the nineteenth century, finding little good between Bodoni and William Morris, apart from the revival of old style types by William Pickering.

Norma Levarie has no such bias. Her vision of what makes a book a work of art is innocent, sometimes naive, but always refreshingly free of any preconceived notion of what things *ought* to look like. She reflects, in her text and illustrations, what they are. Inevitably, the passage of time, the accessibility then of the material from which her choice of examples was made, give her view a slightly different angle from what we might expect today, but, for a book now almost thirty years old, it has worn wonderfully well. The freshness of vision is undiminished, as valid a picture of the subject now as it was in 1968.

What changes might we expect to see in a survey of this sort today? Levarie's view is, predictably, "Eurocentric", or rather based on the system of recording verbally and visually a message which we trace back beyond the familiar book or codex in a continuous sequence to Nilotic inscriptions and papyri and Mesopotamian cuneiform. Now similar recording systems from all over the world, in particular Asia, are more familiar. Although there may

vii

not be much point in comparing unconnected systems of script or traditions of book-manufacture, the problem of marrying words and pictures, the *mise-en-page*, is common to all cultures, and it would be instructive to compare the morphology of the different solutions that have been applied over time in different parts of the world.

A book is a complex construct, appealing as it does to several senses, of which the visual and tactile are only the most important. It exists in three dimensions, not merely the two presented by each page or opening that the eye takes in at one time, which are hard to convey in reproduction. It also exists in a still more elusive fourth dimension, mirrored both visually and intellectually as a message in the mind. Somewhere in this complexity we recognize that part of it which is a work of art, or at least capable of aesthetic appreciation. Within historic and geographic limits that certainly seemed logical at the time, Levarie's account evinces a perceptive feeling for this, balancing it against a larger background of cultural history, simply and without affectation, but rarely falling into the easy trap of over-simplification.

Once on the high road of the transition of Graeco-Roman conventions for the mixture of text and illustration into the needs of the Christian religion, the progress depicted here seems straightforward; the divergence from, and recovery of, common sources remain common features of late antiquity and early medieval books both in the West and the Byzantine East. The fantastic flowering of decorated books in the British Isles from the sixth to the ninth century we would now see as less isolated from the mainstream of European art; in the last generation, the fusion of parts drawn from the decorative arts as a whole, from sources diversely Levantine, Graeco-Roman and Norse, has become a little clearer. Similarly, the sources of the distinctive Carolingian style, in terms of script and decoration, and the imposition of conventions in the form of books which have in some cases lasted to the present day, can be seen more clearly, although their originality and dominance is in no way diminished because we know whence they came. In particular, the Byzantine elements of Ottonian book-design can be directly connected with the entourage of the Empress Theophano, rather than a more remote "inspiration". Equally, the concept of a simple society, "when all intellectual life was in the hands of the monasteries", changing rapidly about the year 1000, needs some revision. Romanesque books seem to evolve more closely from Carolingian and into Gothic.

It would be hard to find a better summary of the diverse trends in late medieval book art, and the links that join them to architecture and panel painting than the chapter on Gothic manuscripts. At the same time, certain limitations in the field of study begin to appear. One is the simple limitation of available resources. In 1968, there were far fewer reproductions of medieval manuscripts than there are now. In one sense this hardly mattered, since there, available in New York, was one of the world's great treasure houses of books, the Pierpont

Morgan Library. The author pays an apt acknowledgement: "much of my research," she writes, "was done among its splendid collection." But even the Pierpont Morgan Library had its limitations: it was a reflection of the collecting taste of its time, that is, from the turn of the present century; and it was, self-consciously and proudly, aristocratic and elitist. Since 1968, its scope has notably broadened. So, too, has our concept of books as works of art, admitting a wider range of material, including popular books as well as those made for potentates, functional books like atlases, natural history, scientific and technical books, children's books, as well as those designed as works of art.

So much is tacitly admitted in the contrast between the chapter on Renaissance manuscripts (where the neglect, or rather ignorance, of examples produced in places other than Florence, Ferrara and Milan strikes us today as astonishing) and that on block books which follows it. Paper, first manufactured in Christian Europe at Fabriano in Italy in 1282, now enters the story. It was the essential raw material of the separate pictorial prints, perhaps originally designed as wall decorations (though many of them owe their existence to being pasted in books), made from wood blocks. They were the earliest examples of graphic art in multiple copies in Europe, dating from the first quarter of the fifteenth century, long after the technique had been in use in the East. The extension of these to provide a continuous text, in which words and pictures were closely interwoven, used to be taken to prefigure the invention of printing from movable type. Thanks to the researches of the late Allan Stevenson, that lonely but titanic figure in the history of bibliographical scholarship of the last generation, we now know that they did not. The paper on which they were printed reveals that the earliest are only just contemporary with the first books printed from type, and that most of them are substantially later. Nor were they "Poor Man's Bibles"; reading and interpreting the complex message, interwoven between text and image, required a sophisti-cated and experienced intelligence. Blockbooks are much more plausibly seen as a derivation of the book printed from type, not its antecedent; they were an attempt to transfer an emblematic devotional device from the wall to the portable, intimate and more elaborate form of the book.

No one will dispute the primacy of Gutenberg, rightly here associated with the beginning of printing. The first datable example of the new art remains, as recorded here, the copy of the 42-line Bible, in which its rubricator, Heinrich Cremer, recorded the completion of his work on 24 August 1456. We are now rather less certain of the order in which the less sophisticated (and fragmentary) works associated with Gutenberg, like the Donatuses, appeared. There is no certainty that any of them preceded the Bible, probably printed some years before 1456; on the other hand, no one now doubts Allan Stevenson's demonstration that the Constance Missal is a late and degraded use of the first large gothic type, not its early imperfect state.

Unexpectedly, the 1457 Psalter, printed in three colours at a single impression, represents a summit of technological perfection, achieved regardless of cost, from which progress could only be downward.

Competition, in terms of volume and price, was now a real, if novel, factor. Both economy and a novelty that would appeal to the market were the motives that inaugurated the tradition of combining type with woodcut. Apart from the exceptional Albrecht Pfister at Bamberg, this can be attributed to Zainer at Augsburg. To do so he had to come to terms with the guild of "wood-engravers and illuminators", a conjunction that predated the press and lasted until the eighteenth century. The transition from one art to the other can be seen in the earliest German illustrated books, but the advantages of woodcut decoration were quickly realized and spread almost as rapidly as the press itself. Here another difficulty emerges, the problem of classifying the work of wandering craftsmen within linguistic and national boundaries that are themselves derived from the political geography of Europe in the nineteenth century. The career of Johann Neumeister typifies the danger of this anachronistic view. He learned the new trade in Germany, went to Foligno in Italy where he printed the first edition of the *Divina Commedia* in 1472, moving back to Mainz, where he printed an edition of the *Meditationes* of Cardinal Turrecremata, illustrated with metal-cuts (a medium that gives it a special integrity); he then went to Lyon, where his typographic style became French, with fine and clearly local woodcut decorations; he ended his career in Albi.

But if it is wrong to imagine cross-fertilization inhibited by modern frontiers, Levarie is quite right to devote a long chapter to the distinctive Italian style of line-engraving, a style which owed little to illumination, and only remotely derived from the work of the great panel painters. The French style, by contrast, was much closer to illumination, and it can be no coincidence that Antoine Vérard, in the special copies he had printed on vellum for Charles VIII of France and Henry VII of England, had the printed decoration painted over by illuminators. Levarie evidently found Caxton's early illustrated books, printed from blocks that came from the Low Countries, unappealing, and likewise illustrated books printed in Flanders and Holland. This, and the short but more sympathetic account of Spanish books, is probably due to the rarity of the books that might otherwise have figured in her account.

Carving up the post-incunabular output of illustrated books by century as well as by country tends further to obscure the extent to which the illustration of books was an international business. Styles and individual pictures or illustration sequences were copied over increasing distances more and more rapidly. The blocks themselves could travel, and multi-lingual editions, especially in Lyon and Antwerp, great entrepôts, were not uncommon. Besides the consciously "artistic" books produced in the sixteenth century, the technical works – Vitruvius and his modern architectural imitators, anatomical works like Vesalius, the many works on natural history that succeeded Fuchs's pioneering herbal, Braun and Hogenberg's city views and, above all, the great atlases of Mercator and Ortelius – not only set the artists of the book their highest challenges but reached a truly international market. This was especially true of the engravers, printers and publishers of the Low Countries, which may explain their poor showing here. Geoffrey Tory, by contrast, the first fully-conscious artist of the book, initiates a vivid account of the French printers whose work has been justly famous from their day to this. It includes two notable achievements in technical book-making, Oronce Finé's *Arithmetica practica* (1542) and Jean Cousin's *Livre de perspective* (1560), arguably the finest as well as most imaginative example of sixteenth-century book-design.

English books were, it is true, a derivative backwater of the mainstream of European book art, but Levarie is right to single out the work of John Day (oddly, she pre-dates the foundation of Oxford University Press by a century). But, derivative or not, English work soon attained a vigour and identity of its own. It is interesting to contrast the examples of the seventeenth century shown here with those in Corbett and Lightbown's *The comely frontispiece* (1979), a pioneering study of the meaning and function, as well as appearance and style, of the work of the great engravers on copper who dominated it. We would not now dismiss Rubens's designs as overblown, while admitting the delicacy of Callot and Bloemaerts's subtle contrasts in the *Tableaux du temple des muses* (1655).

It is equally right to point to the search for unity of text and illustration that typified the development of the rococo book in the eighteenth century. Pine's *Horace* was an eccentric example of a tendency more fairly represented by the merging of the work of Pierre-Simon Fournier (to be distinguished from his elder brother Jean-Francois) and the engravings of Eisen in the *fermiers généraux* edition of La Fontaine. In this, laid paper was not an asset but a disadvantage, and James Whatman's successful invention of the "grainless" wove paper did as much as his revolutionary types to make Baskerville's classics the cynosure of Europe, the first time that British books had achieved such a reputation. Today, too, we would make more of the great Venetian books of Albrizzi and Zatta, of Bernard Picart and the great Dutch printer-publishers, and the baroque and rococo masterpieces of Germany and Austria.

The transition from traditional to neo-classical typography was marked by some of the finest books yet printed by the Didots in France, Bodoni in Italy, Ibarra in Spain, Bell, Bulmer and Bensley in England. But no account of this movement is complete without detailing the revolutionary impact of the Foulis brothers' press in Glasgow, creators of the modern monumental title-page and the conventions of moderate capitalization that we use today. Like the books of Bodoni, theirs were unillustrated, their typography an art in itself. Surprisingly, however, the greatest artist of the book to appear in Britain in the eighteenth century, whose influence spread all over Europe and is alive today, is hardly mentioned. Thomas Bewick's revival of the art of engraving on wood, using the end-grain now rather than the plank, is not only immortalized in his own *Aesop*, the *Quadrapeds* and *Birds*, but in the work of his many pupils and imitators. He, in fact, solved the problem that eluded the rococo artists.

Dorat's *Les baisers* (1770) nearly achieved the match of letterpress text and engraved text. The Abbé Galiani's verdict on it, "Ce poète-là se sauva du naufrage de planche en planche" recalls Lady Blessington's more homely observation on Samuel Rogers's *Italy* (1830), as illustrated by J. M. W. Turner, that "it would have been dished without the plates". But even Turner understood the special art that Bewick had demonstrated of balancing illustration and text, size for size, weight of colour for colour, the two merging in the special and unique artistry of William Blake. It was Bewick's example that infused the great illustrators of the nineteenth century, from Johannot to Tenniel to Toulouse-Lautrec.

Wisely, Levarie does not pursue the technical consequences of the industrial revolution, the exploration of the possibilities of colour printing and the reproductive techniques of photography, in any great detail. She is quite right to attribute to it the final merger of text and decoration begun by Bewick, and judicious in her analysis of those who broke away from its conventions, from Walter Crane and Kate Greenaway to Aubrey Beardsley. We would hardly think of Beardsley's illustrations as "inescapably dated", but her judgement of William Morris's books, lacking the essential simplicity of the fifteenth century he loved, that they "remain thoroughly Victorian, closer to some of Beardsley's pages than to those of a more innocent age" is both perceptive and just.

The extent to which the book as a work of art has ceased to be the prerogative of the rich and entered a new popular market is more obvious now than in 1968. But its further development in the twentieth century is still waiting to be recorded. Here the scene seems to be dominated by the English private press book, the French *livre de peintre*, the German modernism of the Bauhaus (in which Henri van de Velde was a seminal influence) and by Italian and Russian Futurism. A string of names, from the great printer Giovanni Mardersteig to the great wood-engraver Leonard Baskin, ends the story. "The homogenizing forces of our time have broken many barriers of national style, and sometimes it is difficult to tell at a glance the origin of a book." Perhaps the barriers were never quite as high as the author supposed, but no one will dissent from her final summing up:

"For the lover of fine books, nothing can replace the bite of type or plate into good paper, the play of well-cut, well-set text against illustration or decoration of deep artistic value. But an inexpensive edition can carry its own aesthetic validity through imaginative or appropriate design. These are not matters of concern only for aesthetes; if, in an era of uncertain values, we want to keep alive respect for ideas and knowledge, it is important to give books a form that encourages respect. The style and production of books, for all the centuries they have been made, still have much to offer the designer and publisher in challenge, the reader in pleasure."

This is abundantly true of Norma Levarie's own book which she not only wrote but designed with expert eye and hand. The type is Linotype Janson, based, at a certain distance, on the letter engraved by the great Hungarian artist of the book, Nicolas Kis, and transmitted by the Leipzig Janson foundry over most of Europe, even to England. In its American version it was, as the author no doubt intended, a fine example of the best book-production of its time and place. The arrangement and signalling of the plates is faultless. The reproduction of the original pages was equally faultless, a tribute to the photographic skills, and the then new 300-line process screen applied to photolithography, as pioneered by Meriden Gravure. That company, under the gentle direction of Harold Hugo (whose collection provided the example of the 42-line Bible), was the ideal of fine printing thirty years ago. It is now, happily, alive and well, in Vermont, under the eye of Harold Hugo's long-time friend, the partner in many joint enterprises, Roderick Stinehour. It is equally gratifying to think that this book, so redolent of its time, in form as well as style, should have the same power to serve and guide the needs of readers a generation after it was first published under the discriminating eye and imprint of James Heineman.

Bibliographical Note

The list of works consulted by the author was both catholic and up-to-date in 1968. For this edition, it has been decided to retain the original bibliography (pp. 307–310 below), but to provide the reader with information on some of the more significant works published since then.

Two works that notably widen the subject are A. Hyatt Mayor's *Prints and People* (New York Graphic Society, 1971) and Hans Hammelmann's *Book Illustrators in Eighteenth-Century England* (Yale U.P., 1975). Hammelmann's work would have caused the author to enlarge her comment that the classic authors of the seventeenth century had to wait until the next century before receiving appropriate graphic form. Of the many other works that could be added to the list, the most substantial are the late Gordon N. Ray's two magisterial surveys, *The Art of the French Illustrated Book 1700–1914* (New York: Pierpont Morgan Library and Dover Publications, 1986) and *The Illustrator and the Book in England from 1790 to 1914* (New York: Pierpont Morgan Library and Dover Publications, 1991), and the second, expanded, edition of the late David Bland's *A History of Book Illustration* (University of California Press, 1969). The following works will also be of interest: Janet Backhouse, *The Illuminated Manuscript* (London: Phaidon, 1979); Christopher de Hamel, *A History of Illuminated Manuscripts* (London: Phaidon, 2nd ed., 1994); John Harthan, *The History of the Illustrated Book. The Western Tradition* (London: Thames & Hudson, 1981); Edward Hodnett, *Five Centuries of English Book Illustration* (Aldershot: Scolar Press, 1988); Simon Houfe, *Dictionary of British Book Illustrators 1800–1914* (London, 1978); Alan Horne, *Dictionary of 20th Century British Book Illustrators* (Woodbridge: Antique Collector's Club, 1994); Basil Hunnisett, *Steel-engraved book illustration in England* (London, 1980); Janet Ing, *Johann Gutenberg and his Bible* (New York: The Typophiles & London: The British Library, 1990); Alexander Lawson, *Anatomy of a Typeface* (Boston: David Godine, 1990); John Lewis, *The 20th Century Book, its illustration and design* (New York: Van Nostrand Reinhold, 2nd ed., 1993); Mac McGrew, *American Metal Typefaces of the Twentieth Century* (New Castle, Delaware: Oak Knoll Books, 2nd ed., 1993); Eric de Maré, *The Victorian Woodblock Illustrators* (London: Gordon Fraser, 1980); Robin Myers and Michael Harris (eds), *A Millennium of the Book: Production, Design and Illustration in Manuscript and Print 900–1900* (Winchester: St Paul's Bibliographies & New Castle, Delaware: Oak Knoll Books, 1994).

ILLUSTRATIONS

*Book pages are shown in their original size except when
measurements (to the nearest quarter inch) are given.*

[1]From Edouard Naville, *Papyrus Funéraires de la XXIe Dynastie.* Paris, 1912

[2]Courtesy of the Metropolitan Museum of Art, Harris Brisbane Dick Fund, 1923

[3,4,8,9,10]Courtesy of the Spencer Collection, the New York Public Library, Astor, Lenox and Tilden Foundations

[5]Courtesy of the Metropolitan Museum of Art, Dick Fund, 1925

[6]Courtesy of the Library of Congress, Rosenwald Collection

[7]Courtesy of the Metropolitan Museum of Art, Dick Fund, 1918

[11]Courtesy of Ruari McLean, *Victorian Book Design,* University Press, New York, 1963

[12]Courtesy of the Rare Book Division, the New York Public Library, Astor, Lenox and Tilden Foundations

[13,14]Courtesy of Georg Kurt Schauer, *Deutsche Buchkunst 1890 bis 1960,* Maximilian-Gesellschaft, Hamburg, 1963

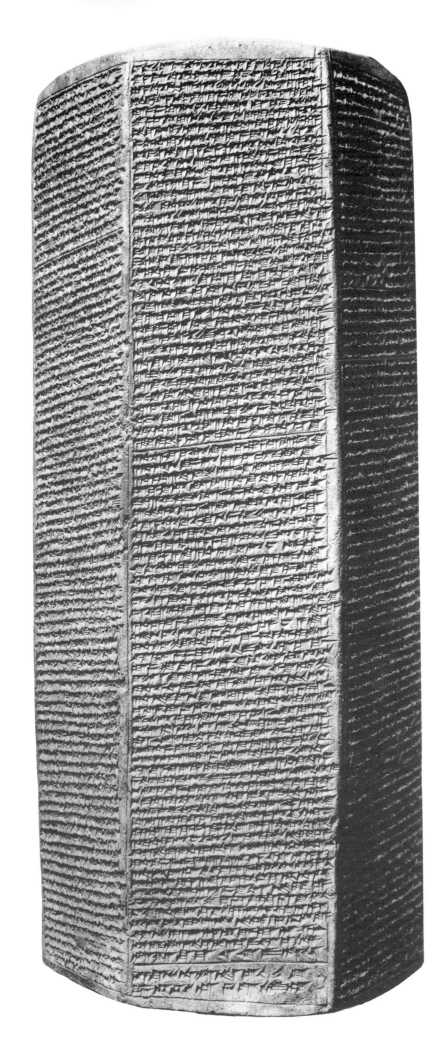

ORIGINS

"...I read the beautiful clay tablets from Sumer and the obscure Akkadian writing which is hard to master. I had my joy in the reading of inscriptions in stone from the time before the flood...." These are the words of Ashurbanipal, the last great king of the Assyrian Empire, in the seventh century before Christ. Books were no novelty to this ancient warrior-king; he had compiled a vast library, for which he sent envoys to search out the old Sumerian and Babylonian texts from millennia before his time. But the works in this library, and indeed the document in which Ashurbanipal's words are recorded, would seem very strange to a modern reader. They are clay objects—flat rectangles or circles, brick shapes, columns, and barreled cones— pricked with characters; some with pictographs, others—the later ones—with the symbols known as cuneiform writing. In the intrinsic sense they are books: they are works of literature, of science, of history and religion, as well as documents of state.

Prism of Sennacherib page xii

There are links between the content of Babylonian-Assyrian literature and ours: some of the clay tablets preserve an account of the Creation and the Deluge related to our biblical version, both probably derived from a common source. But physically our books are in no sense descended from the clay books of Mesopotamia. They have, however, direct lineage from another group of books equally ancient, the papyrus manuscripts of Egypt.

People have from the beginning written on whatever came conveniently to hand. For the Babylonians and Assyrians, living in the Tigris-Euphrates valley, moist clay that later could be baked was the most readily practical material. The word "book," which comes from the Anglo-Saxon word for beech tree, indicates that there was a time when the Saxons and Germans wrote on beech boards. Similarly, the term "codex," by which we designate bound manuscripts, is derived from the Latin "caudex," tree trunk. The concept of "leaves" of a book suggests the use of leaves as writing materials. Pliny, referring especially to Egypt, says that men first wrote on the leaves of palm trees. In India and the Far East trimmed palm leaves, bound at one end like a fan, have long been used for books and continue to be used in some places till this day. Some early book materials have left their vestiges only in names. The perishable nature of the materials has left us with scarcely a trace of whole literatures of such people as the Cretans and the Etruscans.

Prism of Sennacherib. Assyrian, VII century B.C. Oriental Institute, University of Chicago. Height 15 in.

The papyrus that the Egyptians chose as a writing medium is highly perishable, too. We would have no remains of Egyptian papyri were it not for a fortunate combination of circumstances: the preserving quality of the dry Egyptian climate and sand, and the Egyptian religious practice of sealing up objects in tombs. As it is, we have very possibly a biased view of Egyptian literature, because it is mostly the so-called Books of the Dead that have been preserved. These books, whose name is a modern invention, were magical instruction books for the dead to assure their safe conduct into the underworld past demons and other deterrents. Originally the texts were carved on the inner walls of the tombs and on the sarcophagi, or written on the inner coffin lids. Later they were written on papyrus scrolls that were buried with the dead.

Other Egyptian writings are known to us in fragments and in smaller numbers. The earliest preserved papyrus is a fragment dating from the XI or XII Dynasty (c.2150–1775 B.C.); it is a copy of moral and religious treatise said by the text to have been originally written about five hundred years earlier. Rules of conduct and books of wisdom figure among the relics of Egyptian literature. There are also magical texts, books of mathematics, myths and short stories, love songs, poems and ballads, and litanies in praise of the gods.

The Books of the Dead were by far the most frequently illustrated, although the earliest illustrated papyrus roll we have, the Ramesseum Papyrus, is a ceremonial play written for the enthronement of Sesostris I in the early twentieth century B.C. The illustrations consist of thirty little figures running in a strip along the bottom of the roll, executed in a stylized line hardly different in weight and character from the text—plainly meant for clarification and not decoration.

The Egyptians sometimes wrote on animal hides prepared as scrolls, but they had a far more convenient and less costly material in papyrus. Papyrus grew in abundance only in Egypt, and though for centuries it was the writing material of the Greek and Roman worlds, the entire supply came from this one source. The writing sheet was prepared from the sliced inner pith of the plant stem, laid out on a table, moistened with a gluey liquid, pressed and dried. The single sheets of papyrus were made into scrolls by glueing them end to end. According to Pliny, the normal length of a scroll was about fifteen feet. The width of the scroll was determined by the length of the strips of pith. About ten inches seems to have been usual. The Books of the Dead, being of special importance, often exceeded these normal sizes. The Ani Papyrus is fifteen inches wide and runs seventy-seven feet; the Greenfield Papyrus is nineteen inches wide and runs to one hundred and twenty-three feet.

The Egyptian scribe, with his palette of inks and his brushes, is a figure known to us from Egyptian wall paintings and sculptures. He used black ink for his text and red to mark titles and beginnings—a practice that persisted through classical and medieval manuscripts and carried over into the printed book. The early Egyptian scrolls were written in hieroglyphics

Egyptian scribe. c. 650 B.C. Brooklyn Museum

or their simplified form, hieratics, in vertical columns divided from one another by thin black lines. It was natural for the illustrations that accompanied such a text to run along the top or bottom of the scroll, separated from it by ruled lines, as they did in the Ramesseum Papyrus. But as illustration developed in importance, it began to invade the text. In the XVIII and XIX Dynasties (c.1570–1200 B.C.) the most beautifully illustrated Books of the Dead were made, in glowing colors. The Ani Papyrus, the most famous of the XVIII Dynasty, and the Hunefer Papyrus of the XIX Dynasty, are alike in having the horizontal frieze marked off from the hieroglyphic text by double ruled lines that form a rudimentary sort of frame. But the frieze suddenly enlarges for important scenes and figures, which extend freely and irregularly into the text.

The Hunefer Papyrus was a Book of the Dead prepared for Hunefer, overseer of the palace, superintendent of the cattle, and royal scribe in the service of Seti I, King of Egypt about 1300 B.C. It has a frieze of mourners that proceeds to the point where the coffin appears outside the tomb. At this point the frieze enlarges nearly to the full height of the scroll to show the family of Hunefer and the god Anubis, conductor of the dead, holding the coffin. *Book of the Dead of Hunefer pages 4 and 5*

The Book of the Dead of the Priestess Nesikhonsu, made about three hundred years later in the XXI Dynasty, is different in appearance. The text is in hieratics, written horizontally from right to left and arranged in columns. The continuous frieze has been abandoned, and pictures are put in the columns of text where they are related. These unframed vignettes—which are sometimes narrower but almost never wider than the text column into which they are inserted—persist through Greek and Roman manuscripts into medieval and modern books, forming one of the oldest conventions of the format of books. *Book of the Dead of Nesikhonsu pages 6 and 7*

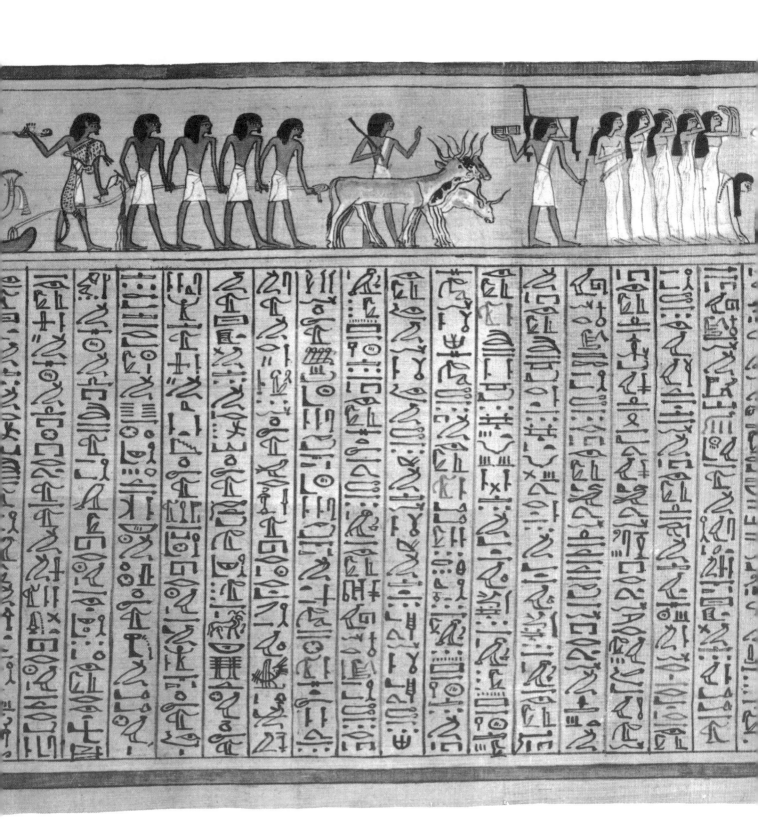

4 *Book of the Dead of Hunefer.* Egyptian, c. 1300 B.C. British Museum, Pap. 9901. Height 15½ in.

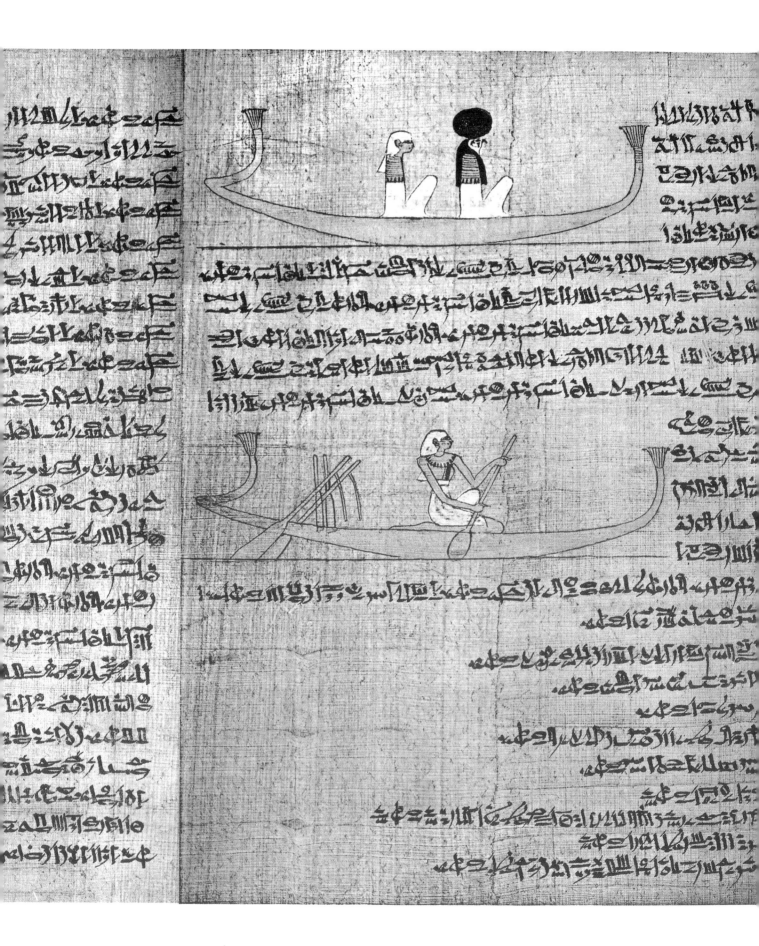

6   *Book of the Dead of Nesikhonsu*. Egyptian, c. 1000 B.C. Cairo Museum. Reduced

With the passing of the XVIII and XIX Dynasties, Egyptian manuscripts had passed their peak of beauty, but their importance extends far later. In the fourth century B.C., when Alexander the Great added Egypt to the vast domain he ruled, Alexandria became the cultural center of the entire Hellenized world. The Ptolemies, Egyptian rulers after Alexander's death, developed the Alexandrian museum and library into an immense institution, said to have held at its peak nearly one million scrolls (among them the present of two hundred thousand scrolls given by Antony to Cleopatra). Scholars flocked to the Alexandrian library from all over the Hellenized world to partake of the gathered wisdom of Greece and Egypt. Scribes were organized into groups for the large-scale production of manuscript copies. The transmission of Egyptian texts into classical culture, along with their illustrations and formats, took place here. But more important, it was at Alexandria, in the dry Egyptian soil, that most of the ancient Greek manuscripts we have today were preserved.

GREECE

What we know of Greek literature we know largely from copies, many times removed from the originals, renewed generation after generation through the ages. However much has been lost to us—and indications are that the loss is great—enough has been transmitted to form the solid nucleus of Western culture.

Our knowledge of the physical appearance of ancient Greek manuscripts is far less than of their contents and must be filled out with inferences. No manuscripts from the classical period of Greece still exist. The Greek manuscripts that have survived are mainly those written between the fourth century B.C. and the seventh century A.D. at Alexandria, where Greek was the scholarly tongue. These precious finds were recovered from refuse heaps, or from tombs where, as waste paper, they had been made into mummy cases. The only other important source of Greek manuscripts is the library discovered beneath the ashes of Herculaneum, preserved intact since the first century A.D.

We know from Greek writers that books were widely read in the fifth century B.C., and that there was a book market in Athens at that time. Xenophon speaks of a wealthy young man who seeks to outdo his friends with a collection of the works of celebrated poets and philosophers. How much further back in Greek civilization books extend is a matter of scholarly conjecture. It used to be assumed that writing was practically unknown in Greece at the time of Homer, about the ninth century B.C. Now it is thought likely that the Homeric poems were written down for the bards to memorize. Evidence in support of this view is found in the division of the Odyssey into twenty books, and the Iliad into twenty-four—a division that seems to indicate the number of scrolls it took to hold the two epics.

Nevertheless, ancient Greece had a primarily oral tradition: the epic poems were recited, the tragedies and comedies were enacted, even historic works were read aloud at festivals. Not until the fifth century—the time of Aeschylus, Sophocles, and Euripides, of Herodotus and Thucydides—were books written and read on a large scale. There is much evidence of the existence of libraries by the time of Aristotle, in the fourth century B.C. Aristotle himself could have scarcely compiled his works without a considerable reference library.

Whatever writing material was used by the earlier Greeks, the historian Herodotus, in the fifth century B.C., could not conceive of civilized men writing on anything but papyrus. The Greek word for "book," *biblion*, is related to the word for "papyrus," *byblos*. Greek scrolls were somewhat smaller than Egyptian ones—nine inches high at the most, seven and a half inches more commonly. A little pocket roll of poetry might be five inches high, and there exists a roll of epigrams barely two inches high—the first miniature book. Greek literary scrolls rarely if ever were more than thirty-five feet long; rolled up, they could be conveniently held in one hand.

The scrolls were written in columns in a way that seems curious to us: continuously, without breaks between words. Punctuation was either nonexistent or haphazard. Breaks in thought might be indicated by an underlining stroke known as the *paragraphos*, or by a small blank space. Unusual as continuous writing is to the modern eye, it persisted in Greek, Roman, and later literatures until the eleventh century.

There were no titles at the beginning of the manuscript, but a blank space was left, to hold on to or to protect the vulnerable first part of the roll. Titles appeared, if at all, at the end of the text in a sort of colophon, as they did earlier in Egyptian scrolls and later in medieval manuscripts and in the first printed books.

There was little standardization of style; the scribe could choose his own column width, which was usually between two and three inches. In poetic texts, the length of the poetic line dictated the column width. No attempt was made in any text to keep an even edge at the right of the columns, which were left "ragged." A space of about half an inch was left between the columns. As in the Egyptian scroll, three columns normally showed when the scroll was in use.

It is clear that the Greek scribes were strongly conscious of the value of white space. Upper and lower margins and the spaces between columns were larger in the more splendid scrolls, which were traditionally made for the most honored books in Greek literature, the works of Homer. The medieval world was to give this special distinction to its Bible.

Besides the formal Greek letter, a more fluent and casual type of script was used in nonliterary and informal writing. This script, known as cursive, runs as a counterpart to formal book hands throughout the subsequent history of books and finds its expression in printed books as the italic.

Illustrations were apparently first used in Greek books for practical reasons: to clarify some part of the text that would be hard to describe in words. Aristotle refers to accompanying illustrations, no longer in existence, in his biological works. A unique papyrus scroll in the Louvre—an astronomical text of Eudoxus usually ascribed to 165 B.C.—is the earliest illustrated Greek scroll extant. The drawings are inserted in the columns of text in the manner of Egyptian column illustrations. Without doubt it is a Greek copy from an Egyptian source, for in

Eudoxus Roll
page 11

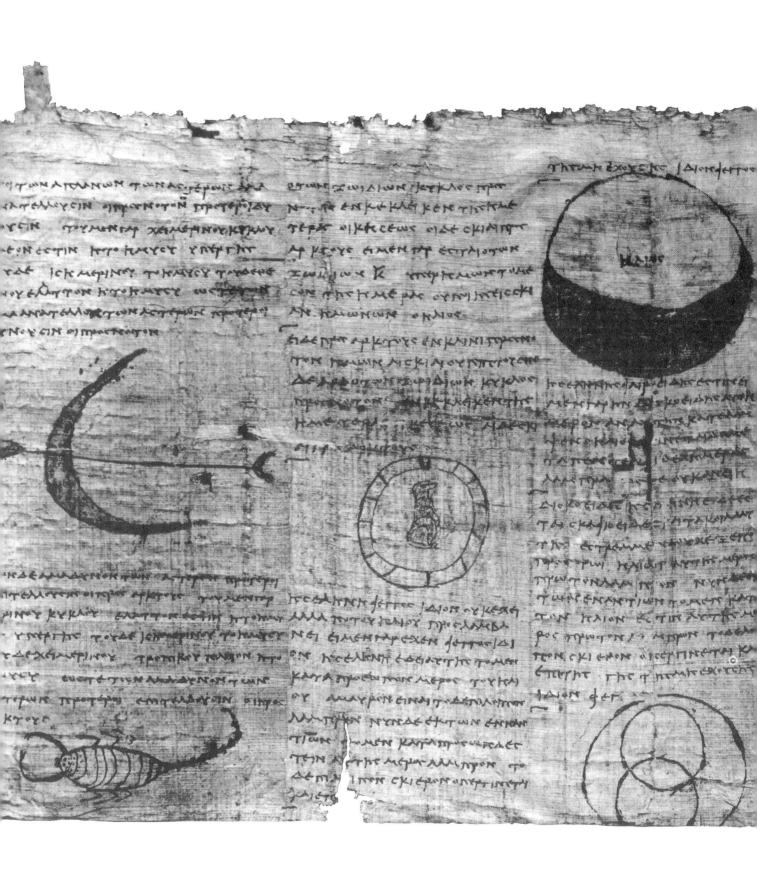

Eudoxus Roll. Greek, ascribed to 165 B.C. Louvre, Pap. Letronne. Reduced

ΙΗϹΟΥϹ
Ο ΤΟΥ
ΝΑΥΗ

ΑΝΔΡΕϹ
ΓΑΙ

ΙϹΡΑ
ΗΛΙ
ΤΑΙ

ΑΝΔΡΕϹ
ΓΑΙ

ΙϹ ΑΝΕϹΤΗ ΙΗϹΟΥϹ ΕΙϹ ΠΑϹΤΟΝΛΑΟϹ Ο ΠΟΛΕΜΙϹΤΗϹ
ΩϹΤΕ ΑΝΑΒΗΝΑΙ ΕΙϹ ΓΑΙ

ΙϹ ΕΞΕΤΕΙΝΕΝ ΙΗϹΟΥϹ ΤΗΝ ΧΕΙΡΑ ΑΥΤΟΥ
ΠΟΛΙΝ ΙϹ ΚΑΤΕΛΑΒΟΝ ΤΟ ΑΥΤΗΝ ΝΙϹΠΕΥϹΑΝΤΕϹ
ΡΟΥΝΤΟΝ ΚΑΠΝΟΝ ΑΝΑΒΑΙΝΟΝΤΑ ΕΙϹ ΤΟΝ ΟΥΝΟΝ
ΞΑΝ ΤΟΥϹ ΑΝΔΡΑϹ ΓΑΙ ΙϹ ΟΥΤΟΙϹ ΕΠΗΛΘΟΝ ΕΙϹ ΤΗϹ ΤΙ

20

ΠϹ ΜΕΝ ΛΑΒ
ΔΙ ΕΙ Ϲ ΤΑϹ

the disk representing the constellation Orion there is a little figure of the Egyptian god Osiris, and a scarab is used as the symbol of the sun.

There is no direct evidence that the ancient papyri of Greece were much illustrated. The earliest surviving manuscripts are all unadorned texts. Though there is no surviving example, some scholars believe that in Hellenistic Alexandria there began, under the influence of Egyptian illustrated scrolls, a period of intensive illustration of certain Greek texts—especially the works of Homer and Euripides. Later manuscripts of these works, still extant, contain illustrations believed to be based on Alexandrian originals. The archaeologist Kurt Weitzmann, of Princeton University, has reconstructed the stages of development of Graeco-Roman illustration from the "simultaneous," in which several actions take place in one picture, through the "monoscenic," one action and one time to a scene, to the "cyclic" illustration, in which a series of actions follow one another without division. According to Weitzmann, the literary illustrations found in Greek vase painting and Greek sculpture are derived from scrolls bearing the friezelike cyclic illustrations.

A manuscript in the Vatican Library, known as the *Joshua Roll*, ascribed variously to the sixth–seventh centuries A.D. and the ninth–tenth centuries A.D., could well be a copy of an Alexandrian cyclic scroll. The scroll, about a foot high, contains delicately colored drawings from the Book of Joshua in a continuous flow of action, which takes place against a suggestive but fundamentally naturalistic background of rocky hills, trees, and walled cities. The style of drawing and the costumes are Hellenistic. Excerpts from the biblical text are written beneath the pictures in a tenth-century script, which could have been added any time after the drawings were made.

Joshua Roll
page 12

An illustrated manuscript of the *Iliad* in the Ambrosian Library at Milan gives a strong indication that the later Greeks illustrated Homer. It also indicates what the illustrations may have been like. The fragmentary copy on vellum, ascribed to the third, fourth, or fifth centuries A.D. contains fifty-eight perfectly classical illustrations. They occur on the verso of the text pages in a Greek script of the era and are enclosed in simple band frames. Sometimes two separate scenes, one above the other, are in one frame. Together they make up the consecutive episodes of the story. Only two of the pictures have background of any sort; the rest are, like Egyptian illustrations, without background.

Graeco-Roman manuscript models, transmitted through later copies, continued to be one of the primary sources of style, costume, and characterization for illustrators of books throughout Byzantine and Western Christendom.

Joshua Roll. Byzantine, ascribed variously to the VI-VII centuries and the IX-X centuries. Vatican Library, Cod. Palat. gr. 431. Height 12 in.

FORSITANETPINGUISHORTOSQUAECURACOLENDI
ORNARECANEREMBIFERIQUEROSARIAPAESTI
QUOQ·MODOPOTISGAUDERENTINTIBARIUIS·
ETUIRIDISAPIORILAETORTUSQUITERHERBAM
CRESCERETINUENTREMCUCUMISNECSERACOMANTI
NARCISSUMAUTFLEXITACULISSTUIMENACANTHI
PALLENTISHEDERASITAMANTISLITORAMYRTOS

ROME

In the three centuries before Christ, Greek literature spread to Rome, as to other parts of the civilized world. There seems to have been no earlier Roman literature, though the Romans had developed their own Latin alphabet, based on their Etruscan neighbors'. Its antecedents were common with those of the Greek alphabet: Phoenician, Old Semitic, and Egyptian hieratics and hieroglyphics.

The recognized father of Latin literature was a Greek schoolmaster, Livius Andronicus, who came to Rome in 272 B.C. He translated the Greek classics of Homer into Latin and wrote Latin plays based on Greek models. Roman intellectual life was thoroughly Hellenic.

In the latter part of the third century B.C. and in the second century B.C. an indigenous Roman literature came into being: the plays of Plautus and Terence, and the encyclopedia of Cato. By the first century B.C. Roman literature was at its height and could boast of Cicero, Caesar, Livy, Catullus, Virgil, and Horace. Lucullus, the Roman general known best for his gourmet tastes, amassed what was probably the first very extensive library in Rome and made it freely available to readers. An organized book trade spread Roman books to the farthest reaches of the Empire.

The Emperor Augustus, ruling at the height of Rome's military and intellectual glory, was the first to found a public library in Rome. Tiberius, Vespasian, and Trajan followed his example. By the middle of the first century A.D. the philosopher Seneca was decrying the ostentatious accumulation of books that were seldom read. He protested that a library had become as standard a part of a patrician house as a bathroom.

For all this abundance of Roman books, which we know of from writings of the time, fewer Roman manuscripts exist today than Greek ones; the earliest is from the first century A.D. or shortly before. But we have a clear idea of the arrangement and contents of a wealthy patrician's library from the preservation intact of such a library beneath the cinders that fell on Herculaneum in A.D. 79. It contained, besides the only Greek scrolls found outside of Egypt, the largest part of the Roman scrolls extant.

The storage of scrolls in a library presented its own problems. They had to be kept lying in cupboards or standing about in vases. They were not differentiated on the outside except for

Square capitals

small projecting labels called *tituli*. But the Romans did what they could to make them decorative, fitting the ends of the rolling sticks with elaborate knobs and wrapping the rolls in purple cloth with scarlet strings and labels.

Roman writing until well into the Christian Era was in majuscules, or capital letters, only. The well-formed square capitals that we know from Roman inscriptions in stone or metal were the basis of formal writing. But these formal capitals are rare in surviving manuscripts. A more casual version known as "rustic capitals" was generally used. Cursive script was used for private or informal purposes. It was most often scratched on the wax-filled wooden tablets that served for notes and letters—hence its disjointed character.

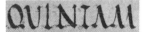

Rustic capitals

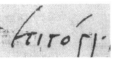

Cursive script

The inscriptions on the walls of Pompeii have been an invaluable source for the study of Roman letter forms. Preserved there are advertisements, recommendations of political candidates, notices of lost articles, announcements of sports events—all drawn with a brush in the formal square-letter style. Along with these are scribblings, often scratched with a pointed object—declarations of love, rude remarks, a few lines of poetry—in the cursive hand.

Papyrus was the most commonly used book material in ancient Rome, as in Greece. But the crude parchment or vellum already known in old Egypt was also occasionally used. In the second century B.C. a major change took place in the preparation of parchment which greatly increased its usability. The historian Pliny tells that at that time the King of Pergamum, in Asia Minor, wanted to build a fine library in his city. King Ptolemy of Egypt wanted no rival to the famous library at Alexandria, so he forbade the export of papyrus to Pergamum. The King of Pergamum was not easily foiled; he ordered experiments to improve the usability of prepared animal skins as a writing surface. The result was a fine, two-sided vellum so successful that a lively vellum trade developed at Pergamum, whose name is preserved in our word "parchment." The library at Pergamum grew to great size and became an important center of culture. It is said to have comprised two hundred thousand volumes when Antony presented it to Cleopatra, who made it a part of the Alexandrian library.

The increased use of the smooth-surfaced parchment, perfect for the pen, no doubt had much to do with the growth of a new rounded majuscule letter form—the uncial—whose main strokes rose and fell from the line of writing. By the fourth century A.D. the uncial was in common use, and it remained the first-ranking book hand until the eighth century. By the fifth century capitals were no longer used as a literary hand and survived only for use in headings and initial letters, or to set off some special part of the text.

Uncials

The Roman Empire carried Roman letter forms to its farthest outposts. When the Empire finally fell, the letter forms began slowly to evolve into local variations in the same way that the Roman language did.

Pliny, whose detailed descriptions provide much of our view of ancient Roman usages, writes of illustrations in Roman books—of plant drawings in herbals and of portrait illustration to a volume of biographies written in 39 B.C. Martial, in the late first century A.D., mentions a frontispiece portrait of Virgil. But no illustrated Roman manuscripts of any sort survive from earlier than the fourth century A.D. The earliest two illustrated Roman manuscripts extant are both Virgils: Virgil was to Roman literature what Homer was to Greek.

The manuscript known as the *Vatican Virgil* was written in the fourth or fifth century A.D. in rustic capitals, in a single wide column to the page. It is embellished with large, column-wide illustrations, the best of which are in a classic style suggestive of an excellent early source. Some of them have naturalistic backgrounds painted in perspective. The pictures are framed in broad bands of color, some decorated with lozenges of gilt. The folds of drapery are also lined with gilt. Six pictures occupy the full page; the others are placed above, below, or within the text, where they relate to it. Raphael knew this Vatican treasure and was influenced by it.

Vatican Virgil page 14

The second Virgil manuscript of early date, the *Roman Virgil,* is also in the Vatican Library. It is in a stiffer and coarser style, but the costumes and furniture indicate a classic model. The existing copy belongs somewhere between the fourth and the sixth centuries A.D. One of its interesting features is that it contains a portrait of the author.

Medieval manuscripts of pagan classics give a strong suggestion of what the Roman tradition of illustration must have been. About a dozen copies of the plays of Terence exist; the earliest of these, from the ninth century, is in the Vatican. Its prototype appears to have belonged to the second or third century A.D.

Terence, Adelphoe pages 18 and 19

At Leyden an eleventh-century translation of Aesop into Latin has many ancient features in its illustrations, which are nevertheless tinged with a later style. Manuscripts of Ovid and Horace in the Vatican Library, dating from about the twelfth and thirteenth centuries, preserve some Graeco-Roman characteristics.

The Middle Ages depended heavily on classical sources for scientific and medical knowledge, and one would expect medieval copies to have kept close to the illustrations as well as the texts of the originals. In Vienna there is a sixth-century copy of a treatise by the first-century Greek botanist Dioscorides, which is considered to be the common ancestor of all the illustrated herbals of the Middle Ages and Renaissance. The manuscript, made for the daughter of the Byzantine Empress Galla Placidia, is the oldest extant to use gold backgrounds for illustrations. Besides six full-page pictures at the front of the book, there are many unframed colored drawings inserted in the text, showing plants and animals. Some may have been newly conceived, but it is likely that many were copied from classical sources.

finonplufoft patre.togopluffilio

aut hoc eft filium effe; si frater: aut sodalif effet qui magif morem gereret. hic nonamandus
                    posset   suabeneficio
hic menongestandus infinu eft.hem. itaq; adeo magná mihi in iecit sua commoditate curá
                              illu   pquáscierit
neimprudens forte faciam.quod nolit sciens.cauebo sed cesso ire intro nemorá eif nuptiis ego
met siem

DEMEA SENEX

demea reuertenf abinquisitione fratrissui delusus abyro
secum loquebatur

                        ó umné
DEM defessus sum ambulando: ut si re te cum tua monstratigne agnusper dat iuppiter.
    circuitu afcendi   ubi bfraé
perreptaui usq; omne oppidum adportam adlacum. quo non nec fabrica illi cullaerat
        meú miserio   apud me uexpectare   tádiu
neq; fratrem homo uidisse se aiebat quisquá; nunc uero domi certu obsidere eft usque
donec redierit

MICIO · SENEX   DEMEA II

i sofert tte i paphile   nuptiarú   i adsuperiorappiner
MIC ibo illis dicam nullá esse in nobis moram; DEM sed eccu ipsú te iam dudú quaero micio
                                                          y roni cos   aeschini
MIC quidnam. DEM fero alia flagitia adte ingentia boni illius adulescentis. MIC ecce autem;

EM noua capitalia; MIC ohe iam; DEM ah nescis quid uir sit; MIC scio; DEM ausculte tu de psal

tria me somnias agere. hoc patitum in uirginem est ciuem; MIC scio; DEM eho scis & patere;

MIC quid ni patiar; DEM dic mihi non clamas non insanis; MIC non malim quidem; DEM puer naturae;

MIC du bene uortant; DEM uirgo nihil habet; MIC audiui; DEM & ducenda indotata est;

MIC scilicet; DEM quid nunc futurum est; MIC id enim quod res ipsa fert illinc huc transferetur

uirgo; DEM o iuppiter istoc in pacto oportet; MIC quid faciam amplius; DEM quid facias

rogitas si non ipsa re tibi istuc dolet simulare est certe hominis; MIC quin tam uirginem

despondi res composita est fiunt nuptiae dempsi metum omnem haec magis sunt hominis;

DEM ceterum placet tibi factum mitio; MIC non si queam mutare nunc cum non queo aequo ani

mo fero; ita uita est hominum quasi cum ludas tesseris si illud quod maxume opus est actu

non cadit illud quod cecidit forte id arte ut corrigas; DEM corrector nempe tua arte uirgin

ti mine p psaltria periere quae quantu potest aliquo abicienda est si non pretio uel gratis;

MIC neque est neque illam sane studeo uendere; DEM quid igitur facias; MIC domi erit;

DEM p diuum fidem meretrix & mater familias erit una in domo; MIC cur non DEM sanu

ne te credis esse; MIC equidem arbitror; DEM ita me diament ut uideo tuam ego ineptia

factu rum credo ut habeas quicum cantites; MIC cur non DEM & noua nupta eadem

haec discet; MIC scilicet; DEM tu inter eas restim ductans saltabis; MIC pbe; & tu nob

cum si opus sit; DEM ei mihi nonne haec pudent; MIC iam uero omitte mea tu istanc

iracundiam atq; ita uti decet hilarum ac lubentem fac te in nati nuptiis; ego hos conue

niam post huc redeo; DEM o iuppiter hanc in uitam hos cine mores. hanc dementiam;

uxor sine dote ueniet intus psaltria est domus sup tuosa adulescens luxu pditus senex

delirans ipsa si cupiat salus seruare prorsus non potest hanc familiam;

SYRUS SERVUS · DEMEA SENEX

A medical manuscript of the tenth or eleventh century at the Laurentiana in Florence contains the earliest copy of a Greek surgical text, a commentary of the first century B.C. on a text of Hippocrates. It also contains Soranus' treatise of the second century A.D. on the art of bandaging. The illustrations in this manuscript are clearly after classical models.

Ptolemy's *Geography* was the standard geographic text until as late as the fifteenth century; the classical sources of the maps and tables have been transmitted along with the text. A ninth-century copy of the astronomical text of the third-century B.C. poet Aratus is patterned after the Greek copy in the Louvre known as the Eudoxus Roll, of the second century B.C., in turn a copy of an Egyptian original. The ancient arrangement of narrow columns with inserted illustrations is preserved through later copies.

These medieval books fill out our image of Roman books through the classical characteristics they preserve. But a major event in the history of the book had taken place between the writing of the prototypes and of their copies. That event was the development of the codex, or, more specifically, of the parchment codex written in uncials that was to be the book of the next thousand years and more.

A codex is a book made of folded leaves bound at one side. The form was doubtless first suggested by the Greek and Roman habit of fastening several wax-filled wooden tablets along one side to provide space for longer notes or letters. The British Museum has two perfect examples of these bound wax tablets, one with seven leaves and the other with six. The six-leaved tablet must have belonged to a Greek schoolboy of the third century B.C.; it has school notes scratched into it and a crude little drawing. The Latin name for the multiple tablets was *codex,* signifying "something made of wood." In the time of Cicero, the first century before Christ, the name "codex" was given to collections of laws or constitutions of the emperors, which for convenience of reference must have been made of side-bound leaves.

The Christian Church began to organize around the preaching of the Apostles shortly after the death of Jesus; by the end of the first century A.D. it had a foothold in every important town in the Roman Empire. The rising church was eager to distinguish its scriptures from pagan writings. The papyrus scroll was associated with pagan literature; the Christian Church chose parchment and the codex format. The advantages, besides identification with the Church, were many: A large body of material could be presented in one unit, reference to any part was easy, and the use of parchment made the whole unit durable. The codex is believed to have been adopted in the second century A.D. From that time survive parts of a leaf of the Fourth Gospel, two leaves from a Gospel no longer known, and parts of codices of the Book of Numbers and Deuteronomy. There are more numerous examples from the third century, including portions of a secular codex: an *Iliad.* Sometime between the fourth and fifth centuries the codex took over completely, and the use of the scroll for general purposes was abandoned.

Codex Sinaiticus. Roman, IV century A.D. British Library, Add. Ms. 43725. 15 x 13½ in.

CΗΣ ΤΗΣ ΤΙΒΕΡΙΑ...
ΕΦΑΝΕΡΩΣΕΝ ΔΕ
ΟΥΤΩΣ ΗΣΑΝ ΟΜ
CΙΜΩΝ ΠΕΤΡΟΣ ΚΑ
ΘΩΜΑΣ Ο ΛΕΓΟΜΕ
ΝΟΣ ΔΙΔΥΜΟΣ ΚΑΙ
ΝΑΘΑΝΑΗΛ Ο ΑΠΟ
ΚΑΝΑ ΤΗΣ ΓΑΛΙΛΑΙΑΝ
ΑΣ ΚΑΙ ΟΙ ΥΙΟΙ ΖΕΒ
ΑΔΙΟΥ ΚΑΙ ΑΛΛΟΙ ΕΚ
ΤΩΝ ΜΑΘΗΤΩΝ ΑΥ
ΤΟΥ ΔΥΟ:
ΛΕΓΕΙ ΑΥΤΟΙΣ CΙΜΩ
ΠΕΤΡΟΣ ΥΠΑΓΩ Α
ΛΙΕΥΕΙΝ ΛΕΓΟΥΣΙΝ
ΑΥΤΩ ΕΡΧΟΜΕΘΑ Κ
ΗΜΕΙΣ ΣΥΝ ΣΟΙ ΕΞΗ
ΘΟΝ ΚΑΙ ΕΝΕ
ΒΗΣΑΝ ΕΙΣ ΤΟ ΠΛΟ
ΟΝ ΚΑΙ ΕΝ ΕΚΙΝΗ ΤΗ
ΝΥΚΤΙ ΕΒΩΠΙΑΣΑΝ
ΟΥΔΕΝ ΠΡΩΪ ΑΣ ΔΕ
ΓΕΝΟΜΕΝΗΣ ΕΣΤΗ
ΕΠΙ ΤΟΝ ΑΙΓΙΑΛΟΝ
ΟΥ ΜΕΝΤΟΙ ΕΓΝΩ
ΣΑΝ ΟΙ ΜΑΘΗΤΑΙ
ΤΙΣ ΕΣΤΙΝ·
ΛΕΓΕΙ ΟΥΝ ΑΥΤΟΙΣ
ΙΣ ΠΑΙΔΙΑ ΜΗ ΤΙ ΠΡΟΣ
ΦΑΓΙΟΝ ΕΧΕΤΕ ΑΠ
ΚΡΙΘΗΣΑΝ ΑΥΤΩ· Υ
ΛΕΓΕΙ ΑΥΤΟΙΣ ΒΑΛ
ΤΕ ΕΙΣ ΤΑ ΔΕΞΙΑ ΜΕ
ΡΗ ΤΟΥ ΠΛΟΙΟΥ ΤΟ
ΔΙΚΤΥΟΝ ΚΑΙ ΕΥΡΗ
ΣΕΤΕ ΟΙ ΔΕ ΕΒΑΛΟΝ
ΚΑΙ ΟΥΚΕΤΙ ΑΥΤΟ
ΕΛΚΥΣΧΥΟΝ ΑΠ
ΤΟΥ ΠΛΗΘΟΥΣ ΤΩΝ
ΙΧΘΥΩΝ ΛΕΓΕΙ ΟΤ
Ο ΜΑΘΗΤΗΣ ΕΚΕΙ
ΝΟΣ ΟΝ ΗΓΑΠΑ Ο
ΤΩ ΠΕΤΡΩ Ο ΚΣ ΕΤ
CΙΜΩΝ ΟΥΝ ΠΕΤ
ΑΚΟΥΣΑΣ ΟΤΙ Ο Κ
ΕΣΤΙΝ ΤΟΝ ΕΠΕΝΔΥ
ΤΗΝ ΔΙΕΖΩΣΑΤΟ·
ΗΝ ΓΑΡ ΓΥΜΝΟΣ

ΕΒΑΛΕΝ ΕΑΥΤΟΝ Ι
ΤΗΝ ΘΑΛΑΣΣΑΝ ΟΙ
ΔΕ ΑΛΛΟΙ ΜΑΘΗΤΑΙ
ΤΩ ΠΛΟΙΑΡΙ
Ω ΗΛΘΟΝ ΟΥ ΓΑΡ Η
ΣΑΝ ΜΑΚΡΑΝ ΑΠΟ
ΤΗΣ ΤΗΣ ΑΛΛΑ ΩΣ ΑΠΟ
ΠΟΠΗΧΩΝ ΔΙΑΚΟ
CΙΩΝ CΥΡΟΝΤΕΣ ΤΟ
ΔΙΚΤΥΟΝ ΤΩΝ ΙΧ
ΩΝ ΩΣ ΟΥΝ ΑΠΕ
ΒΗΣΑΝ ΕΙΣ ΤΗΝ ΓΗΝ
ΒΛΕΠΟΥΣΙΝ ΑΝΘΡΑ
ΚΙΑΝ ΚΕΙΜΕΝΗΝ
ΚΑΙ ΟΨΑΡΙΟΝ ΕΠΙ ΚΙ
ΜΕΝΟΝ ΚΑΙ ΑΡΤΟΝ
ΛΕΓΕΙ ΑΥΤΟΙΣ Ο ΙΣ
ΝΕΓΚΑΤΑΙ ΑΠΟ Τ
ΟΨΑΡΙΩΝ ΩΝ ΕΠΙ
ΑΣΑΤΕ ΝΥΝ:
ΕΝΕΒΗ ΟΥΝ CΙΜΩΝ
ΠΕΤΡΟΣ ΚΑΙ ΕΙΛΚΥ
CΕΝ ΤΟ ΔΙΚΤΥΟΝ
ΕΙΣ ΤΗΝ ΓΗΝ ΜΕΤ
ΙΧΘΥΩΝ ΜΕΓΑΛ
ΕΚΑΤΟΝ ΠΕΝΤΗ
ΤΑ ΤΡΙΩΝ ΚΑΙ ΤΟ
ΤΩΝ ΟΝΤΩΝ ΟΥ
ΚΕΣ ΧΙΣΘΗ ΤΟ ΔΙ
ΚΤΥΟΝ ΛΕΓΕΙ ΑΥ
ΤΟΙΣ Ο ΙΣ ΔΕΥΤΕ ΑΡΙΣΤΗ
CΑΤΕ ΟΥΔΙΣ ΔΕ ΕΤΟΛ
ΜΑ ΤΩΝ ΜΑΘΗΤ
ΕΞΕΤΑΣΑΙ ΑΥΤΟΝ
ΤΙΣ ΕΙ ΕΙΔΟΤΕΣ ΟΤΙ
Ο ΚΣ ΕΣΤΙΝ ΕΡΧΕ
ΤΑΙ Ο ΙΣ ΚΑΙ ΛΑΜΒΑ
ΝΕΙ ΤΟΝ ΑΡΤΟΝ ΚΑ
ΔΙΔΩΣΙΝ ΑΥΤΟΙΣ
ΤΟ ΟΨΑΡΙΟΝ ΟΜΟΙ
ΩΣ ΤΟΥΤΟ ΔΕ ΗΔΗ
ΤΡΙΤΟΝ ΕΦΑΝΕΡΩ
ΘΗ Ο ΙΣ ΤΟΙΣ ΜΑΘΗ
ΤΑΙΣ ΕΓΕΡΘΕΙΣ ΕΚ
ΝΕΚΡΩΝ ΟΤΕ ΟΥΝ
ΗΡΙΣΤΗΣΑΝ ΛΕΓΕΙ
ΤΩ CΙΜΩΝΙ ΠΕΤ
ΔΙΣ CΙΜΩΝ ΑΓΑΠ

ΜΕ ΠΛΕΟΝ ΤΟΥΤ
ΛΕΓΕΙ ΑΥΤΩ ΝΑΙ
ΚΕ CΥ ΟΙΔΑΣ ΟΤΙ
ΦΙΛΩ ΣΕ ΛΕΓΕΙ ΑΥ
ΤΩ ΒΟΣΚΕ ΤΑ ΑΡΝΙ
ΑΜΟΥ· ΠΑΛΙΝ ΛΕ
ΓΕΙ ΑΥΤΩ CΙΜΩΝ
ΙΩΑΝΝΟΥ ΑΓΑΠΑ
ΜΕ ΛΕΓΕΙ ΑΥΤΩ ΝΑΙ
ΚΕ CΥ ΟΙΔΑΣ ΟΤΙ
ΦΙΛΩ ΣΕ ΛΕΓΕΙ ΝΕΤΑΙ
ΤΩ ΠΟΙΜΑΙΝΕ ΤΑ
ΠΡΟΒΑΤΑ ΜΟΥ· ΛΕ
ΓΕΙ ΑΥΤΩ ΤΟ ΤΡΙΤ
CΙΜΩΝ ΙΩΑΝΝ
ΦΙΛΕΙΣ ΜΕ ΕΛΥΠΗ
ΘΗ Ο ΠΕΤΡΟΣ Ο
ΤΙ ΕΙΠΕΝ ΑΥΤΩ Τ
ΤΡΙΤΟΝ ΚΑΙ ΦΙΛ
ΜΕ ΚΑΙ ΛΕΓΕΙ ΑΥ
ΤΩ ΚΕ ΠΑΝΤΑ CΥ
ΛΑΣ CΥ ΓΙΝΩΣΚ
ΟΤΙ ΦΙΛΩ ΣΕ ΚΑΙ
ΛΕΓΕΙ ΑΥΤΩ Ο ΒΟΣΚ
ΤΑ ΠΡΟΒΑΤΑ ΜΟΥ
ΑΜΗΝ ΑΜΗΝ ΛΕΓ
CΟΙ ΟΤΕ ΗΣ ΝΕΩ
ΤΕΡΟΣ ΕΖΩΝ ΝΥ
ΕΣ CΕΑΥΤΟΝ· ΚΑΙ ΠΙ
ΡΙΕΠΑΤΕΙΣ ΟΠΟΥ
ΘΕΛΕΣ ΟΤΑΝ ΔΕ ΓΗ
ΡΑΣΗΣ ΕΚΤΕΝΙΣ ΤΙ
ΧΙΡΑΣ CΟΥ ΚΑΙ ΑΛ
ΛΟΙ ΖΩΣΟΥΣΙΝ CΕ
ΚΑΙ ΠΟΙΗΣΟΥΣΙΝ
CΟΙ Ο ΚΡΟΥ ΘΕΛΕΙΣ·
ΤΟΥΤΟ ΔΕ ΕΙΠΕΝ
ΜΑΙΝΩΝ ΠΟΙΩ
ΘΑΝΑΤΩ ΔΟΞΑΣΙ
ΤΟΝ ΘΝ ΚΑΙ ΤΟΥΤ
ΕΙΠΩΝ ΛΕΓΕΙ ΑΥ
ΤΩ ΑΚΟΛΟΥΘΙ ΜΙ
ΕΠΙΣΤΡΑΦΕΙΣ ΔΕ
Ο ΠΕΤΡΟΣ ΒΛΕΠΙ
ΜΑΘΗΤΗΝ ΟΝ ΗΓΑ
ΠΑ Ο ΙΣ ΚΑΙ ΑΝΕΠΕ
CΕΝ ΕΝ ΤΩ ΔΕΙΠΝ
ΕΠΙ ΤΟ CΤΗΘΟΣ ΑΥ

ΤΟΥ ΚΑΙ ΛΕΓΕΙ ΑΥΤ
ΚΕ ΤΙΣ ΕΣΤΙΝ Ο ΠΑ
ΡΑΔΙΔΟΥΣ CΕ ΤΟΥ
ΟΥΝ ΙΔΩΝ Ο ΠΕΤΡ
ΕΙΠΕΝ ΤΩ ΙΥ ΟΥΤ
ΔΕ ΤΙ ΛΕΓΕΙ ΑΥΤΩ
Ο ΙΣ ΕΑΝ ΑΥΤΟΝ ΘΕ
ΛΩ ΜΕΝΙΝ ΕΩΣ Ε
ΧΟΜΑΙ ΤΙ ΠΡΟΣ ΣΕ
CΥ ΜΟΙ ΑΚΟΛΟΥΘΙ
ΕΞΗΛΘΕΝ ΟΥΝ ΟΥ
ΤΟΣ Ο ΛΟΓΟΣ ΕΙΣ Τ
ΑΔΕΛΦΟΥΣ ΟΤΙ Ο
ΜΑΘΗΤΗΣ ΕΚΕΙ
ΝΟΣ ΟΥΚ ΑΠΟΘΝΗ
CΚΕΙ ΟΥΚ ΕΙΠΕΝ
ΑΥΤΩΙΣ ΟΤΙ ΟΥΚ Α
ΠΟΘΝΗΣΚΕΙ ΑΛ
ΑΝ ΑΥΤΟΝ ΘΕΛΩ
ΜΕΝΙΝ ΕΩΣ ΕΡΧ
ΜΑΙ ΟΥΤΟΣ ΕΣΤΙΝ
Ο ΜΑΘΗΤΗΣ Ο ΜΑΡ
ΡΩΝ ΠΕΡΙ ΤΟΥΤΩΝ
ΚΑΙ ΓΡΑΨΑΣ ΤΑΥΤΑ
ΚΑΙ ΟΙΔΑΜΕΝ ΟΤΙ
ΑΛΗΘΗΣ ΕΣΤΙΝ Η
ΜΑΡΤΥΡΙΑ ΑΥΤΟΥ·
ΕΣΤΙΝ ΔΕ ΚΑΙ ΑΛΛΑ
ΠΟΛΛΑ Α ΕΠΟΙΗΣΕΝ
ΟΙΣ ΑΤΙΝΑ ΕΑΝ ΓΡΑ
ΦΗΤΑΙ ΚΑΘ ΕΝ ΟΥ
ΑΥΤΟΝ ΟΙΜΑΙ ΤΟΝ
ΚΟΣΜΟΝ ΧΩΡΗΣΕ
Τ ΤΑ ΓΡΑΦΟΜΕΝΑ ΒΙ
ΒΛΙΑ:

ΕΥΑΓΓΕΛΙΟΝ
ΚΑΤΑ
ΙΩΑΝΝΗΝ

Parchment, subject to buckling under temperature changes, needed a stiff, heavy cover. The bindings of parchment books were usually of wooden boards, firmly attached to the backs of the sewn leaves and fastened at the open end with clasps. The boards were usually covered with leather. As the desire to enrich the holy books grew, they began to be encrusted with engraved precious metals, carved ivory, enamels, and jewels.

Though radically different in outward form, the early codices were slow to change the internal characteristics of the scroll. The first bound books were square-shaped, to allow the same number of columns per page as normally showed in a scroll in use.

The adoption of Christianity as the official religion of Rome at the beginning of the fourth century brought a great demand for official Christian Scriptures. Complete Bibles were produced for the first time. The Emperor Constantine alone ordered fifty copies. Two magnificent manuscripts of the Greek Bible date from this period: the *Codex Vaticanus* and the *Codex Sinaiticus*. Both show the influence of the scroll: the first is written in three columns of delicate uncials to a page, the second in four columns of uncials, except for the poetic books, which are in two columns.

Codex Sinaiticus page 21

By the fifth century the codex freed itself from the scroll arrangement; the book became taller and narrower, and two columns per page were usual, although sometimes there was only one column. The half-uncial letter was developed, with its long ascenders and descenders. Paragraphs began to be marked by large letters projecting into the margin. Otherwise the writing remained continuous, without breaks between words until as late as the ninth century.

Half-uncials

The earliest surviving example of an illustrated Christian book are a few pages of the Bible, in the old version known as the Itala, ascribed to the late fourth century and now in the Berlin State Library. In style it is very like the *Vatican Virgil*, with classical figures and touches of gold outlining the drapery folds. A single page of illustration is usually made up of four compartments, separated by broad bands of red. The *Vatican Virgil* has one leaf that is similarly compartmented. Christian books were clearly patterned after pagan models in the beginning, and though other influences soon came to mix with and supplant the Hellenic style, it nevertheless remained a strongly recurrent element for centuries.

By the fourth century secular literature was in decline. Sacking and pillaging by barbarian hordes laid waste Roman cities and dispersed the reading public. The Church, after its rise to power, was no more tolerant of pagan literature than it was of pagan art and architecture. What survived of the literature was hidden away in the cloisters, from which it did not emerge for a thousand years. Books and reading altogether disappeared from the common realm and existed only under the aegis of the Church. There in the monasteries, in contrast with the outer darkness, the next millennium saw produced the most splendid books of all time.

BYZANTIUM

The books of the Middle Ages were produced in monasteries, where the monks worked day in and day out at the task of making copies of the Bible and of other sacred writings. In the scriptoria, quiet rooms set aside for this purpose, the scribes received folded vellum sheets, marked out the margins and guide lines with a stylus, then copied the text in careful letters. Some parts of the manuscript called for special distinction: the opening lines of the text, the initial letters of sections, the title and colophon. These parts, lettered in red, were called "rubrics," from the Latin *ruber*, "red"; they were filled in by a special monk, the rubricator. The pages were then sent on to other specialists for decoration and binding.

These books were not thought of as mere texts; as bearers of the Holy Word they were venerated objects themselves. The desire to clothe the holy books in splendor produced a new art of the book: the art of illumination.

Illumination differed from illustration in that its essential purpose was not to clarify or exemplify the text, but to adorn it. The illumination might consist of decorative forms only, in gold, silver, and brilliant color; or it might consist of the painted and gilded illustrations known as "miniatures." The name "miniature" only later acquired its present-day meaning; it came from the Latin *miniare*, "to paint with vermilion."

The art of illumination developed first in the Eastern part of the Roman Empire, principally at Constantinople, the old Byzantium, which Constantine had made the seat of the new Christian Church and of the Empire. Monasticism had its earliest growth there. At Constantinople, the Hellenic, the Roman, and a complex of Oriental cultures came together, and out of their confluence emerged the Byzantine style. It was not an easy partnership; the naturalistic and balanced architectonic quality of Hellenic style was the antithesis of the rhythmic, abstract, decorative Syrian-Persian style. Throughout the long Byzantine period these two elements struggled against each other, the one or the other emerging stronger for a while. But the bizarre and striking results exactly suited the needs of the Church, which was seeking to escape from its reliance on pagan models and to find an emotionally powerful expression of its own. "The main purpose of this art," says David Diringer, Professor of Linguistics at Oxford University, "was theological, liturgical and dogmatic; profoundly anti-realistic, it preferred the static, solemn presentation of mysteries to the representation of events."

The first flowering of Byzantine illumination took place in the reign of Justinian, in the sixth century, at the same time that the great jewel-like basilica of Hagia Sophia was built and the mosaics of Ravenna were made. In books, the Byzantine taste for sumptuousness expressed itself in miniatures whose rich colors were laid against gold backgrounds. The Holy Scriptures were often written in gold or silver letters on purple-dyed parchment. The bindings of these books were of ivory or precious metals, elaborately worked and inlaid with bright enamels and jewels.

The most frequently illustrated books of the Byzantine era were Gospel books. The illustrations to these books were rigidly prescribed by the Church, both as to subject and details of execution. The Church was assiduously developing its iconography—the set of images of the holy personages and events. The earliest depictions of Christ, for example, had followed the Hellenic ideal, and showed him youthful and beardless. But later influences from the powerful Syrian sector of the Church led toward a bearded and more Eastern image.

The standard subjects for miniatures in the Gospel books, particularly after the tenth century, were the four Evangelists. The pictures of the Evangelists, seated and writing, are akin to the portraits of the author that occur in such books as the *Roman Virgil* and the *Vienna Dioscorides* and are probably based on common earlier prototypes. The symbols of the Evangelists —the Ox, the Eagle, the Lion, and the Man—did not enter Byzantine iconography until the fourteenth century, although they early formed a part of the Latin iconography that was developing in the Western sector of the Empire.

The Gospels were usually preceded by Canon Tables—vertical lists of parallel references from the Gospels arranged in columns. These tables were given a particularly decorative treatment. The columns of writing were often divided with architectural columns surmounted by arches. This way of decorating Canon Tables spread to the West and was repeated with increasing elaboration over the centuries.

Rossano Codex *page 25* The *Rossano Codex* is a superb example of a Byzantine Gospel book of the fifth or sixth century, written in silver uncials on purple vellum. Fifteen of its miniatures are preserved. Only one of these is a full-page portrait of an Evangelist, Mark, and it is placed inside the book preceding his Gospel. The other fourteen miniatures are grouped at the front of the book. They represent scenes from the life and parables of Christ, which are arranged on two levels, in what might be called "vertical pairs." Some of the pairs represent two successive actions, but on most of the illustrative pages of the *Rossano Gospels* the action is confined to the upper level, and the lower is occupied by symbolic figures from the Old and New Testaments. A ground line from which the figures and background details rise makes their only separation.

The figures in the scenes of action show a dramatic immediacy that is characteristically Syrian. Background details are conventionalized and limited to what supports the action.

The portrait of the Evangelist Mark is painted in a two-dimensional style whose brilliant color patterns may well have come from mosaics. The geometric frontispiece to the Canon Tables, with four small circular portraits of the Evangelists, also suggests a source in the decorative arts. The first page of the letter from Eusebius, in Greek uncials, is surrounded by a square gold frame decorated with naturally colored flowers, doves, and ducks. The use of a decorative border around the first page of text plays an important role later on in manuscripts and early printed books.

One of the earliest Byzantine manuscripts extant is the *Cotton Genesis*, ascribed to the fifth century. Originally it had 250 miniatures, but the manuscript was all but destroyed by fire in the eighteenth century. Its style is not unlike that of the *Vatican Virgil*, with classic miniatures in frames the width of the text. Touches of gold were used in the *Vatican Virgil*; in the *Cotton Genesis* we have another early example of gold lines used to enhance the folds of draperies. The same device appears in the copy of the herbal of Dioscorides made for the daughter of the Empress Galla Placidia early in the sixth century. The Dioscorides copy is further enriched with gold backgrounds to its brilliant illustrations—a technique much employed in later manuscripts.

The *Vienna Genesis*, ascribed variously to the fourth, fifth, and sixth centuries, is in many respects similar to the *Rossano Codex*. It too is written in silver uncials on purple parchment. A consistent arrangement has been made for its miniatures to fall on the lower half of each page, and to accomplish this the text has been abridged in places. Like the separate grouping of miniatures in the *Rossano Codex*, the arrangement of the *Vienna Genesis* accords the miniatures a separate and distinct importance. The miniatures, more classical than the Rossano ones, are also arranged in the system of vertical pairs. This system is used in other Byzantine books and extends throughout the Romanesque period into Gothic manuscripts.

The seventh, eighth, and ninth centuries, periods of war, brought Byzantine art to a lower state. Iconography received a setback; the threat of an invasion by the Arabs, for whom the human image was forbidden, may have been the ultimate cause of the wave of iconoclasm that swept the Byzantine world. The representation of holy persons and events was replaced by pure decoration in books, either geometric or based on floral forms, worked into intricate interlaces and arabesques of Islamic inspiration. Byzantine painters fled to the Western part of the Roman Empire, which had remained centered around Rome and was thus rather strongly separated from the Eastern Empire.

A long period of political success lasting from the late ninth till the twelfth century brought a second high period of Byzantine art, greater than the first. The iconoclastic controversy had

Greek Lectionary of the Gospels. Byzantine, XI century. Pierpont Morgan Library, M639. 13 x 10 in.

Ο ΜΑΤΘΑΙΟΣ

✝ Τ͞Η ΕΠΑΥΡΙΟΝ Τ͞ΗΣ Η. Η ΓΟΝΗ Τ͞Α Π͞Ν͞Σ ✝

ΕΚ ΚΑ ΜΑΘ

Ε̅ιπωνο̅κ̅σ̅· ὁρᾶτε
μη καταφρονησα
τ̅ ενος τω̅ μικρ̅
τουτων· λεγω γὰρ
ὑμιν· ὅτι οἱ α̅γ̅λ̅

αυτωρ εν ο̅υ̅νο̅ις· δια
παντος μ̅β̅επουσι
το προσωπον τ̅
π̅ρ̅σ̅ μου του εν ο̅υ̅
ρανοις· ἦλθε γὰρ
ὁ υ̅ο̅ς του α̅νου̅ σω
σαι το α̅πο̅λωλο̅ς

been settled. Hellenic sources were turned to anew, and a classic breath entered illuminations. The Psalters that began to be produced for members of the aristocracy were illuminated with miniatures conceived as whole scenes within frames, grouped at the front of the book. After the long repression of the human figure, these scenes were peopled with full, naturalistic figures, animals, and details of nature that might well have been copied from Hellenic models. In the tenth-century *Paris Psalter*, for example, the scene of David playing on his harp is very likely a Christianized version of a Graeco-Roman Orpheus.

Quite different from the Aristocratic Psalters were the Monastic Psalters of Syrian origin that became popular in the tenth and eleventh centuries. They were illustrated with miniatures scattered freely in the margins around the text. The lively little scenes often contained details from daily life. For example, a page depicting, in its lower and right margins, the construction of the Temple, has a partially completed arcade with a ladder against it, leading to a super-structure with little figures busy hauling up building materials in a machine.

Greek Lectionary
page 27

By the eleventh and twelfth centuries the balance in styles had shifted again; earlier Byzantine models were reverted to, and strong fresh currents of Islamic style appeared, especially in elaborate geometric or arabesque headpieces used at the beginning of book or chapter. These decorative devices were usually square or oblong; sometimes they had pendants hanging from their lower sides, and often they were surmounted by peacocks, vases, stylized trees, or other Oriental motifs. As richly patterned as Persian rugs, they were undoubtedly influenced by the textile arts of the East.

Large gilded capitals, painted against backgrounds of pattern, were used at the beginnings of books. These were sometimes so large that a few letters occupied the whole page. Other initials were of the type called "Lombardic"—formed of the shapes of birds, beasts, limbs, or objects—some of them very humorous.

Gospels continued to be the most frequently illustrated Byzantine books and formed an important part of the treasure of the Church. Their usual illuminations were evangelical portraits and decorative headpieces; frequently they had arcaded Canon Tables. Bibles were also illustrated, and in the eleventh and twelfth centuries, liturgical calendars called *menologia*, which included the lives of the saints, were richly decorated.

The Church exercised a strict control over the inconographic scheme of miniatures. It dictated a set of prescriptions that covered every detail, down to the placement of objects, the position of bodies, and the color of hair. There was no possibility of reference to nature; prototypes were to be copied and recopied. They were not meant to suggest living beings, but, as deeply symbolic art, to represent the sacred mystery of Christianity in the same way that the liturgy did.

The rigidly imposed restrictions of Byzantine illumination, which at best produced an effect of exaltation and otherworldliness, in the long run drained it of all vitality. The tradition continued, with a brief renaissance in the fourteenth and fifteenth centuries. After Constantinople fell to the Turks in 1453, the center of Byzantine art moved to Russia, where it remained.

The West, disrupted by barbarian wars, was nevertheless receptive to the Byzantine arts from the earliest times. Byzantine architecture and mosaics alone made an overwhelming impact in Ravenna as early as the fifth century, and later in Venice (crowned by St. Mark's), Rome, and Palermo. But there were numerous other contacts as well. Monks brought Byzantine manuscripts to the West; the *Rossano Codex* is believed to have been in Italy from the sixth century on. Textiles and church objects of precious metals, carved ivory, and enamels contributed to the spread of the style. Byzantine painters and mosaic workers came to the West when the iconoclastic period made it impossible for them to work in Byzantium. Byzantine manuscript models were not only copied in Italian monasteries, and, during the reign of Charlemagne and his sons, in French and German ones as well, but the whole spirit of the many aspects of Byzantine style became so absorbed in the West as to form an inseparable part of Romanesque art.

HIBERNO-SAXON MANUSCRIPTS

From the late seventh till the early ninth century, at a time when the greater part of the Western world was vitiated by struggle and invasion, an isolated corner of the Continent produced a flowering of the arts of the book. Ireland had been off the track of both Roman and Germanic invasions. When Christian missionaries brought their faith to the island in the fifth and sixth centuries, that faith rooted strongly. Irish missionary monks spread their religious zeal to Scotland, England, and the Continent, founding monasteries where they went. In these monasteries books were produced in a new style that owed much to the pre-Christian Saxon arts of jewelry and metalworking. They were written in a round half-uncial hand developed by the monks and known as "Irish majuscule."

The earliest of these manuscripts known is the *Book of Durrow* (c. 675), a Gospel book not very large in size but with a primitive majesty in its decoration. Eleven full pages of pure ornament known as "carpet pages" are its most remarkable feature. They are in vivid colors, each different from the others. Some are filled with curved and interlaced bands, like Chinese ceremonial knots; others are in geometric patterns like those of Oriental rugs. The interlacement that is the keynote of the manuscript comes directly from Saxon metalwork and *cloisonné*. Its use of stylized animal forms comes from the same source. These Gospels have no portraits of the Evangelists; Matthew, Mark, Luke, and John are represented by enamel-like figures of the Man, the Lion, the Ox, and the Eagle. The evangelical symbols stand against plain backgrounds, but each is surrounded by a broad border of the same interlaced or geometric style that is found in the purely ornamental carpet pages. Among the interlacements are elongated animals stretched into ropelike forms that twine, knot, and bite at each other. The text in Irish majuscule flows through the manuscript, spacing out the splendor of the ornamented pages. But in the text itself initials grow, some of them very large, thrusting paisley-like whorls and scrolls into the lines of letters. The colors of the *Book of Durrow* bear out its effect of primitive vigor: brick red, yellow, and green are used against brownish black to brilliant effect.

Book of Durrow page 30

The *Lindisfarne Gospels* is the masterpiece of Northumbria, written in the late seventh or early eighth century. A much larger volume than the *Book of Durrow*, it is at once more delicate and more intricate in ornament and color. The origins of its style are more complex: the Saxon influence, with its twisted bands called "strapwork" and interlaced animal forms, is combined with a Roman influence, drawn perhaps from provincial monuments still plentiful in Britain, or from manuscripts brought by Roman missionaries. The Saxons, even in pre-Christian times, traded with the countries of the Eastern Mediterranean, and jewelry, objects of precious metal, and pottery of Eastern design contributed their share to the art that finds expression in the *Lindisfarne Gospels*. The Canon Tables, for example, which in the *Book of Durrow* are contained in neat linear boxes, in the *Lindisfarne Gospels* are framed by highly decorated columns surmounted by round arches, as they often are in Byzantine manuscripts. The portraits of the Evangelists are based on late antique models; their hard linear treatment of drapery folds and hair indicates a source in relief sculpture. The evangelical symbols that accompany them, on the other hand, have much in common with the *Durrow* animals.

The essential effect of the *Lindisfarne Gospels* is that of bejewelment. The carpet pages are finely worked in a myriad of delicate colors; gold is used for backgrounds (as it never is in Irish manuscripts of the period); the initial letters that begin each of the Gospels are increased to great size and surrounded by a scintillating aura of tiny dots of color that sometimes takes in the whole first word.

The illuminator of this manuscript is known by name: Eadfrith. The same monk wrote the text in a mixture of uncials and half-uncials with a particularly fine black ink. A solidly filled-out text page was sought in all Hiberno-Saxon manuscripts. Eadfrith achieved this by a frequent coupling of letters and by filling in short lines with various devices.

Book of Kells
pages 33 and 34

The most celebrated of all Hiberno-Saxon manuscripts is the *Book of Kells*, now, like the *Book of Durrow*, at Trinity College in Dublin. This manuscript, believed to have been written toward the end of the eighth century in Ireland, carries the effect of intricate bejewelment to the most incredible extremes of richness and minute precision. A multiplicity of designs decorates every aspect of this immense Gospel book. The range of their inspiration is immense —from Saxon ornament to Coptic manuscripts and textiles and Egyptian Cufic inscriptions. The theme that underlies the dazzling mass of colors and forms is the celebration of the Evangelists as the Four. This theme recurs throughout the Canon Tables and the Gospels with ever-fresh invention.

At the beginning of each Gospel is a massive page with a symbolic portrait of the Evangelist so stylized and so densely surrounded by decoration that figure and ornament all but merge. Facing the portrait page the Gospel begins, introduced by an initial letter that has grown so large that it takes up almost the entire page and allows for only the first two words of the Gospel. Borders sprout from the great initial and partially wrap around the page, binding its contents into one. These borders break off irrationally, ending up sometimes as an animal

Book of Kells. Hiberno-Saxon, late VIII century. Trinity College, Dublin. 12¾ x 9¼ in.

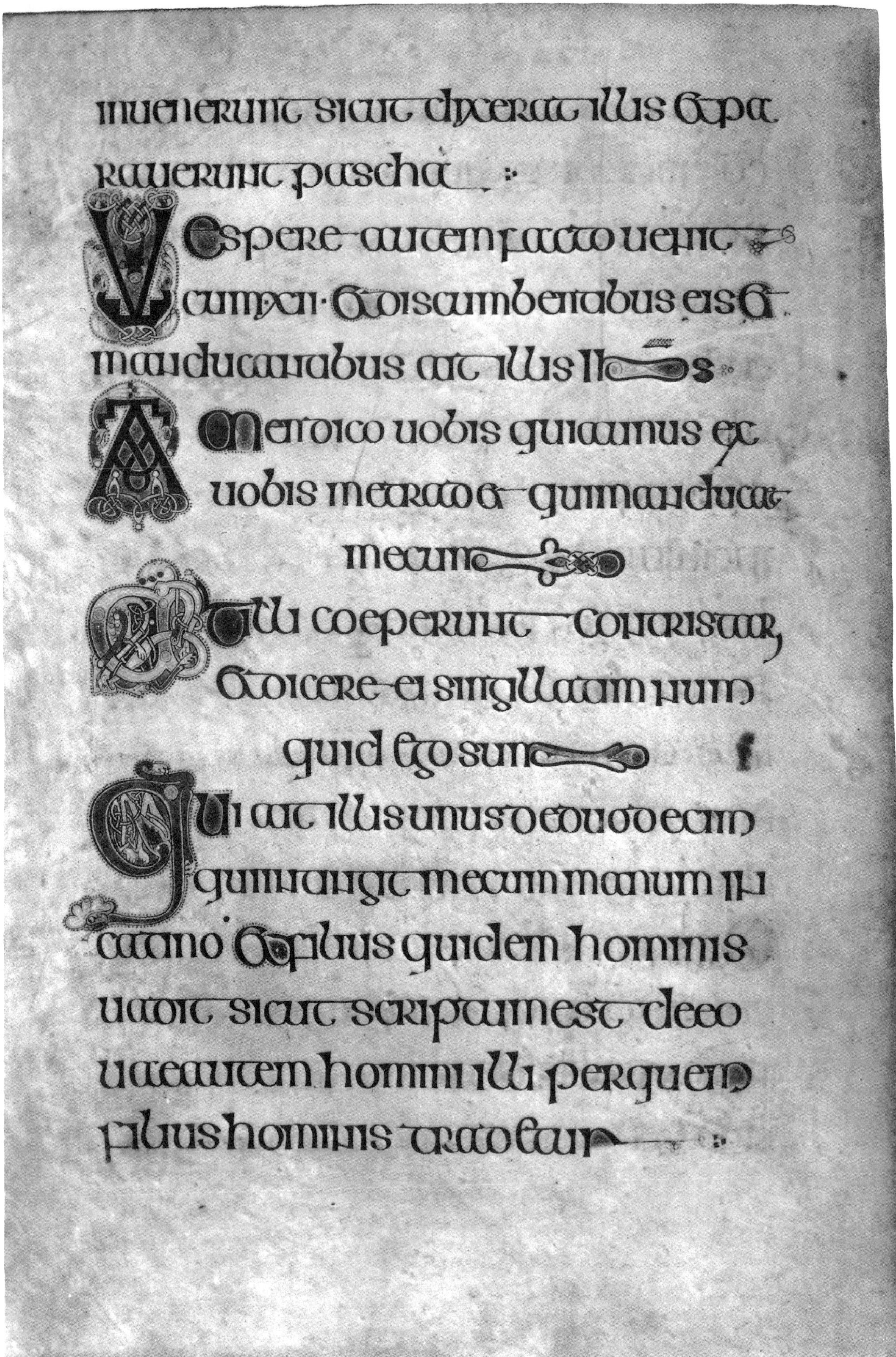

inuenerunt sicut dixerat illis & pa.

rauerunt pascha :

Vespere autem facto uenit

cum XII · & discumbentibus eis &

manducantibus ait illis IHS

Amen dico uobis quia unus ex

uobis me tradet · qui manducat

mecum

Illi coeperunt contristari

& dicere ei singillatim num

quid ego sum

Qui ait illis unus de duodecim

qui intingit mecum manum in

catino · & filius quidem hominis

uadit sicut scriptum est de eo

uae autem homini illi per quem

filius hominis tradetur :

head or leg. Every particle of space is accounted for, the negative areas between letters or designs as well as the positive forms themselves, so that the sense of the page begins to founder in the rich effect.

Of these pages, E. H. Alton, Provost of Trinity College from 1942 till 1952, wrote, "They speak of an instinct deeper than decorative art and mere ornament; they exemplify the ancient principle of esoteric mysticism, *sancta sanctis.*" These entrances to the Gospels, then, obscured by ornament, function as veils that only the initiate can penetrate.

The *Book of Kells* would be famous for its majuscules alone. Writing, known only to a few initiates in the North, partook of mystery itself. This was especially so when it embodied God's Word. A consistent evenness of letter form flows through the more than six hundred text pages. The letters are often linked, to keep the sense of flow, and they are sometimes ingeniously extended to fill out a line. Throughout they are enlivened with small brilliant ornaments and with initials that sprout whorls, limbs, heads and animal forms.

The colonnaded Canon Tables that precede the text prepare the reader for the wealth of ornament beyond. A great many carpet pages complete the ornamentation of the *Book of Kells*, their motifs running the entire gamut: systems of spirals springing from one another, animal interlacements, geometric patterns based on Roman mosaic floors or Eastern Mediterranean bookbindings.

Other important Hiberno-Saxon manuscripts were produced in Ireland, Northumbria, and the south of England, and still others at the Benedictine monasteries founded on the Continent by Irish monks, at St. Gall in Switzerland, Bobbio in Italy, and Fulda in Germany. Each had its individual character. Some went much further in the abstraction of the evangelical portraits, but none approached the richness of the *Book of Lindisfarne* and the *Book of Kells.*

Book of Kells. Hiberno-Saxon, late VIII century. Trinity College, Dublin. 12¾ x 9¼ in.

CAROLINGIAN
AND
ROMANESQUE
MANUSCRIPTS

The dissolution of the Roman Empire and the division of Western Europe among rival Germanic tribes brought Western culture to an ebb. But even during the Dark Ages some books were produced by the Christianized tribes. The Roman scripts, like the Roman language, began to develop strong local idiosyncracies. In France, the Merovingian hand became compressed and contorted, full of ligatures and contractions. The Visigothic hand in Spain and the Lombardic in Italy went their own divergent ways. The books produced at this time represented a low stage of art. The crabbed texts were generally decorated only by initials in bright colors, mostly formed of twisted birds, beasts, and serpents. These initials, known as Lombardic, are similar to initials that appear two centuries later in Byzantine books and are assumed to have a common origin.

When in 768 Charlemagne became king of the Franks, the destiny of Western Europe took a new turn. The ambition of this warrior and statesman was a renaissance of the Roman Empire. Politically, he acted out this ambition by the series of conquests that culminated, in the year 800, in his being crowned Emperor of the West. Culturally, he sought a return to the high civilization of the past by importing books and scholars to his court at Aix-la-Chapelle, and by establishing schools and monasteries throughout his empire. He brought the scholar Alcuin from his Northumbrian monastery to organize the educational system and to oversee the rewriting of the church books and the ancient classics in a clear form. A standard script was developed: a miniscule in which each letter was fully formed and separated from the others. Roman majuscules or uncials were used for titles and other such purposes. The Carolingian script, spread by the monasteries, became the standard book hand of Western Europe for the next three centuries. After submergence for two centuries during the Gothic period, it was revived by the Italian Renaissance to become the humanistic script and finally the basis of roman type.

Pliny,
Historia naturalis
page 39

The most striking books produced under Charlemagne's reign and that of his immediate successors were devotional books written for the royal family. Full of a heavy, Byzantine splendor, they were written in gold letters on purple vellum and ornamented with large initials in the Hiberno-Saxon tradition. The Gospel book made for Charlemagne and his wife around

Gospel Book
of Charlemagne
page 36

Gospel Book of Charlemagne. Carolingian, late VIII century. Bibliothèque Nationale, Ms. lat. 1203. 12½ x 8½ in.

781 is written in golden uncials, but a poem at the end is in Carolingian miniscules—one of the earliest examples of the new script. Its full-page illuminations against gold backgrounds are grouped on facing pages at the front of the book, as they were in the Byzantine *Rossano Gospels*. They include portraits of the Evangelists accompanied by their symbolic beasts, Christ in Glory, and also one of the subjects newly introduced in the Carolingian era: the Fountain of Life, markedly Syrian in origin, with its curious little roofed colonnade and the peacocks and drinking stags that surround it.

Charlemagne's son, Louis the Pious, had a Gospel book made for him in which the portrait of each Evangelist appears at the beginning of his Gospel. The Canon Tables at the front of the book are decorated with columns bridged by half-round arches, the tympanum above them filled in with a biblical scene.

*Vivian Bible
page 40*

The sons of Louis had other fine books made for them: Lothair, a Gospel book bearing his portrait, and Charles the Bald, two Bibles that are among the earliest complete illustrated Bibles to survive. One of Charles's Bibles known as the "Vivian" Bible was probably made at Tours at the beginning of the ninth century under the care of Alcuin, and later presented by the Abbot Vivian to his king. It contains a full-page miniature that shows Vivian and the monks and canons of St. Martin de Tours offering homage to Charles the Bald. Some of the illustrations of the biblical text are on full pages divided into two or three lateral strips; along these the friezelike illuminations depict successive scenes of action that must derive from the picture cycles of earlier scrolls. An unusually gay full-page miniature that shows King David with his harp, surrounded by fellow-psalmists, bears out the classical inspiration of the illustrations.

Charlemagne's ideal may have been a return to classical forms, but other current influences were bound to have their effect. Several Carolingian schools developed, some more influenced by Byzantine models, some by Graeco-Roman models, others by the approach of Hiberno-Saxon art. At Metz a beautiful manuscript, the *Sacramentary of Bishop Drogon*, was produced with ornamental initials grown over by tendrils of foliage; many of the initials enclosed a little biblical scene. Initials containing scenes, known as "historiated" initials, occur in a few other early examples. They later played an important role in book decoration.

At Rheims the *Utrecht Psalter* was illuminated in a new style that had a more immediate and profound effect on Northwestern Europe. The sketchy pen-and-ink drawings, uncolored and purely illustrative, make no attempt at decoration. They move about—little crowds of people, groups busy in action—against a background of windswept barren hills, with an occasional detail of architecture or tuft of tree. The hallmark of the style is the quality of windy motion—blown draperies, gesticulating hands and feet—which gives it a sort of excited gaiety. Though the *Utrecht Psalter* appeared to be entirely new against the static, gilded style of the

PLINY, *Historia naturalis*. Carolingian, IX century. Pierpont Morgan Library, M871. 13½ x 10¼ in.

Mundum et hoc quod cumque
nomine alio caelum appellare libuit
cuius circumflexu degunt cuncta
nomen esse par credi par est aeternum himen
sum · neq; genitum neq; interiturum umqua ·
huius extera indagare · nec interest hominum
nec capit humanae coniectura mentis · sacer est
aeternus himensus totus in toto · immo uero ipse
totum infinitus ac finito similis omnium reru
certus est insimilis incertus est extra cuncta
complexus intse idemq; rerum naturae opus
& rerum ipsa natura furor est · mensuram eius
animo quosdam agitasse · atq; prodere ausos
alios rursus occasione hic sumpta aut bis data
innumerabiliter tot didisse mundo · ut totide
rerum naturas credi oporteret · aut si una
omnes incubaret · totidem tamen soles · toti
demq; lunas · & cetera etiam in uno & inmensa
& innumerabilia sidera · quasi non eaedem quaes
tiones semper inter mino cogitationis occursura
& siderio finis alicuius aut si hoc infinitas naturae
omnium artifici possit adsignari · Non idem illud
in uno facilius sit intellegi; tanto praesertim opere
furor est · profecto furor egredi ex eo · & tamqua
interna eius cuncta plana iam notas int · ita ex
cruciari extera · quasi uero mensuram ullius rei

possit agere qui sui nesciat · aut mens or hominis
uidere quem mundus ipse non capiat · Formam eius
in speciem orbis absoluti globatam esse · nomen in
primis & consensus in eo mortalium orbem appel
lantium · sed & argumenta rerum docent · Non
solum quia talis figura omnib; sui partib; uergit
in sese · ac si ipsa tolerandast seq; includit & con
tinet · nullarum egens compagum · nec finem
aut initium ullis sui partibus sentiens · nequi ad mo
tum quos ub inde uert mox apparebit talis aptis
sima est · sed oculorum quoq; probationem quod
conuexus mediusq; quacunq; cernatur · cum id

accidere in alia non possit figura ·

Hanc ergo formam eius aeterno & inrequieto ·
ambitu inenarrabili celeritate xxiiii horarum
spatio circumagi solus ex ortus & occasus ·
haud dubium relinquere an sit himensus ·
et ideo sensum aurium excedens ante molis
rotatae uis tagine adsidua sonitus · non qui
dem facile dixerim · non hercule magis ·
quam circum actorum simul tinnitus sideru
suosq; uoluentium orbis · And ulcis quidam
& incredibili suauitate conceptus · nobis qui
intus agimus · iuxta dieb; noctibusq; tacitur
labitur mundus esse innumeras ei effigies ·
animalium rerumq; cunctarum inpressas ·
nec ut in uolucrum notamus ouis · leuitate
continua lubricum corpus quod dixi uti simul
auctores dixere teneru · argumentis iudicat ·
Qm inde deciduis rerum omnium seminibus ·
innumeris in mari praecipue ac plerumq; ·
confusis monstrifice gignantur effigies ·
praeterea uisus probatione · alibi ut restauri alibi ·
alibi litterae figurae candidior · medio per uer
ticem circulo · & quidem consensu gentium ·

Immo ueron amq; & graeci nomine ornamenti
appellauere · cum & nos a perfecta absoluta
q; elegantia · mundum caelum quidem haud
dubie celati argumento diximus · ut inter
pretatur · in uarrone · adiuuat rerum ordo
discripto circulo · qui signifer uocatur · in
duodecim animalium effigie · sed per illae
solis cursu congruens tot scit ratio ·

Nec de elementis uideo dubitari · iiii esse · ignuum
summo · inde tot stellarum illos tot con lucen
tium oculos · proximum spiritus · quem greci
nostriq; eodem uocabulo aera appellant · uita
lem · hunc & per cuncta rerum me abilem
totoq; confertum; huius ui suspensam cum
quarto aquarum elementa librari medio ·

day, in actuality it harked back to some early classical manuscript—a fact attested to by its text in Roman rustic capitals, arranged three columns to a page.

The monastery of St. Denis, founded by Charles the Bald, had the greatest monastic library in France in the ninth century. The books produced there reflected all of the Carolingian schools, combining classic forms with Celtic intials and the mannerisms of the Rheims school.

The high period of the Carolingian manuscript approached its end with the split of Charlemagne's Empire at the end of the ninth century. The splendid, austere books associated with the pomp of the Carolingian court were no longer made. New tribal invasions reduced all the aspects of civilization, including the production of books. When a revival finally took place, it was in the Carolingian monasteries in the Germanic Eastern half of the old Empire. The Pope decreed this land the new Holy Roman Empire in 962, under Otto I.

The Ottonian era produced rather stiff and solid manuscripts. They were illuminated with darkly serious figures of Byzantine inspiration, which often had a peculiar intensity of expression and action. As in earlier Carolingian manuscripts, the miniatures usually occupied a separate page. Sometimes they were arranged in pairs of scenes one above the other in a single frame, and often the action broke through from one level to the other. The backgrounds of the miniatures made no attempt at realism; they contained what was useful in furthering or explaining the action or were filled in with purely decorative repeat patterns. *Lectionary page 44*

Initial letters made of tightly interlaced strapwork were characteristic decorations in Ottonian manuscripts. The tendency toward closely woven initials produced dense monogram pages for the initial pages of the Gospels.

Northern Italy was closely connected with Germany at this time, and its manuscripts had German characteristics. France and England were still under the influence of the gay linear style of Rheims. England, which was experiencing a revival of monastic activity, produced especially fine manuscripts, slowly adding subtle color to the drawings and inventions of her own. The most notable of these was a type of border formed of a bright, straight frame, from which foliage sprang with naturalistic vigor. Toward the end of the tenth century the drawing of the Anglo-Saxon Winchester school surpassed that of the Continent. *Latin Gospels pages 42 and 43*

The name "Romanesque" is loosely applied to a variety of artistic styles found in the Western world from the sixth century until the thirteenth. It is the art of an essentially feudal and rural era, when all intellectual life was in the hands of the monasteries, and men's eyes were fixed on salvation. About the year 1000 sweeping changes were beginning to take place. Populations were increasing, communications were reopened, trade grew wider. Towns were beginning to be established and in them an entirely new sort of life. But men's deepest tenets are slow to change, and the simple piety of the past lived on for a while.

Vivian Bible. Carolingian, before 851. Bibliothèque Nationale, Ms. lat. 1. 19¼ x 14¾ in.
Latin Gospels. English, XI century. Pierpont Morgan Library, M709. 11½ x 7½ in. →

LIBER GENE RATIO NIS IHV

XPI FILII DAVID
FILII ABRAHAM

pax hominibus· bonɛ uolun
tatis·

44

The spiritual and material strength of the monasteries was high in the eleventh and twelfth centuries. Abbeys and abbey churches were being built in a massive style based on the round Roman arch and barrel vault. For more than five hundred years there had been little large-scale building and almost no monumental sculpture. The sculptors employed to embellish the new edifices looked to manuscripts for decorative devices and storytelling images.

The Romanesque art found on the curved lintels and capitals of the abbeys and in the manuscripts of the time shows a fusion of the linear Anglo-French style with the more solid Germanic forms. The series of Crusades launched in 1096 brought fresh Islamic influences to mingle with these.

The huge illustrated Bibles produced during the twelfth century in England, France, the Netherlands, Germany, and Italy express the strength, dogmatism, and internationalism of the era. England, which had recovered from the Norman conquest, produced the most splendid of them all: the Winchester Bible. It was illuminated with compartmented full-page illustrations embodying several scenes at once, drawn in outline and filled in with deep color. Made by more than one hand, some of the illuminations show a Byzantine tendency, others the Anglo-French tradition inherited from Rheims. The cycle of Bible pictures authorized by the Church had been enlarged to include such subjects as the Last Judgment, the Tree of Jesse, and scenes from the lives of the saints. It also included a new dogmatic instrument which remained a central preoccupation of manuscripts for a long time—parallel scenes from the Old and New Testaments.

Besides its full-page miniatures, the Winchester Bible has immense initials elaborated with interlaces and foliage motifs, and terminated in grotesque or animal heads. These initials extend the full depth of the page, almost twenty inches. Within the loops and spaces of the letters are figures or scenes from the Bible. Historiated initials, first known in early Carolingian manuscripts, were destined to play a highly important role in Gothic and Renaissance manuscript illumination, and to persist for centuries in the printed book.

GOTHIC
MANUSCRIPTS

In the course of the twelfth century the Gothic style evolved in architecture. The surge of energy, at once spiritual and worldly, that led to the building of Chartres and Notre Dame brought the illuminated book to its greatest heights.

The book had been related to architecture in the past: The solid forms of Romanesque architecture had their counterpart in the manuscripts of the period, which displayed the same tendency to massiveness and concentrated decoration. The round arch that supported the vaults of the church enclosed Canon Tables and miniatures, or appeared in depicted architectural details. Iconographic and decorative forms were alike in sculpture and illumination.

The Gothic book reflected Gothic architecture even more. The pervading architectural principles of unification, of lightness and soaring height, were expressed in manuscripts by a smaller, more graceful format, and by a close unification of text and illumination. The separate full-page miniature all but disappeared for a while, and the historiated initial letter took over the function of illuminating the text, at once penetrating it and surrounding it with bars and appendages. The letter forms themselves became narrow and broken, reflecting the Gothic arch; their even, close-woven texture gave them the name "textura." Details of Gothic architecture were made part of the illuminations, which were often set inside a Gothic arch or niche, or even framed inside a little cathedral form. Sometimes the page was compartmented into a number of vaulted "rooms" in each of which a separate scene was taking place. Illuminations were painted in the jewel-like colors of stained-glass windows and made more gleaming still with burnished gold. *Psalter page 46*

An indirect contribution of Gothic architecture to the art of the book was that its diminished wall space left little opportunity for mural painting and thus made illumination the most important function open to the painter.

France, which brought into being the Gothic cathedral, also developed the Gothic style in manuscripts and gave it its fullest realization. In the mid-thirteenth century—the time of Saint Louis and of the founding of the Sorbonne—France took over from England the leadership in manuscript production. The historiated initial had been a central Anglo-French ornament for the past century; its descending bar, extended in branchwork and leaves, enlivened

Histoire
de Saint Louis
page 54

with dragons, animals, birds, and droll little perched figures, gradually crept farther around the page. By the end of the fourteenth century a complete ivy border depended from the initial. By the fifteenth century the border had freed itself from the initial and become an independent entity.

Old Testament
page 49

Bibles and Psalters were still the most frequently illuminated books in the thirteenth century. The "moralized Bible" was newly popular. In it, scenes from the Scriptures were paralleled by symbolic applications to point up a moral. These books were richly illuminated on every page with series of roundels containing small scenes, set into a patterned and gilded background—an effect clearly derived from stained-glass windows.

The story of the Apocalypse, in the Commentary of the eighth-century Spanish monk Beatus, was a favorite from the eleventh century on, accompanied by illustrations showing the many-headed beast, the descent of the angels with their trumpets and vials of calamity, and other bizarre and colorful aspects of the immense catastrophe. In Spain, under the influence of Moslem art, and in France at St. Sever, near the Spanish border, the most striking Apocalypse manuscripts were produced, darkly mysterious in all their brilliant color.

A group of illustrated popular religious books appeared in Germany and the Netherlands in the fourteenth century, with such titles as *Biblia pauperum* and *Speculum humanae salvationis*. A central theme of theirs was the "harmonization" of the Old and New Testaments through the presentation of parallel episodes in pictorial form.

Roman de
Lancelot du Lac
page 53

Liber Floridus
pages 50 and 51

Secular reading increased considerably. From the thirteenth century on, monasteries were no longer the only patrons of books; the nobility and even wealthy merchants began to collect libraries. New types of literature became popular. Stories such as the *Roman de Lancelot du Lac* and *Tristan und Isolde* appeared in illuminated manuscripts written in the vernacular. Encyclopedias or compendia of knowledge began to be made, such as the *Liber Floridus*, compiled by the monk Lambertus in the twelfth century from various earlier sources, and preserving ancient characteristics in its illustrations.

Books of history were prepared for royal patrons. The monks of St. Denis wrote the *Grandes chroniques de France* for King Charles V in the second half of the fourteenth century. A history of Alexander the Great was prepared for the court of Burgundy. In these medieval history books, historical accuracy in illustration was completely ignored. Alexander appears in Burgundian armor before a group of tents from a contemporary scene of battle, and the mother and wives of Darius are presented to him in the latest fashions of the court.

Among scholars, from the eleventh and twelfth centuries on, interest grew in the writings of Greece, Byzantium, and Islam. An attempt was made to reconcile this newly gained pagan knowledge with the theological tenets that until then governed all intellectual life.

The monasteries, no longer the only patrons of books, ceased also to be the only producers of

Old Testament. French, XIII century. Pierpont Morgan Library, M638. 15¼ x 11¾ in.
Liber Floridus, French, XIII century. Bibliothèque Nationale, Ms. lat. 8865. 14 x 10¼ in. →

valr rex Jerlm, audita fama Josue, regens sibi et regno suo, cum quatuor alijs regibus comunit. et ante

joi aggredif Sabaon cuntate qa cum Josue fedus freat. Gabonite aut imploraint auxilium Josue ob

los quinq reges qui uenies ei excitu magn pho co uicit. et umes ne nox supueies uictori i ipediret igni a fiducia

ixepit soli et lune ut starent. et stetert nec unqua tam longa dies fuit. obediente dro homini uoci

Ualiter interfectis fere omnibus de exercitu regum. cum iam nunciatum esset Josue reges ipsos quinq latitare in spelunca. fecit eos inde extrabi et jcepit principibus Israel ut eorum colla pedibus conculcarent:~

creatione. Opacio diuina q̃ sc̃a creauit ⁊ gubnat quadrifozmi ratõe distingũ. pzimo q̃d h̃ in illo dĩ dispensatõne n̄ fc̃a
ſ; et̃a ſuit qui nos apl̃o teſte ante tēpa ſc̃laria p̃deſtinauit in regnũ. Sc̃o q̃d in mat̃ia pariť elemẽta ĩdi ſc̃a ſc̃
uit qui mat̃ ſecinum creauit ꝯ̃ ſimul. Tercio: q̃ eadem mat̃ia ſc̃dm cauſas ſimul creatas. n̄ iam ſimul ſʒ diſtinctè
ſex pzimoz dierum in celeſtem ĉreſteʒq; fo̷rmatõnem fꝯaťur. Qito: q̃ ex eiuſdem creature ſeminub; ⁊ pzimoꝛdijs ab
his cauſis tocius ſc̃li tēpus natali curſu pagiť. ubi pat̃ uſq; nc̃ opaťur ⁊ fili̅ſ n̄ ⁊ coꝛuos paſcit ⁊ lilia ueſtit.

Aquarius in ianuario cu-
ius nox habet hoꝛas xvi.
Dies uo. viij. Januarius a
iano idolo nomen accepit
ut ab eo q̃ ſit ianni ianua
hoc eſt pzincipiũ.

Capricoꝛnus i decenbri cuius nox hoꝛas h̃t xviij. dies
u. vi. Decemb a numero nomen accepit eo q̃ decim̃ ſit in
uerſu a matio. hic ap̃ ma-
cedones i pzincipio ãn poniť.

Sagittarius in nouẽbri cui-
nox hoꝛas habet xvij. dies
uero. vi. Nouember autē
pzopterea diciť: eo quod
nouus ĩ imber ſit a mat-
tio.

Scoꝛpius in octobꝛi cuius
nox hoꝛas h̃t xiiij. dies u
x. October a numero nom̃
accepit: eo quod octauus ſit
imber a matio. ideſt ap̃
oꝛientales.

Piſces ı februario cui
nox hoꝛas h̃t xiiij. dies
iij. februaria a februo idolo nom̃ accepit. l'a febri-
h̃ ea fꝛigoꝛe. pp̃ fꝛigidũ tp̃s
ipius menſis.

Libra in ſeptembri ci-
uis nox h̃t hoꝛas. xij
dies u. xij. ſeptẽb a nõ
nom̃ accep. eo q̃ ſepti-
mũ ymb̃ ſit a matio. q̃
miſis ap̃ romanos. i. fiut.

Aries ı matio cui nox
h̃t hoꝛas. xij. dies u. xij.
a matte part ro-
muli nom̃ accep̃ q̃ pzo-
mul pzim̃ mẽſem ap̃
romanos ꝯſtituit.

Virgo i augſto c̃ nox
hoꝛas h̃t x. dies u. xiiij.
auguſtus a ĉeſaĩe auguſto
nom̃ accepit eo q̃ kl'ãs
augti iniat ãtonui̅. n̄
antea uocabř ſextil'.

Taurus ı apꝛili cui nox
hoꝛas h̃t x. dies uero xiiij.
Apꝛilis a uenere nom̃ accepit
affron de ſpuma. un̄ uenus
oꝛta creditur. l'ab apiendo ſe-
nitate fugatis nubib;.

Gemini in maio cuius nox
hoꝛas h̃t viij. dies uo. xvi.
Maius a maia matre mer-
curij nom̃ accepit. l'a maioꝛ
maioꝛub; quoꝛ ꝯſilioꝛes pu-
blica augebatur.

Cancer ı iunio cuius nox
hoꝛas h̃t vi. dies uo. xviij.
Junius a iunone filia ſatur-
ni dictus eſt: ul a iunio bru-
to pzimo & romanoꝛuṃ
conſul e.

Leo ı iulio c̃ nox hoꝛas h̃t
viij. dies u. xvi. Julius a
iulio ceſare nomen accep.
quia octauo idus iulij ceſar
creatus ẽ. nam antea uoca-
batur quintilis.

De oꝛdine ⁊ poſit̃õe ſignoꝛ.

Polus diciť maioꝛ h̃t ſtellas in capite vij. ſingulas huius ſingulas. i armo. i. i pectoꝛe. i. i pede
poſt claras. ij. ı ſuma cauda. i. i uentre clara. i. i ſetute po-
ſterioꝛ. ij. ı extimo pede. ij. i cauda. iij. fiut uiginti due.
E noſtra arctus minoꝛ h̃t ſtellas i utno late iiij.
claras i qdꝛo poſitas ı cauda claras. iij. ſub his
polus apparet circa q̃ ſidus tocius oꝛbis uti putať.
Serpens q̃ int̃ arctuos media iacet h̃t ſtellas v. in
capite claras ⁊ in toto coꝛe decem.

Hercules h̃t ſtellas ı capite i. ı
bꝛachio i. ı humis ſingulis claras.
i cubito ſiniſtro i. ı manu i. in
utroq; ilib; idʒ ı femoꝛe ij. i pede
ſub dextram manũ idʒ ı pelle leonis iiij. fiut xiij.

Iouis. Saturnus. sol. is.
Septem planete.
Lucifer. luna. mercurius.

Vrsa maior. Serpens. Vrsa minor.
polus sub cauda urse minoris.

stella leonis. Hercules.

50

Corona hr stellas viij. in orbe positas qñ quatuor clare contra caput serpentis septentrionalis.

Boetes auth'ophilax hr stellas in dextera manu iiij. que ñ occidunt. in capite i. in singlis humis i mamill' sigla i dextro cubito i. in genua i. in singlis pedibz singlas. Boetes post tgum urse maioris uersis pedibz ad uirginem uidetur.

Serpentarius sub h'cule posit' e. Serpentari' in capite i. in singlis pedibz i humis i. i sinistra manu iiij. in dextra iiij. i cubitis singlis. i genibz singlas. i crure i. i tibiis i. oms clare. Serpens i ore ij. i capite iiij. uidz ad manus se tenentes. i flexu corporis xv.

Scorpione calcat serpentarius.

Scorpius hr stellas in singlis cornibz ij. i fronte iij. claras. in dorso iiij. i uentre iiij. in cauda v. in aculeo ij. fiut xxij. i spaciu duor signor partitus.

Virgo hr stellam i capite obscura i. i singlis humis singlas. i sinistra ala i. i singlis cubitis singlas. in singlis manibz singlas. sz i sinistra clariore q uocatur spica. i tunica obscuras vi. i singlis pedibz singlas. suma xviij.

virgo sub pedibus boetis e contam priores pedes urse maioris.

Leo hr stellas in capite iij. i collo ij. i pectore i. i spina

in cauda media i. i summitate caude i. claras sub uentre i. sub pectore ij. i pedibz pon bz claram i. in me dietate uentris i. i tlibz i. in postiori genu i. Summa xvij. uidz i alia ad cauda et vij.

Cancer hr stellas i pec tre ij. qs appellant asinos int qs e nubicula candidi coloris q presepiu appellat. in dextris uertisz pedibz iiij. obscure. in sinistra pede petori ij. i sed'. ij. i trio una. i q̃rto i. in dextro corniu ij. i sinist' ij. summa xxvij.

Co uir cru uirginem occiret e uxor boeten.

Canc uixta geminos posit' e. h'is in dorso presepiu.

Geminor uniũ qui uixta cancru e hr stellam i capite i. claram. i singlis humis singlas cla ras. i dextro pede i. i singlis getibz singlas. in pedibz singlis sex gulas. Alt' hr ca pite i. i mamillis singulas. in sinistro cubito ij. i manu i. i sinistro getu i. in pedibz singulas. uixta sinistru pedem i. que uocatur pps. Summa xviij. Gemini h'ut ã leuo latere agitatorem.

Agitator comitaturi sinistru tangit.

Taur' hr stellas in u troq cornu i. uidz octo i. i naso i. h'et v. h'iades uocat. i ungla iiij. i collo iij. i dorso iij. sub uentre i. i pectore i.

Taurus orione tangat qñ sub illo e situs.

Sut xxvij. stel le athalautides ul pliates i cau da tauri posite. sed septima obsca e.

Orion hr stellas i capite iij. claras. in singlis humis singlas claras. i dex cubito i. obscura. i dextra manu i. in balteo iij. i ech'indicu iij. claras. i getibz sigtas. i pedibz singlas. fiut xvij.

Orion sub tauro e.

them. Outside artisans had always been called into the monastic scriptoria for needed specialties. In the middle of the twelfth century, with the decline of monastic power, book production began to pass into the hands of lay craftsmen altogether. Even when books of a religious nature were ordered, the more worldly interests of the lay artists expressed themselves. Religious figures that in earlier times had been portrayed as elderly or ascetic began to have a youthful charm and to assume more human attitudes. Little details or scenes from daily life found their way into the illuminations—a circumstance not surprising in view of the prevalent belief that all that had been created by God was worthy. But the delicate balance between the spiritual and the temporal could not be maintained long, and the scales were tipping slowly in the direction of the temporal.

In the second half of the fourteenth century and the first half of the fifteenth, wealthy and noble patrons commissioned books of devotion for themselves—Psalters and the newly-desired Books of Hours—which brought the illuminated manuscript to its very height in France. The Psalter had been, since the ninth century, the personal prayer book of faithful Christians. The Book of Hours grew out of a group of prayers and litanies that began to be added to the Psalter. The exact composition of a Book of Hours might vary somewhat according to personal preference or usage, as would the illuminations that were lavished on them, but they had the same general content.

Of the many noble patrons of books, the Duc de Berry, in particular, amassed a library of volumes that surpassed even that of his book-loving brother, King Charles V. Among his illuminated books were the *Livre des Merveilles,* an account of travels in the Orient; the works of Guillaume de Machaut; and the plays of Terence. He is best known, however, for the devotional books that were made for him. The makers of these books were among the finest artists of the time, brought chiefly from Flanders. They painted for Berry a Psalter and the *Grandes heures,* the *Petites heures,* the *Belles heures* and the *Très riches heures.* The range of approach, technique and ornament in these books is immense. The Duc had a taste for both richness and cool perfection.

Belles heures of the Duc de Berry page 55

In the *Très riches heures,* begun for the Duc de Berry at the end of his life and finished after his death in 1416, the illuminators, the Limbourg brothers, made a great step in the direction of realism. In the calendar section they portrayed the activities of the months against realistically detailed backgrounds that showed interior scenes of the Duc's palaces or views of the towns and chateaux that belonged to him. The customs of both peasant and courtly life are depicted: peasants plowing the fields and tending the vines near one of the Duke's vast castles, or a noble cortege riding past another castle deep in forests.

In the late fourteenth and the fifteenth centuries exquisite Books of Hours were made for other members of the nobility—the *Bedford Hours,* the *Laval Hours,* the *Rohan Hours* among the

Roman de Lancelot du Lac. French, XIV century. Pierpont Morgan Library, M805-7. 13¼ x 10 in.

celle fay que uos me deuez
li dame tant il bien uos
dizpul me uenit dire Da
me ce estes uos Je fui elle fiuoz
ne peocliaster uos une letiun la
cele que ma pucelle uous porta
ie ci ie metloie tuit hors dou
mandement Dame le fil s'elles
ce que ie dui Et fui us sirge ce
que ie pos Or me dittes le ciholz
z les prouedez que uos auez fautz
s cui lez tentes uos Dame fait
il s'uos comeut fait elle ame
me uos dou tant z dit me faut
celle amoz Dame fait il de que
ie fui primesapelles chlr z
ne le estoie me J ces parler tui
touth la dame de malohaut acu
ciaut Et le ua la teste quelle a
noir embzuncha ue Et cil uent di
tautout car maistez fui lauote
aie Et il la reigard fi la couuen
si bit ceil dolez z ceil anguist

Et il s'eltoice plus quil pue de p
ler Dame le tor que ie uos ai dit
comeut fui ce dont fait elle Da
me fait il uos feutez de moi ui
ami tu uit bouche ne me uit
montant fait elle z qui t
Dame qui ie ai pzant congie
a mon signor le Roy Artu
ie uing deuant uous z ie estoie
tout armez fozs dou chuef z de
mains si uous comanday adieu
z dique ie estoie uil chlr en
quel que fui que ie fuil z s
dutter que uit ami z uos elsir
uoiez uit bien que ie fuil z
ie di dame guc micl z plui apar
dame adieu uos çmant z uos
ditte adieu biau douz amis
onquez puil li uos dou euer ne
ne me puit iffir Qfti limot q
preudome me fera se ie fui mil
long ue me nt se onquez puil
ne fui au gnt meich rez que sa

for le duc Et uitz peuser ne
fu mie uilanu Jluis fu douz de
bonauez z u oz euest bit auenu
qui preudome uoul el faire et
ns fault la coutume ne ilt me
celle amaut chlr qui fuit eu
ceudaire manieze chose amat
tez danes doue uit soz est petit
bzef euez z uos tremblant une in
uultre que uos auez une de cez
dames la plui que uos ne faute
moi car uos auez plore ue de
pzun uitez uos uit reigard uerr
elle adcuez si uoz bit que le bzef
peuser ne ilt me si amoz çme
uos fautez le semblant Et par
la fay que uos me dtez la quele
ilt ce que uos auez tait Hai da
me s dien mei çluit mait dtz
nulle delles u a mon euez cede na
meth fait la Ronne uos ne uie
poez rienz embler car ia uout
maistez chose uncelez Et ie çnoit

tilton euer que il ne pooit respou
dire a ce que la Ronne disoit si qil
ca alonsinpzer uilt durement
z lez lez mez li coule ut contreual
lez uols si que li haims quil auo
te uestit euts tout mouillez Et q
plui reigardeut la dame de malo
haut z plui eltout amalaise
De cette chose se pziut gar
de la Ronne Et uit quil res
garde uilt pzoim met les dames
uitez moi fait elle dont elle a
amee mene que ie uoul de mat

cel mot ne me souueut euls ui
mor ma conforte eutout mes a
mui euls erazt ma conl mes maui
gari euls moz ma coul amui
fait oublier euls mai ma saoute
eucutes mez faius euls moi ma
fait Riche eucutez mez poure
tez par foi fait la Ronne euls moz
fu dit de boue euze Et dtz çune
loure z qui si dire le me fait
gare ie uelpziut pasi acertez ce
çme uos feutes Et amaut chlr
luge dir on ne penst onquer

bien bit euer qui est la plui ql
ueit ci Et dez seit elle por uoir
quelle le puet mettre amalaise
car elle cuidoit bien sauoir qil
ne pensoit dames selli non
jamar eust il fait s gla uirier
dit uouez ar mez Maselle se
dltiout eusa malice uenir z cel
fu si anguiseus que par i pau
quil ne se pasine Et la Ronne le
pziut par la chemize quil ne
cheut z apella fisal z il fuit
ment deuant li si uoit que ses

Son bon
seigneur
loois fil3
du roy de
fraunce, par la grace de
dieu roy de nauane,
de champaigne et de bri
e conte palazin. Jehan
sur de ioinuille son se
neschal de champaigne.
Salut et amour, et .i.

lonneur, et son sentl
se appareille. Chier sur
re uus ssoit a sauoir
que ma dame la roy
ne uostre mere qui .i.
moult mamoit a cau
dieu bone merci face:
me pria si a certes co
me elle pot que ie li fe
isse faur .i. luure des sai
tes paroles, et des bons

Sapp= A. n° 2016

JOINVILLE, *Histoire de Saint Louis*. French, XIV century. Bibliothèque Nationale, Ms. 13568
Belles heures of Jean, Duc de Berry. French, XV century. Metropolitan Museum, Cloisters

Celauitq̃ se ranam donec uidic angelos ro
tas cũ tanco impetu diuelleret q̃. iiij. milia
gentiluũ mortua cecidenunt unde statim se
manifestat qui eam statim decolari iubet.

finest of them. All of these books are characterized by a perfection of finish and a working-together of the parts: the miniature, the text, the embroidered initial embedded in it, and the border surrounding and binding all together.

From the thirteenth century on, much of Europe was under the spell of French Gothic books. England, still close to France, absorbed the style fully and at the same time kept, in some of its manuscripts such as the *Psalter of Queen Mary* (c. 1330) a continuation of its own earlier Winchester style. Animal grotesques in borders were a particular English contribution; they may have derived from the bestiaries popular in England in the twelfth and thirteenth centuries. But by the middle of the fourteenth century the plague and subsequent wars had drained England's energies, so that her manuscript production became negligible.

In some parts of Italy, particularly around the university centers, the French Gothic style was adopted, but it was transmuted by the Italian sense for the classic, which imparted some of the monumentality and dignity of fresco and panel painting to Italian miniatures. The Byzantine influence remained strong, especially in the region of Venice and in the South, and showed itself even in Gothic illuminations in the peculiar little truncated hills that appeared in backgrounds. Duccio, Cimabue, Giotto and their followers left their stamp on Italian manuscript illumination.

Other books besides Bibles and devotional books were illuminated in Italy. In university towns like Bologna, for a long time the most important center of manuscript production, and in Padua, law books were illuminated with drolleries and other Gothic decorations. It was customary to produce splendidly decorated membership books for the guilds. Petrarch had the frontispiece to his own copy of Virgil painted by none less than Simone Martini. But liturgical books received far more attention than all others. From the thirteenth century to the sixteenth, among Italy's most characteristic productions were gigantic choir books meant to be visible *Antiphonarium* from some distance. They were illuminated with historiated initials so large that the miniatures *page 57* they contained were often the size of a full-page miniature. Partial or full borders extended from these initials in a peculiarly Italian composition of large, loose acanthus leaves combined with round beads, sometimes strung on a rod and often sprouting stylized flowers and little heads. These borders grew richer and more rolling as Italian taste grew more luxurious.

Germany and Spain were slow to absorb Gothic style and just as slow, later on, to abandon it. Burgundy and Flanders, on the other hand, had a fluent interchange of influence with France. Flanders at that time belonged partly to France and to Burgundy, and the royal houses of France and Burgundy had the closest ties of blood. Philip the Bold of Burgundy, brother of Charles V and the Duc de Berry, was an ardent collector of books. Notable in his collection *Roman de la Violette* were a great many tales of chivalry, written in the dashing Gothic hand known as *bâtarde*. *page 58* Flemish artists illuminated most of the books for the court of Burgundy as they did for the

Antiphonarium. Italian, XIV century. Pierpont Morgan Library, M653. 23¼ x 15¾ in.

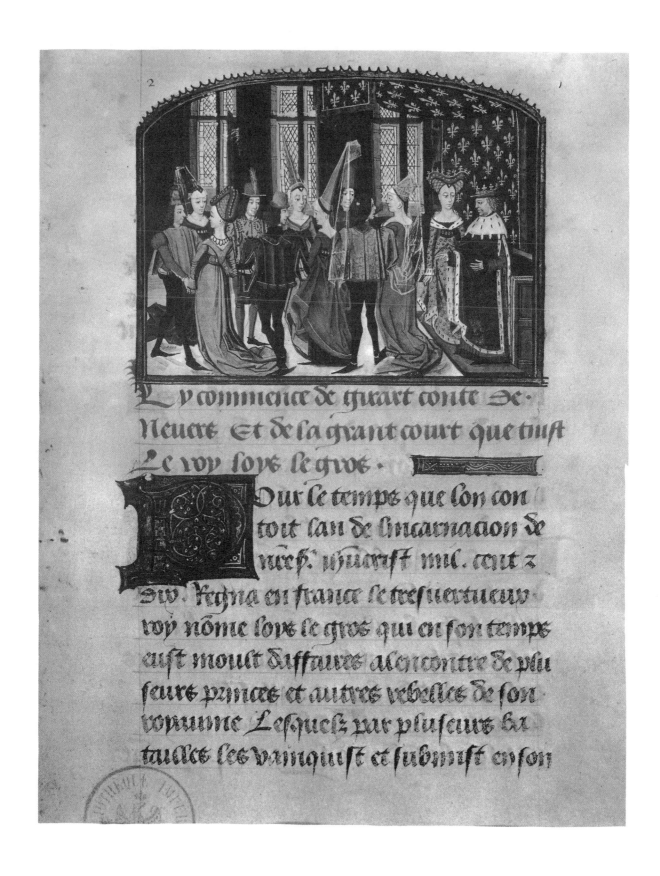

Ici commence de Gérart conte de Nevers. Et de la grant court que tint Le roy loys le gros.

Pour le temps que lon contoit lan de lincarnacion de nostre seigneur ihucrist mil. cent z xix. Regna en france le tresvertueux roy nomme loys le gros qui en son temps eust moult diffaires a lencontre de pluseurs princes et autres rebelles de son royaume. Lesquelz par pluseurs bataillez les vainquist et submist en son

Roman de la Violette. Burgundian, xv century. Bibliothèque Nationale, Ms. fr. 24378

en cellur qui fu tirsdesiretu Lit prepare
au fil du roy des rops

Burgundian scribe (portrait of Jean Miélot, from *Miracles de Notre Dame*), xv century. Bibliothèque Nationale

court of France. Early Gothic books in Flanders, while made in the French style, had shown a charmingly earthy fantasy all their own. In the fourteenth and fifteenth centuries an astonishing technical proficiency in painting was emerging in Flanders, along with a passionate interest in objective nature. This delight in the minute sensual impressions of the material world, grafted onto the French Gothic concept of the book, brought Flemish manuscripts to the forefront toward the end of the fifteenth century at a time when French books were beginning to lose their vitality. Out of the school of Flemish miniaturists arose in the fifteenth century the group of panel painters that began with the Van Eycks and went on to include Van der Weyden and Memling. Ties between these painters and the miniaturists remained close; the influence of the best Flemish painters was felt in the miniatures, with their delicately airy and minutely observed backgrounds. According to the British art historian Sir Kenneth

Maestricht Book of Hours page 60

Hours of the Virgin page 61

Maestricht Book of Hours. Flemish, XIII century. British Library, Stowe 17

Clark, the "sense of saturating light" for which the Flemish painters are famous grew out of miniature painting.

In well-organized Flanders, not only miniature painting and the writing of texts but also the various aspects of book decoration were separate specialties, controlled by their various guilds. The border-painters evolved a new type of border to go with the realistic miniature: a flat broad band, usually of gold, strewn with the most tangible blossoms and insects, painted with artful cast-shadows that make one feel that one could pick them up off the page. Sometimes the border went even farther and depicted a still-life setting in the midst of which, seen as though distantly through an arched window, the miniature was set.

A swiftly broadening realism was to be found not only in Flanders, but also in fifteenth-century Italy, where the forces of the Renaissance were at work. In France, not only the books produced by imported Flemish artists partook of the new realism but so did an indigenous school founded at Tours in the middle of the fifteenth century by the painter Fouquet. Fouquet spent some time in Italy and imbibed the classic sense of posture and of composition, along with details of Renaissance architecture. He added these to his own skill in landscape painting (the dreamy landscapes of his own Loire Valley often fill the backgrounds of his

Hours of the Virgin. Flemish, xv century. Pierpont Morgan Library, M6

miniatures) and to his mastery of crowd scenes. His illustrations for Josephus' *Les antiquités Judäiques (Jewish Antiquities)* are among his masterpieces, although they have the effect of large-scale paintings compressed into a small space and surrounded by an ivy border.

By the fifteenth century illuminated manuscripts were being produced in great numbers not only for the nobility but for the wealthy bourgeoisie. In France, Books of Hours were made not only at the express order of patrons, but also to go into the general stock of booksellers. Flanders had an atelier producing Books of Hours for export in the first quarter of the fifteenth century; by the second half of the century almost all the products of her busy book craftsmen were intended for export. In the midst of this full activity, the manuscript book was approaching its end.

RENAISSANCE
MANUSCRIPTS

In Italy, the Greek and Latin classics, studied increasingly over the past several centuries, had come to be considered the absolute spring of all knowledge. The afterlife was no longer the only goal; the pagan classics exalted the value of man and his temporal possibilities. The fervor for the classical past reached a climax in Florence in the early fifteenth century and spread to all the intellectual and cultural centers of Italy. The men who collected, translated, studied, and promulgated the classics were called "humanists," because of their emphasis on human goals.

Copies of Greek and Latin texts began to multiply, and, as if to indicate the value attached to the unadorned word, even the finest copies were unembellished except for a border framing the first page of text. Such borders had been seen in Byzantine and Romanesque books and were probably considered to be of classical origin.

The writing itself was likely to be in the humanistic script developed some time before 1429 in Florence and perfected a decade or two later. The script combined Roman capitals with a neat round miniscule based on the Carolingian hand, in which the classics had for the most part been preserved. This clear hand became, late in the century, the basis of roman type. In both manuscript and type it followed the spread of humanistic literature across Europe.

The border that framed the first page of Renaissance manuscripts was made up of an assortment of classical motifs: putti, garlands, vases, candelabra, busts, medallions, architectural elements. These were grouped together in a rich variety of ways, usually within a rectangular gold frame. In Florence, a white interlaced vine motif was characteristic, worked against a background of alternating blue, green, and crimson and scattered with rayed disks of gold. The Florentine workshops produced manuscripts not only for the renowned library of the Medici but also for wealthy patrons in other cities, and even such foreign patrons as the King of Hungary. The copy of St. Augustine's *De civitate Dei* now in the New York Public Library was illuminated in Florence around 1470 with an elaborate border around the first page of text. A scene is embodied in the base of the border and another in the large historiated initial,

St. Augustine,
De civitate Dei
page 64

63

which shows St. Augustine writing and dreaming of the City of God, here depicted in the shape of Florence.

The decorations of the Florentine masters for devotional books were in the Renaissance style, more fully applied than to the classics. The script in which sacred (and legal) books were written remained the gothic black letter—a conservative distinction that continued for a long time after the invention of printing.

The names of Attavante and Del Cherico are prominent as much-sought-after masters of Florentine illumination. The Book of Hours made by Del Cherico in 1458 for Lorenzo de' Medici is in small format. The miniatures are surrounded by borders of putti (little angels) with festoons painted in brilliant spots of color and gold against white vellum—an effect at once full of detail and of lightness.

Attavante, working for Duke Federigo Montefeltro of Urbino, owner of one of the most magnificent libraries of the Renaissance, collaborated in the illumination of the Urbino Bible in 1475–78. Its fantastic and profuse borders are a riot of delicate color and gold and combine chandeliers, gems, and putti with many medallions containing complex and dramatic scenes on a minuscule scale.

Painters of the stature of Botticelli and Fra Angelico in Florence occasionally painted miniatures and greatly influenced the style of others. In Ferrara, at the court of the d'Este, Piero della Francesca as court painter had a strong influence on the painting of miniatures. The Borso d'Este Bible was illuminated between 1455 and 1461 by Crivelli and others in a light, brilliant, and elaborate manner, in which borders of floral rosettes interspersed with many fantastic details, Renaissance architectural framework, and scenes from the Bible flow together. A highly original set of illustrations for Dante's *Divina Commedia* was produced at the same court around 1480.

Fine manuscripts were eagerly sought by the King of Naples and in Rome by the Pope and others, but no local schools of importance developed at those places, or in Venice. However, in Milan, under the patronage of the Sforza, notable work was done. The finest Milanese manuscript, the *Sforza Book of Hours*, was made around 1490, with miniatures at once sharply brilliant and expressive, in a typically Lombard manner.

The highest period of Italian manuscript production had begun around the middle of the fifteenth century. A tendency toward excess present even in the fifteenth century got more and more out of hand in the sixteenth century. The attempt was made—and made brilliantly—to squeeze into the compass of a page the exuberant, massive effects of late Renaissance painting, sculpture, and architecture.

At the height of organization and virtuosity in the production of manuscript books, the rapid increase of printing sapped their vital existence. Illuminated manuscripts continued to be produced for special patrons and special occasions throughout the sixteenth century; hand-painted borders and miniatures were not infrequent in fine copies of early printed books. But these were only phenomena of the transition period between one epoch and another. The long glory of the manuscript book was over.

THE
BEGINNING
OF
PRINTING

BLOCK BOOKS

Books were scarce in the fifteenth century. Copying manuscripts by hand was laborious and costly work. The books that existed were concentrated in the libraries of monasteries and universities, or in the rare private libraries that were the privilege of the very wealthy. A university such as Cambridge had only a hundred and twenty-two volumes in the year 1424. A private library at the end of the fifteenth century might boast of perhaps twenty volumes.

A bound manuscript at that time cost as much money as an average court official received in a month. A scholar or student who was not exceptionally wealthy could only acquire books by copying them himself. The typical manuscript of the Middle Ages was not the splendid ornamented volume we know from reproductions or exhibitions; it was a hastily written copy made for practical use.

In this time of scarcity, the need for books was mounting. An intellectual ferment seemed to be at work all over Europe. In the North, the religious questioning had begun that led to the Reformation. In Italy, the rediscovery of the pagan classics, stimulated by the stream of Greek refugees fleeing the Turks, had released an excited inquiry into man's worldly self. People needed books, and this need perhaps more than anything else brought about the beginning of printing.

There already existed in fifteenth-century Europe, as yet uncombined, the essential components necessary for printing books in large quantity. Paper, made from rag pulp, had been known in China since A.D. 105. It came circuitously into Spain through the Arabs during the Moslem conquests and around 1150 was being produced there. Shortly afterwards France began producing paper, and in 1276 the mills at Fabriano, Italy, began a production that soon outdistanced other European mills. By the fifteenth century large supplies of paper were available and were widely used for manuscripts as a cheaper substitute for vellum.

The printing of textiles from wood blocks was an art that had been known to the West throughout the Middle Ages. The screw press was an instrument commonly used by paper-makers and bookbinders, and it had already been employed to print textiles. Oil-based pigment

had been used for more than a century for decorative purposes; soon after 1400 it was being used by Flemish and Italian easel painters as well.

The most difficult requirement for printing was a means of producing large quantities of accurately formed type. Steps toward this means were to be found in the techniques of engraving and casting used by the goldsmiths and bookbinders, who made casting molds in fine sand. Bookbinders had since the thirteenth century engraved letter forms on wood or metal to form such casting molds for letter stamps.

These techniques and materials were at hand, but it still required a particular genius to combine and adapt them for the purpose of printing books.

The first harbingers of printing to appear in Europe were single-page prints of religious subjects made from wood blocks, which sometimes included a few lines of text. They originated mainly in Germany and the Netherlands; some seem to be of French origin. It is difficult to attach firm dates to the earliest of these prints. A *Rest on the Flight into Egypt*, a *St. Jerome*, a *St. Dorothy*, and a *Martyrdom of St. Sebastian* were judged by Arthur M. Hind, a leading authority on woodcuts, to have been made around 1410. The first dated print is a *St. Christopher* that depicts the Saint carrying the Christ Child through the water between one craggy shore and another. A Latin couplet at the bottom of the print, carved into the same block, is a sort of charm against death. It is followed by the date 1423.

These prints were probably hung on the walls of houses as little shrines or talismans. Many of them were no doubt brought back from the pilgrimages which were still widely popular. (Luther complained, a century later, that the revenue from monasteries selling pictures to pilgrims often went into some cardinal's pocket.)

The first woodcuts were made in broad flowing outlines, which were meant to be filled in with color as a cheap substitute for painted pictures. Some of these religious prints must have been made inside the monasteries, but records indicate that some were produced by the woodcutters who cut wood blocks for textiles. These same woodcutters also printed playing cards. There is an early record in Bologna, from the year 1395, of one Federico di Germania who sold "*cartas figuratas et pictas ad imagines et figuras sanctorum.*" The cause of the document was that the versatile Federico had also manufactured false money. There is altogether a faint savor of counterfeit connected with this earliest printing. The woodcutters were not held in high regard, and they remained anonymous. Inside the monasteries they had a free hand, but outside they were restricted by the painters' guilds, who tried to keep them from copying paintings.

Block books were a natural development from the pictures of saints. Made up of pages of illustration and brief text printed from wood blocks, they provided a simple and popular means

legit in genesi xxxvij ca ϙ
cu tres Joseph vellet eu hys-
maelitis vedere ipm tunica
sua spoliauert z eu i cister-
na vetere miserut: Joseph
iste cristu sigt qui missus
fuit in cysternam hoc e in
sepultura cum eu amici de
cruce posuert

legit in libro ione ij ca ϙ cu
ipe Jonas ascedet naui vt
iret thasi i citate quada fa-
e tepestas magna i mari cu
misset sorte iue se ϙ erat in
naui sois cecidit sup Jona ϙ
illi aphetes miserut in mare
z pistis magn⁹ stati eu de-
glutiuit i cui⁹ vetre fuit trib⁹
dieb⁹ z trib⁹ noctib⁹: Jonas
cristu sigt qa fuit i vetre ire
tribus dieb⁹ z trib⁹ noctib⁹

Euolat⁹ e teip dormies dꝰ teip ꝓphes sepulur⁹ a dio .g.   Ego dormio et cor meu vigilat

Dauid   cantico⁹ .v.

Mittans cu in cisternu vetere   Mitte me i mari

                                                                Hui coplebitr daps sepulchr

Ysaias Erit sepulchr Mirra oditus: et ab hijs cristus sepltr
 li.   eius gloriosu   vs Jonas glutit̄   genesis Requies
vs Hac i cysternā: detru-   tame illes⁹ repertr xlix. cubauit
ditur iste vetexrū   sicut leo

of instruction in the stories of the Bible and the conduct of spiritual life. They were made by the same workshops that produced single prints and playing cards.

The earliest block books, like the earliest single prints, are elusive as to date. They probably antedate the typographic book by at most two or three decades. It has been argued, and with reason, that there is no direct, but only stylistic, evidence that they antedate printing from type at all. Both forms of book continued to be printed through the rest of the fifteenth century. Many of the texts and pictures of the block books were based on existing manuscripts, but the technical conditions of the woodcut gave them a character very much their own. Because the carving of texts was a difficult task, the medium was best suited to the simple picture story. The letter forms were based on gothic script but were altered in character by the cutting.

One of the most popular of the block books was a little volume of twenty-four pages: the *Ars moriendi (The Art of Dying)*. Its subject was close to the medieval heart at a time when the plague made death an ever-present threat. It deals with a man on his deathbed resisting the devils' temptation to impatience, avarice, and other evils. The eleven full-page illustrations, faced by full pages of beautifully cut text, are in the vigorous and draftsmanly style that is associated with the early Flemish masters. There is great variety from page to page: violent demonic scenes alternate with scenes of angelic comfort. In the final picture the soul of the dead, in the form of a tiny figure issuing from his corpse, is received by the waiting angels, while the devils roll and howl in frustration below.

Ars moriendi page 68

The wide appeal of this book took it through at least twelve different editions in three languages: Latin, German, and French. The first edition appeared about 1450, at a time when Gutenberg was already printing from type. Our illustration is from the fourth edition, thought to have been published at Augsburg, Germany, in 1465–70. The block-book printers were quick to take advantage of the printing press after its invention; the sharpness of the impression and the blackness of the lines in this edition show it to have been printed on a press with printers' ink.

The *Biblia pauperum (The Poor Man's Bible)*, must have been as popular as the *Ars moriendi*. One of the earliest block books, it was probably intended for the instruction of the poor clergy. Its forty pages show scenes from the Life and Passion of Christ compared with similar scenes from the Old Testament. These comparisons were a favorite device of the Middle Ages. The designs in the *Biblia pauperum* have been attributed to the schools of Dirk Bouts and Van Eyck. Each page is organized by an architectural framework producing panels very much like niches. The central panel holds the scene from the New Testament, flanked by its Old Testament counterparts. Small niches above and below contain pairs of prophets. All of the figures are in medieval costume, and the houses and landscapes in the background are contemporary Flemish. The text is very limited in this book, appearing only in the upper corners

Biblia pauperum page 70

Biblia pauperum. Netherlands, c. 1470. Pierpont Morgan Library and on decorative banners. It was intended, as in the single prints, that the pictures be colored. But shading, to give plasticity, was used for the first time in these woodcuts.

The early block books shared certain features. They were printed from blocks arranged in pairs, so as to make facing pages when folded. The method of printing was to ink the blocks with a watery ink, to lay the paper over the blocks, and to make the impression by burnishing the back of the paper. This method made such a deep impression that it was impossible to print on both sides of the paper. As a result, when the printed sheets were made up into books, two facing pages of print were followed by two facing blanks. In some cases the blanks were pasted together to overcome the difficulty. The problem disappeared when it became possible to print the blocks on a press.

Popular block books went through successive changes from the early method of printing to editions printed on the press; still later their illustrations might appear with a text set in type. A few examples of an earlier stage survive, in which the woodcut illustration is accompanied by a text in manuscript.

Apocalypse
page 73

Ars memorandi
pages 74 and 75

Among the earliest block books are the first editions of the *Apocalypse of St. John* and of the *Ars memorandi (The Art of Memorizing)*. The *Apocalypse* is based closely on an illuminated manuscript telling of the revelations of St. John. There is a direct, primitive power in its pictures accompanied by a scanty text. The *Ars memorandi* consists of large symbolic pictures intended to help impress on the memory of the clergy the Gospels of the four Evangelists. A handsomely cut page of text faces each of the full-page pictures.

The *Canticum canticorum* has delicately attenuated, Gothic illustrations. Each of its sixteen pages contains two engravings that treat the Song of Songs as an allegory of the Virgin Mary. The *Speculum humanae salvationis (The Mirror of Human Salvation)*, has again the favored device: the comparison of the life of Christ with events from the Old Testament and from traditional history. It exists only in a mixed edition in which woodblock illustrations printed by friction are combined with a text set in type and printed on a press. It is considered likely that earlier woodblock editions once existed, especially as both text and illustrations are based on a manuscript from the late thirteenth century.

Other block books dealt with the appearance of the Antichrist, the life of David, the Seven Deadly Sins; one was a guidebook for pilgrims to Rome.

The introduction of typographic printing did not at first interfere with the popularity of the block books, which continued to be produced throughout the fifteenth century. The explanation for this is thought to lie in the fact that a text carved in wood, though laborious to produce, far outlasted the earliest types, which were apparently cast in a soft metal. The earliest type-printed editions consisted only of one hundred to three hundred copies; apparently after

Apocalypsis sancti Johannis. Germany, 1460-65. Pierpont Morgan Library

Ars memorandi. Germany, 1460-70. Pierpont Morgan Library. 12½ x 8½ in. →

Domicianus Johane crox uroz conteptore i pathmos insula exulo

A

velegant eum pathmos.   hic s. iohe

Septimum · Capitulu̅
De penitencia ma
rie magdalene que vnx
et pedes ihe̅su̅ · Octauu̅
Capitulum · Loquitur ihe̅sus de
semine ⁊ de tempestate qua̅ ccū
tus se dauit in ba̅u̅ ꝛc̅ · Nouū
Capitulum · De tra̅sfiguraci
one visa de quinquꝰ panibꝰ Et
de petri respo̅sio̅e ad cristum Tu
es filius ꝛc̅ · Decimum · Capi
tulu̅ · De duabus sororibus
scilicet martha et maria magda
lena · Et incidit quidam inter la
trones ꝛc̅ · Vndecimum · Ca
pitulu̅ · Domine doce nos
orare ꝛc̅ · Et de eiectione demo
nium ꝛc̅ · Duodecimum
Capitulum · De fideli seruo ⁊
vbi thezaurus ibi et cor tuum · ꝛc̅

that it was necessary to cast a new set of types. For a book with a limited text and a steady popularity, it would have been worth the trouble to cut the text as well as the pictures in wood.

The existence of woodcut versions of brief, unillustrated school texts bears this out. The most popular early school text was a grammar, *De octo partibus orationes (Of the Eight Parts of Speech)*, by the fourth-century grammarian Donatus. This brief work provides a dramatic if obscure link between the woodcut text and the full-fledged printed book, for besides the woodcut versions there have been found a number of Dutch specimens printed on both sides of a vellum sheet in an uneven and imperfect type. The name of Laurens Coster of Utrecht figures in the disputes that these unidentified and undated Donatus prints have caused. Speculations have been made as to whether they were perhaps made by flat, shankless types glued into position on a paper or board. Whatever the case, they may form part of the shadowy group of unperfected experiments that came before the dawn of printing.

GUTENBERG

An event of primary importance to the history of civilization took place in Mainz, Germany, in or shortly before 1455. A large, two-volume Bible, as fine as a very fine manuscript, was printed from type. It has been conjectured that the edition consisted of about two hundred copies, some on vellum, others on paper. (Twelve copies on vellum, thirty-six on paper are still extant.) This Bible, consisting altogether of 643 leaves printed in double columns of large, closely woven type, is known by several names: the "42-line" Bible, from the number of lines of type in a column; the "Mazarin" Bible, from the seventeenth-century French cardinal in whose library it came newly to attention; and the "Gutenberg" Bible from the belief that it is essentially the creation of Johann Gutenberg. It has the reputation of being the first substantial book printed from movable type.

Bible page 79

It seems impossible that a book of such unsurpassed perfection could have come into being as Pallas Athene did. Yet that is very nearly the case. We know the approximate date of its printing from the circumstance that the rubricator and binder of one of the copies, Heinrich Cremer, vicar in Mainz, left in it his signature and the statement that he had completed his work on August 24, 1456. The printing of the Bible must have been finished at least a year prior to that.

What led up to the production of this splendid book has been deduced from fragmentary evidence consisting of a few surviving printed leaves thought to antedate the Bible, a number of civic records, and the written comments of persons contemporary or nearly contemporary with the event.

The early printed examples consist of a fragment of a leaf from what must have been a sizable volume of sibylline poems, and parts of three different editions of Donatus' little grammar. None of these bears a printer's name or a date, but by comparisons of type and correlation with the information given by documents they have been attributed to Johann Gutenberg at a period when he was experimenting with printing in Strassburg. (The *Constance Missal*, the only copy of which is in the Morgan Library, remains controversial.)

There are thirty existing official documents pertaining to Gutenberg, most of which give us only glimpses of his personal life (a suit for breach of promise of marriage, a litigation for unpaid taxes on wine). Of the thirty, three documents have direct bearing on the art of printing. It is known that Gutenberg was born in Mainz about 1400, and that when he was a young man his family were political refugees in Strassburg. The first evidence of his experiments in printing occurs in a Strassburg document of 1437 recording a suit against Gutenberg by the brother of a deceased partner of his. The brother claimed that the deceased had gained partnership in the working of an invention in exchange for a sum of money, for which the heir now wanted restitution. In the description of the enterprise the words "press" and "printing" occur.

A few years later, in 1441 and 1442, there are records of loans made to Gutenberg, apparently for further work on his invention. About 1445 Gutenberg returned to Mainz and once more borrowed money. The book of sibylline poems, the remaining fragment of which is now known as "The Fragment of the World Judgment," is thought to have appeared at this time, followed by the Donatuses.

We hear for the first time of Gutenberg's relationship with Johann Fust, then a goldsmith, in connection with a loan to Gutenberg of 800 gulden made by Fust in 1450. Another loan of 800 gulden in 1452 carried the proviso that Fust be made a partner in Gutenberg's enterprise. These were not small sums that Gutenberg borrowed; his debt to Fust, including interest, amounted to at least $50,000 in today's money. In 1455 we have the record of the final stages of a suit in which Fust claims his money or else the forfeit of the equipment in which it was invested. Among the names of the witnesses is listed that of Peter Schoeffer, a former scribe employed in the enterprise. Fust won the suit, and from then on there exists the prospering firm of Fust and Schoeffer, printers.

The 42-line Bible was very likely printed at a time when Gutenberg, Fust, and Schoeffer were working together with the backing of Fust's funds. From the same period we have the first printed matter to bear an actual date—a papal bull of 1454 against the Turks, who had the year before taken Constantinople. In 1454 there were also printed papal indulgences granting authority to raise money for a campaign against the invading infidels, one of them, the "30-line" indulgence, using the type of the Bible for its headings and "incipits."

The clear attribution of the printing that came immediately after the 42-line Bible is often difficult; in some cases the best evidence is afforded by the similarity of types. The new Bible, which was printed around 1458, was copied after the 42-line Bible but printed in a larger, less refined type with only thirty-six lines to a column. The type had appeared earlier in one of the Indulgences of 1454 (the "31-line" indulgence), and again, slightly modified, in a series of

Bible. Mainz, Johann Gutenberg, 1454-55. Collection of E. Harold Hugo. 15 x 10¾ in.

et temptauerūt me iam ꝑ decem vices
nec obedierunt voci mee · nō videbūt
terram pro qua iuraui patribus eorū:
nec quiſꝗ eҳ illis qui detraxit michi
intuebitur eam. Seruū meū chaleb ꝗ
plenus alio spiritu ſecut⁹ eſt me indu-
ram in terram hanc quā circuiuit · et
ſemen eius poſſidebit eam: quoniam
amalechites ⁊ chananeus habitāt in
vallibus. Cras mouete castra: ⁊ reuer-
timini in ſolitudinē ꝑ viam maris ru-
bri. locutuſꝗ ē dūs ad moyſen ⁊ aaron dicens. Vſquequo multitudo hec
peſſima murmurat contra me? Que-
relas filiorū iſrahel audiui. Dic ergo
eis. Viuo ego ait dominus: ſicut lo-
cuti eſtis audiente me · ſic faciā vobis.
In ſolitudine hac iacebunt cadauera
veſtra. Omnes qui numerati eſtis a
viginti ānis ⁊ ſupra · ⁊ murmraſtis
contra me · non intrabitis terram ſup
quā leuaui manū meam ut habitare
vos facerem: preter chaleb filiū iephone · ⁊ ioſue filiū nun. Paruulos autē
veſtros de quibꝫ dixiſtis quod prede
hoſtibus forent introducam: ut vide-
ant terram que vobis diſplicuit: vꝛa
cadauera iacebūt in ſolitudine. Filij
veſtri erunt vagi in deſerto ānis qua-
draginta: ⁊ portabunt foꝛnicationē
veſtram · donec conſumenꝫ cadauera
patꝛū in deſerto: iuxta numerū ꝗdra-
ginta dies quibus conſideraſtis terrā.
Ann⁹ pro die imputabitur. Et qua-
draginta ānis recipietis iniquitates
veſtras: ⁊ ſcietis ultionem meā. Quoniam ſicut locut⁹ ſum · ita faciā oī
multitudini huic peſſime · que conſur-
rexit aduerſum me: in ſolitudine hac
deficiet ⁊ morietur. Igitur oīes viri
quos miſerat moyſes ad cōtemplan-
dam terram · ⁊ qui reuerſi murmurare

fecerant contra eū omnē multitudinē.
Detrahentes terre ꝗ eſſet mala: moꝛ-
tui ſunt atꝗ percuſſiꝫ in conſpectu do-
mini. Ioſue aūt filius nun ⁊ chaleb
filius iephone vixerunt eҳ omnibus
qui pergerant ad conſiderandā terrā.
locutuſꝗ eſt moyſes uniuerſa verba
hec ad omnes filios iſrahel: et luxit
popul⁹ nimis. Et ecce mane primo
ſurgentes · aſcenderūt verticem mōtis
atꝗ dixerunt. Parati ſum⁹ aſcendere
ad locum de quo dominus locutus
eſt: quia peccauimus. Quibus moyſes. Cur inquit tranſgredimini verbū
dūi · quod vobis non cedet in proſpe-
rum? Nolite aſcendere · non enim eſt
dūs vobiſcum: ne corruatis coꝛā ini-
micis veſtris. Amalechites ⁊ chananeus ante vos ſunt quoꝫ gladio corru-
etis: eo ꝗ nolueritis acquieſcere dūo:
nec erit dominus vobiſcū. At illi con-
tenebrati · aſcenderūt in verticem mon-
tis. Archa autem teſtamenti dōmini
et moyſes non receſſerūt de caſtris. De-
ſcenditꝗ amalechites ⁊ chananeus ꝗ
habitabāt i mōte: et percutiens eos atꝗ
cōcides · pſecut⁹ ē eos uſꝗ hoꝛma. XV

L ocutus eſt domin⁹ ad moyſen
dicens. loquere ad filios iſrl · ⁊
dices ad eos. Cum ingreſſi fueritis terram habitationis vꝛe quā ego dabo
vobis · ⁊ feceritis oblationē domino
in olocauſtum · aut victimam pacifi-
cam vota ſoluetes · vel ſponte offeretes
munera · aut in ſolemnitatibꝫ vꝛis a-
dolentes odorem ſuauitatis dūo: de
bubus ſiue de quibꝫ offeret quicunꝗ
immolauerit victimam: ſacrificiū ſic
decimam partem ephi cōſperſam oleo ·
quod menſurā habebit quartā partē
hin: et vinum ad liba fundenda eiuſdem menſure dabit in olocauſtū ſiue

small printed pieces—grammars and calendars. After its use in the 36-line Bible, the type appeared in 1460 in the hands of one Albrecht Pfister, printer, in the city of Bamberg. It has been reasoned that after the loss of his equipment in Mainz, Gutenberg may have set up partnership with Pfister in Bamberg and printed the Bible there. Fragments of press waste found in Bamberg strengthen this contention.

The last major printed work tentatively attributed to Gutenberg is the *Catholicon*, a large encyclopedic dictionary printed at Mainz in 1460, in a small, imperfectly cut type. For reasons of sentiment one would like to think that Gutenberg printed the *Catholicon*, for it ends with a colophon that reads: "By the help of the Most High, at Whose nod the tongues of infants become eloquent, and who ofttimes reveals to the lowly that which he hides from the wise, this noble book Catholicon, in the year of the Lord's Incarnation 1460, in the bounteous city of Mainz… without help of reed, stylus or pen, but by the wondrous agreement, proportion and harmony of punches and types has been printed and brought to an end."

In a matter of such world-shaping importance as the invention of printing, especially when the evidence is incomplete, disputing claims drawn along national lines were bound to arise. There are factions that claim that Gutenberg was not the inventor of printing at all, but that Laurens Coster of Holland was. But fifteenth-century sources seem to indicate that Gutenberg was accepted in his own century as the inventor. The earliest of these, a letter written in 1470 by Guillaume Fichet, a professor at the Sorbonne instrumental in bringing the first printers to Paris, says that "a certain John, surnamed Gutenberg, first of all men thought out the printing art, by which books are fashioned not with a reed (as people used to do it) or pen (as we do it), but with letters of brass.…"

The *Cologne Chronicle*, printed in 1499, says of the invention of printing that, "This right worthy art was invented first of all in Germany, at Mainz" and that "the first inventor of printing was a Burgher at Mainz… called Yunker Johann Gutenberg." For this information the writer credits Ulrich Zell, a printer still working at the time of the Chronicle, who had been the first printer in Cologne.

The statement would seem conclusive enough, had it not gone on to say: "Although this art was invented at Mainz, as far as regards the manner in which it is now commonly used, yet the first prefiguration was invented in Holland from the Donatuses which were printed there before that time. And from out of these the aforesaid art took its beginning, and was invented in a manner much more masterly and subtler than this, and the longer it lasted the more full of art it became."

Endless debates have risen out of these words, which have seemed to those who wished it to support the claim for Laurens Coster. But the facts seem to indicate that Coster's attempts, even if real, were at best abortive. The actual bringing-together and development of the equipment needed for the successful printing of books—a workable press, an oil-based ink, a system for the accurate casting of large quantities of type (the adjustable hand mold with punch-stamped matrices), and a metal alloy that would perform well—was accomplished by Johann Gutenberg. The city of Mainz was the origin of the explosion of printing that sent German printers, in the decade beginning in 1465, to every important city in Europe.

An early representation of a printer's shop. This woodcut, from a *Dance of Death (La Grand danse Macabre)* printed in Lyons in 1568 by Pierre de Saint-Lucie, is based on the earliest representation, in the Lyons *Dance of Death* of 1499/1500. Metropolitan Museum

FUST AND SCHOEFFER

If Johann Gutenberg is to be credited with the invention of the art of printing, Johann Fust and Peter Schoeffer, printers, were the men who first made it a successful enterprise. In contrast to the anonymity of Gutenberg's press, the firm of Fust and Schoeffer began at once to advertise themselves in their books. In 1457, when they had finished their great Psalter, they ended it with the following colophon: "The present book of the Psalms, decorated with beautiful capitals and with the proper rubrics, has been thus fashioned by an ingenious invention of printing and stamping without any use of a pen. And to the worship of God has been diligently brought to completion by Johann Fust, a citizen of Mainz, and Peter Schoeffer of Gernsheim, in the year of the Lord, 1457, on the eve of the Assumption."

*Psalter
page 83*

The Psalter thus became the first printed book to carry both the name of the printer and the date of publication. Fust and Schoeffer made it a practice to put their names at the end of all the major books they printed. With their names they used a pictorial device of the sort hitherto used only by tradesmen to give their products an identifying mark. The printer's mark of Fust and Schoeffer was a double shield hung from a branch. It was much used in altered form by later printers, when self-advertisement became more common, along with other devices such as elaborated initials, coats of arms, printers' implements, and ingenious pictorial plays on names.

When the 42-line Bible was printed, some time before 1456, an attempt was made to print the rubrics also. The attempt was quickly abandoned, however, because of the difficulties encountered. The Psalter printed by Fust and Schoeffer was the first book to carry out the printing of not only rubrics, but also elaborate initials in one and two colors—red and blue or gray. The two-color initials, aside from their great beauty, were so perfectly executed as to have caused much wonder about how they were printed. Study of the ten surviving copies of the Psalter, in all of which the two-color initials vary, has led to the conclusion that the initials and text were for the most part printed at one pull of the press. To accomplish this, the 292 metal-cut initials and their arabesque backgrounds had to be picked out of the form and

Psalter. Mainz, Fust and Schoeffer, edition of 1459. Pierpont Morgan Library. 13 x 8¼ in.

Eatus
vir ā Seruite dño. Euouae
qui nō abijt in cōsilio im=
piox: ꝗ in via peccatox nō
stetit: et in cathedra pestilē=
tie nō sedit, Sed in lege
dñi volūtas eius: ꝗ in lege ei⁹ meditabiꞇ die
ac nocte, Et eit tanꝗ̇ lignū qd̄ plantatū est
secus decursus aꝗrū: qd̄ fructū suū dabit in
ꞇpe suo, Et foliū ei⁹ nō defluet: ꝗ oīa quecūꝗ
faciet ꝓsꝑabunꞇ, Non sic impij nō sic: sed
tanꝗ̇ puluis quē ꝓicit ventus a facie terre,
Ideo nō resurgūt impij in iudicio: neꝗ̇ pctō=
res in cōsilio iustox, Qm̄ nouit dñs via iu=
storū: et iter impiox ꝑibit, Gꞁia pꞇi, Gfdd

Vare fremuerūt gētes: ꝗ ꝓꝓꞁi meditati
sūt inania, Astiterūt reges ꞇre et prin=
cipes ꝯuenerc in vnū: aduūsus dñm ꝗ aduūsus
ꝟpm ei⁹, Dirūpam⁹ vincꞁa eox: ꝗ ꝓiciam⁹
a nobis iugū ipox, Qui habitat in celis irri
debit eos: et dñs subsannabit eos, Tūc lo
queꞇ ad eos in ira sua: et in furore suo cōtur
babit eos, Ego aūt cōstitutus sū rex ab eo

inked separately for each impression. Occasionally one finds a second impression and some details stamped in by hand. The Psalter, printed in red and black on vellum in two sizes of clearly cut type, and completed with the initials, lacks nothing in perfection or richness. But its method of production was apparently too laborious to go on with. Fust and Schoeffer used two-color initials in two other books but then abandoned their use except in new editions of the Psalter, in 1459 and later.

Peter Schoeffer became the son-in-law of Johann Fust, as a reward, Schoeffer's son later said, for his services. Those services are thought to include important steps in the perfecting of the manufacture of type. Type is made by driving an original letter form or punch into a receiving substance to form a hollow matrix. Molten metal is poured into this matrix to form the printing type. We do not know how Gutenberg made his punches. He may have carved them directly in wood or brass, or even have cast them in fine sand as the makers of bookbinders' punches did. Whatever his method, Schoeffer is thought to have improved it radically by cutting punches in soft steel and then hardening it. This would make it possible to cut a more perfect letter which, hardened, had the strength to be driven into copper, forming a perfect matrix. The finely cut type of the indulgences printed at Gutenberg's press in 1454–5 is thought to have been made by Schoeffer.

The firm of Fust and Schoeffer combined business acuity with the highest craftsmanship. They turned out fine books regularly and soon had business connections with a number of other European cities. In these early books they sought even more than rich effects and perfect printing; they were looking for new solutions to the problems of printing. In 1459 they made an important advance with the production of the *Rationale diuinorum officiorum* (a work that explained the meaning of the ceremonies used in church services) by setting the lengthy text in a small type that made it the first example of inexpensive printing. Schoeffer was the first printer to use a separate title page: four even lines of large type set high on the first page of a papal bull, giving its title and the author's name. But this remained a unique example.

In 1461, in the mounting struggle between two rival archbishops in Mainz, printing found a new application: Fust and Schoeffer produced eight political placards. By 1462 the crisis broke; it was no longer possible to continue work in the bitter fighting that ensued. The press of Fust and Schoeffer was practically silent for the next three years. The last product of their great early period was a magnificent Bible with headings printed in red, and many red and blue capitals and chapter numbers, finished in August 1462 just before the political conflict disrupted the city.

THE
FIFTEENTH
CENTURY

GERMANY

The conflict in Mainz may have brought printing to a temporary standstill in that city, but it gave impetus to the spread of the art. The journeymen and apprentices trained in the workshops of Gutenberg, Fust and Schoeffer moved on to more promising towns, taking their knowledge with them. Prior to 1462 two printers were known to be working outside of Mainz: Johann Mentelin in Strassburg and Albrecht Pfister in Bamberg. By 1464 there were German printers at work in the Benedictine monastery at Subiaco in Italy, by 1467 at Rome, by 1469 at Venice, by 1470 at Paris. In five more years books were being printed in every major city in Europe. These first printed books have been given the name *incunabula,* from the Latin *incunabulum,* cradle. Latterly the name has come to apply to all fifteenth-century books.

Some of the earliest printers can be traced back to their origins. Conrad Sweynheym, one of the two printers who introduced the art to Italy, was from Mainz. Ulrich Zell, the first printer at Cologne, also seems to have been trained in Mainz. But however large the printing operations of Gutenberg, Fust and Schoeffer may have been, it is difficult to conceive of how so many men acquired enough information and skill to set up their own printing shops far from any source of aid or supply. Setting out to work in a strange town or country, the first printers had to manufacture their own presses, cut their own type punches and cast sufficient type before they could begin to print. Except where they were specifically engaged to print for a monastery, a university, or a noble patron, they had to function as printer, publisher, and bookseller in one. The amount of capital such a venture called for was large, and the risks proved great. Not more than ten per cent of the 350-odd printers who set up before 1480 lasted out twenty years in their trade. The wildfire spread of printing quickly led to ruinous competition; many printers were forced to take to the road as itinerant printers to escape their debts, while others returned to the trades from which they had come.

The aim of all these earliest printers was to turn out copies of the books of the past for which there was a large unsatisfied demand that the producers of manuscripts could not fill. Books

pꝛimo inuenerunt. Non enim erat iuris ꝙ homo cru
ci cum daue annectaretur. Sed vt funibꝰ suspenderet
voner moꝛeret. Bene etiam inuentoꝛ melodie ihesum
cꝛistum pꝛefigurabat. Quia ipe pꝛimus erat qui talem
melodiam decantabat. Xpus nō solum p crucifixo/
ribus exoꝛauit. Sed p salute totius mundi patrem
suum efflagitauit. Et quamuis multi olim p pecca/
to hominis oꝛauerunt. Tamen nec p oꝛationes nec p
sacrificia exauditi fuerunt. Xpus autem oꝛauit cum
lacrimis ꝛ clamoꝛe valido. Et exauditus est pꝛo sua
reuerentia·id ꝙ petijt impetrando.

   Scda figura.

¶ Hanc etiam crucifixionem xpi ysaias pꝛefigurauit.
Quem gens iudaica nimis inhumaniter mactauit·
Iudei enim ipm cum secra lignea xpm p medium di
uiserunt·Quia animam eius ꝛ coꝛpus p cruce abin/
uicem separauerunt. Quamuis auc aiaꝫ in carne abin
uicem diuidebant. Nunꝗ auc deitatem a neutra ea
rum diuidere valebant. Deitas enim a carne moꝛtua

of a religious nature figured largely among these; almost half of the books printed in the fifteenth century were theological or liturgical. For the first printers, printing was a way of reproducing manuscripts more quickly and more cheaply. The manuscript remained the ideal; its styles and formats were closely adhered to, and types were modeled after local manuscript hands. It took sixty years or more for the book to liberate itself from this tradition. There were no title pages in use yet. Like the scribes, the early printers put the author and title of the book at the top of the first page of text in the same size, and after a short space began with *Incipit*—"Here begins."

The division of labor that prevailed in monastic and lay scriptoria was at first respected by the printers, who saw themselves as replacing only the scribes. After the early experiments of Fust and Schoeffer with stamping colored initials in their Psalter, both rubrics and decoration were for a while left to be added by hand, and only the running text was printed. This may have been due to inherent difficulties in printing in more than one color, but it was even more likely because of pressure from the rubricators' and illuminators' guilds. Competition against the scriptoria, which continued to be active throughout the century, and the excellent examples of format provided by manuscripts made early printing of the highest quality.

Almost from the beginning popular illustrated books were produced side by side with the more stately volumes. While Johann Mentelin in Strassburg was printing his Latin Bible around 1460, Albrecht Pfister was turning out the first of a small series of illustrated books, *Der Ackerman aus Böhmen (The Farmer from Böhmen)* in Gutenberg's type with five full-page woodcuts. The second of the books, a group of German fables named *Der Edelstein (The Gem)*, came out in 1461, illustrated with many small oblong cuts, beside each of which was a little figure of a man pointing. The woodcuts in all Pfister's books were in simple outline with only the slightest amount of shading. Like the block books and most German illustrated books of the fifteenth century, they were meant to be colored.

After Pfister's few books, there were no illustrated books produced in Germany for five or six years. Then at Augsburg and Ulm, the centers of the woodcutters who made religious pictures and playing cards, there began the great period of German woodcut illustration, when text and woodcut achieved their most harmonious balance. Augsburg and Ulm were probably the most highly developed towns in Germany at that time. Germany was in a disorganized period, and life centered in the separate provincial towns. Provincialism shows itself in the naive qualities of illustrations, which kept a strong local flavor.

The high period of German illustrated books was initiated by the two Zainers—Gunther and Johann—relatives who had worked at Strassburg but who moved on to Augsburg and Ulm respectively. Originally scribes and illuminators, they had probably received their training as printers at the workshop of Johann Mentelin.

Speculum humanae salvationis. Augsburg, Gunther Zainer, 1473. Yale Beinecke Rare Book Library. 12 x 7¼ in.

Chmid werck iſt das ander handt=
werck · vnnder dem · waffen ſchmid·
goldſchmid · kanttengieſſer · rotſch=
mid · vnd wölche mit eincherley me
tall vmb gand · müntzmeyſter · ſtein=
metz · maurer · zimerleüt · ſchreyner ·
vnd ir geleychen begriffen werdent ·
Ir notturfft iſt groß · Wañ wo die bew nit wärent ·
ſo möchtent die mēſchen · in ordenlicher gemeynſame
nit bey ein ander wonen · vnd vergienge menſchliche
einmütigkat vñ aller gottes dienſt · Wañ woz möch
teſt du lieplichs oder luſtlichs auff erden finden · wañ
weder ſtett · ſchloß dörffer · oder heüſer wärent · vor auß
kein tempel gotes · Die mēſchen müſtent in dē hölern
wonē · als die wilden tier · Der gold ſchmid håtwerck
vñ irer nachfolger · die mit andn metallen ire künſtē
treibent · ſeind nit allei erlich vñ luſtlich ſy ſind auch
nutzlich · wañ ſy machent · geſchirz zů der zierlicheit d
gottes dienſt · vnd der menſchen · Von den ſchmiten
werdent getreüwe waffen vnd harnaſch gemachet ·
durch die das vatterland beſchirmet · vnd die feind
vertriben werdent · Vñ andre tauſentfältige nutzung

When Gunther Zainer came to Augsburg to print, he immediately got into difficulties with the woodcutters' guild. Zainer wanted to use woodcut illustrations in his books, and the guild prohibited him from doing so. With the intervention of the Abbot of SS. Ulrich and Afra, a man of local importance interested in printing, Zainer was at last permitted to use illustrations provided that the designs and cutting were done by members of the woodcutters' guild. Zainer printed his first two illustrated books in 1471 and 1472, improving both his blocks and his technique. In 1473, working at the press established at the monastery of SS. Ulrich and Afra, he produced an extremely fine edition of the *Speculum humanae salvationis*. The subject *Speculum humanae salvationis* page 86 was the same as in the block book printed at about the same time: a harmonious comparison between episodes in the Old and New Testaments, but Zainer's treatment of it was quite different. He set his own beautiful rounded gothic type in a single column of comfortable width and had the 176 illustration blocks cut to the same width. The type is one size, chapter headings and all, with red initials drawn in by hand. The oblong woodcuts with their regular hatching blend with the texture of the type; their action is fresh and direct. Much of the appeal of the book comes from the variety achieved with simple means and the snugness of the type-and-woodcut area within ample margins.

Two years or so later, in 1475–6, Gunther Zainer printed the *Spiegel des menschlichen Lebens* *Spiegel des menschlichen Lebens* page 88 (*Mirror of Human Life*), a vernacular edition of one of the most popular medieval texts, which described the advantages and disadvantages of every career and station in life. Zainer had printed an unillustrated Latin edition in 1471, before he had the right to use woodcuts. The German edition of 1475–6 was set in Zainer's even gothic type to the same column width as the *Speculum humanae salvationis* and illustrated, as it had been, with column-wide woodcuts (these more sophisticated in drawing) bordered by a double line. To the new book Zainer added large printed block capitals in the design known as "maiblumen," lilies of the valley, that came to be widely used in Augsburg, Ulm, and wherever else the books of these two towns were emulated. The initials, the type, and the illustrations in the *Spiegel des menschlichen Lebens* fit together in perfect unity. The black backgrounds of the initials, and the areas of pure black used in the illustrations along with scanty and confined areas of shading, produce a rich and colorful effect.

In the same year as the *Spiegel des menschlichen Lebens* Zainer produced one of the first printed illustrated Bibles, its illustrations contained mainly in large historiated initials.

Gunther Zainer died in 1478, but in his few years of printing in Augsburg he produced an enormous number of books. Thirty-six thousand copies came off his press—over a hundred editions—and he became one of the wealthiest citizens of the commercial city of Augsburg.

Nearby Ulm was the center of production for playing cards distributed all over Europe. It became also a center of illustrated books second only to Augsburg. Johann Zainer began there

Boccaccio,
De mulieribus claris
page 91

in 1473 a less fortunate but no less distinguished career than his relative with an edition of Boccaccio's *De mulieribus claris (Of Famous Women)*. Its eighty woodcuts of women are all in contemporary German dress, whether they represent Cleopatra or a Greek goddess. But the illustrations have a very decorative, overall quality—a conscious filling-out of the space. They are set in close relation to Johann Zainer's lighter, smaller type and embellished with fantastic little capitals shaped of serpents, birds or twisted leaf-forms after the Lombardic capitals of earlier manuscripts.

The book begins in manuscript style: with a simple statement of the title and contents in the same size of letters as the rest of the text. The first page of the text is marked by an elaborate woodcut half-border also taken from manuscript style, showing the Serpent, Adam, and the first famous woman, Eve, handing down the fateful apple. The curves of the serpent form the initial "S" and then end in a scroll of foliage in whose tendrils are depicted the seven deadly sins. William Morris said of this ornament: "The great initial 'S' I claim to be one of the very best printers' ornaments ever made, one which would not disgrace a thirteenth-century manuscript."

Aesop,
Vita et fabulae
pages 92 and 93

Aesop's *Fables* were a great favorite in the fifteenth century and were printed in innumerable editions. Johann Zainer's edition is certainly the most delightful of them all. Zainer printed it around 1476 in a good-sized gothic type with simple but effective uncial initials. Besides a full-page frontispiece with an imaginary portrait of Aesop, he used nearly two hundred woodcuts the width of the type and something less than half a page deep. The drawing, faithfully preserved in the woodcutting, is of a fluent, easy grace; the cuts are often unbordered, so that the lines and spaces flow into the large white space of the margins. The name of the illustrator is not known; the Aesop is the only book he illustrated at Ulm, but his distinctive style has been traced in various other places.

The Aesop was reprinted at Augsburg by Gunther Zainer and copied later in Germany, France, the Netherlands, and England. But despite the popularity of his work, Johann Zainer seems to have had financial difficulties from about 1478 on. He became a miscellaneous printer and from then on produced no more first-class illustrated books, though many of his otherwise unillustrated books had beautiful half-borders and woodcut capitals.

The production of illustrated books was taken over by other printers in Ulm in the last two decades of the century. Conrad Dinckmut was especially prolific. Occasionally he sinned rather heavily in the matter of reusing the same cuts to produce the effect of a richly illustrated edition. In one book, the *Seelenwurzgarten*, he repeated nineteen blocks to make 134 illustrations, reusing a full-page "tortures of the damned" no less than thirty-seven times. But he is

Terence,
Eunuchus
pages 94 and 95

justly famous for his edition of Terence's *Eunuchus*, printed in 1486 with twenty-eight nearly full-page cuts illustrating the scenes. The backgrounds of most of these scenes are perspective

BOCCACCIO, *De mulieribus claris*. Ulm, Johann Zainer, 1473. Pierpont Morgan Library. 11½ x 7¾ in.
AESOP, *Vita et fabulae*. Ulm, Johann Zainer, 1476. Pierpont Morgan Library. 12 x 8¼ in. →
TERENCE, *Eunuchus*. Ulm, Conrad Dinckmut, 1486. Pierpont Morgan Library. 11¼ x 8 in. →

De Marsepia & Lampedone reginis amazonū. C. ri

Arsepia seu marthesia & lampedo soro res
fuere Amazonum inuicem regine/ & ob il=
lustrem belloꝛ gloriam sese martis vocauē
filias Quaꝝ qm peꝛgrina sit historia paulo
altius assumēda est/ e scithia ergo ea tēpestate siluestri &
fere in accessa exteris regione/ & sub artheo se in occea
num vsꝗ ab eusino sinu ptendente/ Siliscus & scolo=
picus (vt aiunt) regij iuuenes factione maioꝛ pulsi cū
parte ipsoꝛ iuxta thermodohontē cappadocie amnem
deuenē/ & tirps occupatis aruis raptu viuē & incolas
latrocinijs infestare cepē. A quibus tractu temporis p
insidias fere omnes trucidati sunt homines. Qo cum
egreferent viduate coniuges/ & in ardoꝛē vindicte de=
uenissent feruidē/ cum paucis qui supuixerint viris in
arma ꝓrupere. Et primo impetu facto hostes a suis
demouere finibus/inde vltro circumstantibus intulere
bellum/demum arbitrantes hūitutē potius ꝗ ꝺiugiū/
si exteris adhererent hoīnibus/ & feminas solas posse

Die erst fabel von dem Han vnd dem bernlin

Ain han súchet syne spys vff ainer miſ
ty·vñ als er ſcharzet/fand er ain koſt-
lichs bernlin an der vnwirdigen ſtatt
ligende·wo er aber daz alſo ligend ſach
ſprach er· O du gútes ding wie ligſt
du ſo ellenglich in dem kátt:hette dich ain gytigé
gefunden/wie mit groſſen frôden hett er dich vff
gezuket· vnd wereſt du wider in den alten ſchyn
dyner zierde geſetzet worden·So aber ich dich fin
de an der ſchnôden ſtatt ligende· vnd lieber myne
ſpys fúnde·ſo biſt du weder mir nútzlich noch ich
dir ¶ Diſe fabel ſagt eſopus denen·die in leſent vñ
nit verſtant·die nit erkeñent die krafft des edeln
bernlins· vnd das honig vß den blúmen nit ſugñ
kúnent·wañ den ſelben iſt er nit nútzlich ze leſen ·

Primus
De Gallo ⁊ iaspide

Dū rigido fodit ore, dū queritat escam
Dū stupet inuenta iaspide gallus, ait
Res vili preciosa loco, miriq; decoris
hac i sorde iaces? nil mihi messis hēs
Si tibi nūc esset, q debuit eē repertor
Quem fimus sepelit, viueret arte nitor
Nec tibi conuenio, nec tu mihi, nec tibi prosum.
Nec mihi tu prodes, plus amo cara minus
Tu gallo stolidum, tu iaspide zona sophye
Pulcra notes, stolido nil placet illa seges.

Fabula Secunda de Lupo et agno.

Esopus de innocente ⁊ improbo, talez
retulit fabulam. Agnus ⁊ lupus si-
cientes, ad riuū e diuerso venerūt, sur-
sum bibebat lupus, longeq; inferior a-
gnus. Lupus vt agnum vidit, sic ait
turbasti mihi aquaz bibenti, agnus patiens dixit,
quomodo aquā turbaui tibi que ad me de te recur-
rit, lupus non erubuit veritatē, ac maledicis mihi
inquit, agnus ait, nō maledixi tibi, at lupus et an
sex menses ita pater tuus mihi fecit, Agnus ait,
nec ego tunc natus eram. At lupus denuo ait ag
rum mihi pascendo deuastasti, Agnus inquit, tū
dentibus careā, quomodo id facere potui, lupus de
mū ira concitus ait, licet tua nequeam soluere argumenta, cenare tamen opipare intendo, agnūq;
cepit, innocentiq; vitam eripuit ac manducauit
Fabula significat qp apud improbos caluniat o
res, ratio et veritas non habent.

Phe.

As thun ich nun ⁊
wird ich auch noch
nit gan · so ich vnbe
gerend bin berieffet⁊oder
will ich mich allso stellen
das ich der bulerin schma
chait nit verdulde⁊ Sie
hat mich aus geschlossen
Sie beriefft mich wider ·
wird ich widerumb hin
gan⁊ Nain ⁊ob sie mich
flechnete · Par · Bei
hercle so ist nuntz fordrer
noch sterckers ob du das
thun macht · aber wirdest
du das anfachen vnnd nit
weislich volbringē so du
es nit mer erleiden macht
in vngemachtē fride wir
dest vnberieffet zu ir kum
men · ertzaigende sie lieb
haben · vnd dein abwe-
sen nit mügen erleidenn ·

N disem ersten tail Pro
thesis wirt gezaigt wie
gar verirret vnd ayges
willen vngewaltig ain
yeglich mensch in bul-
schaft verwickelt ist · vñ
wie wyß ð sich dar vor
bewaret ·

⁊Was thůn ich nun ·
Magst du wol dar ans
mercken das der Jüng-
ling mēgerlay gedacht
hat ee das er i dise trau
rige wort gefallen ist in
zweiflnng ·

⁊Wird ich noch nicht
gan ist ð sin · das er zwei
felet ob er sich durch
ir entschuldigen vnd ge
nůg tůn versönen wöll
oder sie gantz nicht mer
süchen · besunder ir ent-
schlahen ·

⁊Der bulerin smachait
Klagt von allen vnd ist
doch nun über aine er
zürnet ·

⁊Außgeflossen · Macht
es grösser wann sie flos
in nit auß · Aber sie wolt
in nit ein laffen die weil
der ritter bei ir was ·

⁊Beriefft mich wider

ist aber mer wañ sprech er sie begeret mein · ⁊Nain ob sie mich
flechnete · Ob er spräche · weder von gebet noch von berüffes we
gen noch von flöhen · das grösser ist wird ich zů ir komen · ⁊Her
cle · Er schwört als so wir sprechen by got · ⁊Vordrer · Loblicher
⁊Sterckers · Wann ainem mannß gemüt zů gehöret das er vn-
ordenlicher lieby mügte krefftigklichen widerston ·   b ij.

uidebatei dimna:contra eius dignitatem . Nunc autem quicumcp vestrum penes se
aliquod haberet testimonium. aut nouerit aliquid super hoc.referat nobis illud. vt z
nos omnia regi referamus.quoniam non est sui propositi interficere quemcp: nisi p⁹
acquisitionem diligentem et sufficientem examinationem. Non enim vult ipse iudi/
care secundum propriam voluntatem. nec faciem cognoscere in suo iudicio. Et ait iu
dex. Respicite et attendite bene omnia:que legalis leopardus locutus est . nec aliquis
vestrum occultare debet quod nouit de ista materia.siue causa . z hoc propter multas
causas. Prima quidem est:quia nullus vestrum dedignari debet sententiam que la /
ta fuerit.siue bona.siue mala. Nec velitis aliquid mutilare de eo quod scitis Na mo/
dicum veritatis maximum est.et precipue apud deum. vt rex non interficiat innocen/
tem et absq culpa verbis seductoris et mendacis . Secunda causa est . quia quando
punitur peccator iuxta peccatum suum:reliqui audientes:rimebunt et cauebunt sibi .
ne in simili incidant peccato. z hoc redundat in bonum regis exercitus et populi. Ter
tia causa est.quia quando perditur malus et seductor exercens mendacia et dolum:est
maxima tranquillitas regi:et exercitui suo. Nam sua conuersatio cum eis in maximū
et grauem turbationem redundat . Nunc igitur dicat vnusquisq vestrum quod no /
uit. necp celet veritatem.et confirmet:falsitatem. Cumq audissent viri exercitus ver/
ba hec:respiciebant vnusquisq ad inuicem et tacebant. Dixit dimna . Quare tacetis?
dicat vnusquisq vestruz quod nouit. quoniam non credatis mixi displicere.si omnia
que scitis dixeritis. Nam si ego deliquissem gauderem vticp pro vestro silencio: Uer/
tamen scio me esse innocentem. Et ideo in eo quod scitis loquamini. Scitote tamē cū
veritate.quia ad omnia est responsum.Et ideo cauete:ne aliquod quod nescitis:profe
ratis. Nam ei qui putat vidisse quod non vidit:et audiisse quod non audiuit: dignū

views of the streets of a medieval town, and obviously represent stage sets. The text of the play is set in large type with commentary in much smaller type running in a narrow column beside it.

Strassburg, where Johann Mentelin had been printing his large, dignified volumes since 1461, produced no pictorial books until around 1476 when Heinrich Knoblochtzer began to print there. His books were mostly of a popular nature, and their illustrations followed the style of Augsburg and of Ulm. Nevertheless, they added something of their own. When Knoblochtzer copied Johann Zainer's Aesop, for example, he added a fine woodcut border in illuminated style, with interlaced branches full of flowers, birds, and insects. Knoblochtzer printed over fifty books in Strassburg before 1484 and was next heard of at Heidelberg where he printed about twenty more.

Johann Prüss of Strassburg is another printer whose books, while lacking the controlled beauty of the Zainers' best books, had often a vitality of their own. His 1488 edition of Bidpai's *Directorium humanae vite*, a book of ancient fables, is set in an extremely fine, even, but black gothic type whose texture is repeated in the cutting of the curious woodcuts. The similarity of these textures, and the contrast provided by the heavy borders to the cuts and the heavy, large type of the headings, produce a fresh, vivid effect.

Bidpai, Directorium humanae vite page 96

The city of Basel, a university town, from the outset printed books for scholars and clerics. Berthold Ruppel, the first known printer there, turned out Latin Bibles and other large books. Michael Wennsler, who began printing shortly after Ruppel, was obviously an admirer of Peter Schoeffer's books.

In the wake of all these large, heavy volumes Johann Froben made a landmark in 1491 by producing as his first book a small printed Bible. All Bibles had hitherto been either folio or quarto size. Froben made his octavo (4½″ x 6⅝″ bound) and only 2½″ thick by printing it in the first very small type. The initials were left to be filled in in color by the rubricator, but in minute type references to parallel passages were printed in, for the first time.

Froben's books, like those of his predecessors, were mainly addressed to the scholars at the university. He was closely connected with the humanist Erasmus, whose writings were prominent among Froben's publications after 1513.

A scholar at the University of Basel took an uncommon interest in illustrated books and had much to do with stimulating their production in Basel and elsewhere. Sebastian Brant, one of the most distinguished humanists of his day, wrote the *Narrenschiff (The Ship of Fools)* and supervised its illustration and printing in 1494 at the press of Johann Bergmann. The format and presswork of the book are not fine, but the illustrations are Basel's best, thought to have been made by the youthful Albrecht Dürer, who spent some time there in his early travels.

Brant, Narrenschiff page 99

Dürer's style is detected also in another Basel book, the *Ritter vom Thurn*.

Before the end of the year, pirated editions of the *Narrenschiff* appeared at Nuremberg, Augsburg, Strassburg, and elsewhere. Bergman printed a number of new editions in German and also in Latin, and the book quickly became the best known in Europe.

Brant's influence on illustrated books extended to Strassburg, where he went about 1494. Johann Grüninger was the most prolific of Strassburg's printers. He had begun work in 1483 but produced no noteworthy illustrated books until he came under the influence of Brant. The result was his edition of the comedies of Terence published in 1496, illustrated in a rich Gothic style in which many close parallel lines gave the deep tonal quality of engraving. The full-page frontispiece showing the interior of the theater is very fine, though the theater is a fanciful version of a contemporary Gothic one and not the classical theater of Terence's time. The smaller illustrations are made up in a curious way by various combinations of a set of separate cuts—an attempt that was made a number of times in fifteenth-century books with little success. A Horace and a Virgil edited by Brant followed, in the same rich style—the Virgil more successful because it contained no combination cuts.

At Cologne, printing had begun early—some time before 1466—with Ulrich Zell, later the informant of the *Cologne Chronicle* about the invention of printing. Zell printed in an excellent even type, mostly quarto volumes of practical use to priests. A local rival to Zell rose in Arnold ther Hoernen, apparently a self-taught printer who became a fine craftsman and something of an innovator. In 1470 Ther Hoernen used a separate title page for Rolewinck's *Sermon for the feast of the presentation*—eight and a half lines set as they fell at the top of the page. He also used pagination, for the first time in printing history, in his edition of Rolewinck's *Fasciculus temporum* in 1474. But he did not follow up these innovations, which remained merely precursors of a development to come later. The use of a separate title page did not begin continuously until the 1480's and was not really general until the end of the first quarter of the sixteenth century.

The *Fasciculus temporum* printed by Ther Hoernen was the first of the printed epitomes of history that became immensely popular thereafter. These books lumped together biblical and mundane history, beginning with the Creation and ending with local affairs of the time. Another printer, Gotz, brought out an edition in the same year at Cologne, but Ther Hoernen's book, with a fair number of cuts, was the prototype for the many copies that appeared in Germany and elsewhere.

Cologne Bible
page 100
Cologne's most important illustrated book was the Bible printed in 1478–9 by Heinrich Quentell, which influenced Bible illustration all over Europe for generations. It was issued in two editions, one Low, the other High German, in two large folio volumes. The use of one size of type throughout, with divisions in the text marked by white space and large red and blue

SEBASTIAN BRANT, *Narrenschiff*. Basel, Johann Bergmann, Latin edition of 1497. Yale Beinecke Rare Book Library.

De Antiquis fatuis.
Ad ſtructũ q̃uis langueſ declino ſepulchrum.
Triuerit & metã iam mea vita datam.
Non tamẽ antiquos fatuoꝛ deſero mores.
Stultitięꝗ vias inueteratus amo.

De antiquis
fatuis.

Inueterata meę dementia craſſa ſenectę:
Non ſolitos linquit mores:vitamve priorem:
Sum puer:& centũ tranſacti temporis annos
Connumerare queo:nec enī ſapientior vſꝗ

god dat wy gheſtoruen weren dorch de hant
des heren in dem lande van Egipten · do we ſe
ten by den duppenen des vleſches · vnde eten
broet in ſadicheit Warumme heueſtu vns ge
leydet in deſſe woſtenyge · dat du alle dat volk
hůgs wylleſt dode · Vn do ſprak de hē to moy
ſen Se ik ſchal iw regenen broet van deme hē
mel · dat volk ga vth vnde vorgadere dat dat
en ghenoch ſy dorch alle de daghe vp dat ik
ſe temptere efft ſe wanderen in myner ee efft
nicht Des ſeeſten daghes ſcholen ſe bereyden
dat ſe in brengen · vnde dat ſy dubbel mer wē
ſe plaghen to vorgaederen vor eenen ytlike
dach · Vnde do ſpreken moyſes vnde aaron to
alle yſrahels kinderē · tho auent ſchole gy we
ten dat de here hefft iuw gheleydet vth deme
lande van Egipten · vn vroge ſchole gy ſeē
des heren glorie Ik hebbe ghehort iuw mur
mureren teghen den heren Men wat ſint wy
dat gy teghen vns ghemuſmurret hebben ?
Vnde moyſes ſprak de here ſchall iw des auē
des gheuen vleſche to etten vnde des morgēs
broet i der ſadicheyt · wēt he iuw murmurē
ghehort hefft · dar mede ghy ghemuzmuret
hebben men wat ſint wy? Juwe murmureren
en is nicht teghen vns · men teghen den herē
Vnde do ſprak Moyſes tho aaron · Segge alle
der vorghaderinge der kindere Iſrahels Gaet
vor den heren wente hee hefft iuwe murmure
ren ghehoet Vnde do aaron ſprak to alle der
ſcharen der kindere iſtahel · ſe ſeghen to d wil

teniſſe wert vnde de glorie des heren apen
de ſik in dem volke Vnde de here ſprak to
ſen ſegghende Ik hebbe der kindere iſta
murmureren ghehoert Spreke tho en des
des ſchole ghy vleſche eten · vnde des anerē
ſchole ghy gheſadyghet werden myt br
vnde gy ſchole weten dat ik iuw got iuwe
re bin Als dat auent wart quamen de w
telen vnde bedeckede ere Tenten · vn des
ghens lach de douw omme alle den vmint
tenten · vnde als de douw dat vterſte der
bedecket hadde · do vorſcheen he ghemyn
in der woſtenighen · recht efft he in eenē
teer to wreuen were · gheliker wijs als de
vp der erden · vnde als dat ſeghen de ki
iſtahels · do ſpreken ſe vnder een anderen
huſdat ys bedudet wat is dat? Se en wu
nicht wat dat was vnde moyſes ſprak t
Dyt is dat broet dat iuw de here hefft ge
uen tho etten Dyt is de rede de iuw de her
bouen hadde · vorghader een ytlick van
alſo vele als hee ghenoch hebbe th o ett
eene mate vor eenen ytlicken mynſche · G
ſcholen yt nemen na dem ghetale iuwer ſ
de wonen in den tabernaculen · Vnde alſo
den yſtahels kindere · vnde vorghader
der eene mer · der ander myn · Vnde mētm
nae der maten ghomor · noch de meer vor
dert hadde · hadde meer · noch de es myn
reyt hadde en vant myn · ſunder een iur
lick daer nae he etten mochte vorghader

initials put in by hand for contrast, makes a book of harmonious simplicity. Widely spaced in the text are 113 woodcuts that span both columns. The design of the woodcuts is Netherlandish in character, with stiff, heavy outlines and parallel shading, used in decorative wavy lines for water and hair. They show the hand of more than one designer: some are very primitive and expressive, others haxe extraordinarily fine groupings of figures; still others, an Italianate sense of order and space. Poor planning, or a shortage of time or funds as the work went on, produced a state of affairs not uncommon in early printed books: almost all of the cuts are in the first half of the book. Toward the end of volume two a one-column cut is suddenly introduced and repeated nine times, as if a desperate attempt had been made to make up for the lack. But this small shortcoming did not diminish the impact of the Cologne Bible. It remained the source of inspiration for Bible illustrations for a long time to come. The illustrated Malermi Bible of Venice in 1490 based its woodcuts on the Cologne Bible, and Hans Holbein, working in Basel a generation later, turned to it for ideas.

At Lübeck in 1494 Stefan Arndes printed a Bible with illustrations of exceptional merit, far more sophisticated than those of the Cologne Bible. But as a whole the Lübeck Bible was less successful than the Cologne Bible, and had less effect on subsequent Bible production.

By 1472 Mainz had lost the leadership in printing to other German cities. The firm of Fust and Schoeffer had broken up when Fust on a business trip to Paris succumbed to the plague. Peter Schoeffer continued printing alone until 1505, when he was succeeded by his son. His books were of very high quality and interest, but they never attained the magnitude of the firm's early books.

The three most important herbals of the fifteenth century were printed at Mainz, two of them by Schoeffer. Herbals, descended with little change from Greek sources, continued to be important books of medicine in the fifteenth century. Schoeffer printed the *Herbarius latinus* in 1484. The following year he brought out the *Gart der Gesundheit (The Garden of Health)* with a large number of illustrations, mostly of plants. The author, a Frankfurt doctor named Joannes de Cuba, claimed not only to have compiled the standard ancient herbals but also to have traveled with an artist to Italy, Greece, the Holy Land, Arabia, Babylonia, and Egypt in search of herbs. Some of the illustrations in Schoeffer's book were probably copied from the manuscript sources, but many of them were obviously drawn directly from nature—an unusual thing at that time.

Gart der Gesundheit
page 102

Schoeffer's *Gart der Gesundheit* was the most popular herbal of its day, but from the point of view of bookmaking it is rivalled by the *Ortus sanitatis* published in 1491 by the Mainz printer Johannes Meydenbach. The *Ortus sanitatis* was based on Schoeffer's popular herbal but added sections on animals, birds, fish, stones, and minerals to produce a hefty book of

Flores frumentoꝛ kornblomen Cap·lrcij

Lores frumentorũ latine.   Die meister sprechen daz disse
blomẽ wachsen in dẽ korn·vñ der synt etlich an der farbe blae
etlich brün vnd etlich wyß. Diß blomen krut oder würtzel
nutzet mã gar wenig zũ artznyn dẽ mẽschen in dẽ lyp·Aber vßwẽdig
des lybes mag man die nutzen in dryerley wege nach dẽ sie dry farbe
haben·Zũ dẽ ersten die blaen gemischet mit spangrün vñ die vff eyn
fule fley schicht wũden geleyt verzeret das gar balde·Die brunẽ korn
blomen gemischet mit bolo armeno vñ vmb die wũden gestrichen be
ny mpt die hitze dar vmb·Die wyssen korn blomẽ gemischet mit bly
wyß vñ baumöle vñ darvß gemacht eỹ plaster kület vñ heylet alle
hitzige blatern.   Item die blaen vñ brunen korn blomẽ gedorret
das puluer machet dem zucker hübsch farbe·Das zucker do mit gez
macht mag man nutzen on schaden in den lyp·

454 leaves. The plants and the frontispiece are copied after Schoeffer's book, but the figures in the new parts of the text are in a different style, identified by some authorities as that of the illustrator of the Ulm Aesop.

By far the most important of the illustrated books of Mainz, and one of the most important of the fifteenth century, is the *Peregrinationes in montem Syon* (*Travels in Mount Syon*) written by Bernardus de Breidenbach and published by the artist Erhard Reuwich in 1486, using Peter Schoeffer's type and probably his press. Breidenbach was a wealthy nobleman who reputedly had led a loose life until the time of his pilgrimage, which he undertook in penance. He brought with him on his travels the artist Erhard Reuwich to draw the cities and sights they saw along the way. This was the first time that the name of the illustrator of a printed book was recorded.

Briedenbach, Peregrinationes page 104

Reuwich was the first medieval woodcut designer to have a truly modern spirit. He observed closely from nature and recorded his observations in a clear and beautiful style. Most of his pictures in the *Peregrinationes* are views of places visited: Venice, Corfu, Candia, Rhodes, and others. Some of these are double-page views with fold-out flaps, affording a large panorama of the towns in their crenelated battlements, with many little scenes of life visible here and there. The most extensive (and the best known) is the view of Venice, which folds out to a leaf fifty-seven inches long plus its facing page—room for the entire island with its chief buildings, set in the surrounding sea and islands. A map of Palestine is almost as long.

Reuwich made drawings of the types of people he met in his travels—Saracens, Greeks, Jews, Indians—all in carefully detailed costume. He also drew the strange beasts of the Holy Land— some so strange they must have been meant as jests. In the illustrations in this book, Reuwich used cross-hatching for the first time in woodcut history. He used the direction of the line with consummate skill in modeling.

The German printer most renowned at the end of the century was Anton Koberger of Nuremberg. He carried on an immense trade in books, doing business with Paris, Milan, Florence, Bologna, Venice, Lyons, Vienna, and Krakow, besides many German cities. He is said to have had twenty-four presses and a hundred craftsmen working for him. Nuremberg had printers at work from 1470 on, and some of them developed substantial trades. But Koberger's large, ambitious volumes far surpassed any others published in his city. Even in the eighties, when other publishers found it necessary to give up printing large-sized books, Koberger kept up a prosperous business in them.

Koberger's two masterpieces are the *Schatzbehalter*, a religious treatise, and the *Nuremberg Chronicle*, both illustrated by the artist Michael Wolgemut, for a time Dürer's teacher. Both books are immense, heavy tomes, richly made and illustrated. The Schatzbehalter was printed

Hec est dispositio et figura
templi dñici sepulchri abextra

Ante templu sepulchri dñi locatq. & lapis iste supq. quo xp̃s cruce baiulãs cecidit.

¶ De ingressu in templum dñici sepulcri et processione inibi facta
ad loca sacra.

Ie·xij. Iulij hora vesperarũ in ipm venerandũ dñici sepulcri templũ a paganis·id est rectoribus ipius ciuitatis sancte
Ierosolime suim⁹ admissi et numerati·ostijs p eos apertis·
pro qua re vnusquisqz nostrũ quinqz exsoluit ducatos·nec
vnqz alias hoc aperitur templũ ab eis·nisi vel propter aduenientes pere-
grinos·vel fratres mutandos qui ibi pro custodia deputãtur. Moxqz
nobis intromissis templũ clauserũt. Intrauerũt autẽ nobiscũ Gardia-
nus ipe et plures suoz cõfratrũ. Quaprimũ aũt deuotus quisqz xp̃ia-
nus vel peregrin⁹ in templũ hoc pedem posuerit·plenariã cõsequitur
remissionem.

¶ Est autẽ hec dispositio templi eiusdem sacratissimi. Ecclesia ipa rotũ-
da est·et habet p diametrũ inter columnas septuaginta tres pedes·ab-
sidesqz que habẽnt p circuitũ a muro exteriori ecclesie decẽ pedes super
sepulcrũ dñi·qd in mediũ eiusdem ecclesie est apertura rotunda ita vt
tota cripta sancti sepulcri sit sub diuo. Galgathana autẽ ecclesia adhe-
ret isti·et est oblonga loco chori ecclesie sancti sepulcri adiũcta·sed parũ
demissior·sunt tamẽ ambe sub vno tecto. Spelunca in qua est sepulcrũ
dñi habet in lõgitudine octo pedes·in latitudine similiter octo vndiqz
tecta marmore exteri⁹·sed interi⁹ est rupes vna sicut fuit tpe sepulture

104

in 1491, when Koberger had been twenty years in business. It followed an ambitious scheme which was only partly realized: There are ninety-two full-page woodcuts in the first half of the book; in the second half of the book there are only two. The illustrations, mostly scenes from the scriptures, are in a rich engraving technique. Perhaps the most characteristic is the one which shows Christ kneeling before God the Father, a scene as decorative as a Gothic tapestry. The intensely curled hair and beards are typical of Wolgemut's style.

In startling contrast are two hands, larger than life-size, that suddenly cover two facing pages near the front of the book, their joints covered with roman numbers. Later in the book there are again hands, this time bearing a tiny portrait of the saints, the apostles and the Holy Family on each joint. The hands were, in the Middle Ages, natural devices for numbering or memorizing.

The illustrations in the *Schatzbehalter* appear among simple pages of large, flowing gothic type set in two columns which run continuously, with paragraphs indicated only by printed marks. A large running head is used over the right-hand page, and the same heavy type appears over the pictures in written-out numbers. Rubrics and large illuminated letters were put in by hand.

Even more elaborate in plan is the *Liber chronicarum* or *Nuremberg Chronicle* which Koberger printed in 1493—a book of monumental ambition carried out with masterful technique. The text itself ventured nothing less than a total world history—biblical, classical, and traditional. The illustration scheme was immensely complex, embracing large double-page topographical cuts of cities which break across the pages in a variety of formations, and figures scattered in and among the text in every imaginable way, sometimes connected by richly coiling vines: over eighteen hundred pictures in all.

Nuremberg Chronicle page 107

The illustrators were apparently inexhaustible, but closer examination shows that among the large blocks of cities, twenty-two illustrate sixty-nine different subjects, and of the figures of kings, popes, and other personalities, ninety-six cuts are used to produce 598 illustrations. Cities and persons, regardless of epoch or place, are all in the prevailing German style. Alfred Pollard, the British authority on incunabula, has said of Koberger's two masterpieces, "Both books, fine as their best work is, must be regarded rather as the crown of German medieval craftsmanship in book-building than as belonging to the period of self-conscious artistic aim which is heralded by the Mainz *Breidenbach*, but really begins with Dürer."

Dürer, one of those giants who straddles two eras, embraced the end of Gothic and the beginning of Renaissance style in German illustration. What is thought to be his early work in Basel—the illustrations to Brant's *Narrenschiff* and to the *Ritter vom Thurn*—provided the high point in illustrated books in that city. After his travels, which took him to Italy, Dürer's style had matured into that powerful blend of Gothic and Renaissance which made him the greatest of all woodcut designers. In 1498 he produced his *Apocalypse,* with fifteen enormous woodcuts. So faithfully do the woodblocks convey his tempestuous line that it has often been assumed that Dürer cut his own blocks. Hind believes it more likely that he drew directly on the blocks and supervised their cutting.

The text in the *Apocalypse* was set in Koberger's black-letter type and printed in two columns on the reverse of each large woodcut, facing the next illustration. It was undoubtedly printed at Koberger's press, although the colophon reads, "Printed by Albrecht Dürer, painter."

HARTMANN SCHEDEL, *Liber chronicarum.* Nuremburg, Anton Koberger, 1493. Pierpont Morgan Library. 19 x 12½ in.

Iaphet tercius filius noe habz septem filios q̇ et europam fortitus eſt. Iſte iaphet a p̄e bn̄dictus ē
ꝓpter ingenuā nobilitatem dilatatiōnéq̇ ei impcabat . ꝉ ab eo deſcenderūt generatōnes. xv. Septē
aūt gētes per iaphet filios inſtitute fuerūt.   Gomer p̄mogenit⁹ iaphet in europam venienſ gome|
ritas inſtituit:q̇ poſtea a grecis galathe nūcupati ſunt: ꝉ a q̇bus galatia regio. Ḣec quippe biſpanie ꝉ luſi
tanie cōtermina quā a meridie bz. Ab occidēte v̇o ꝉ ſeptētriōe occeanū. Et ab oriēte flumē ſequaue ꝉ ger
manie puicias. Gomer q̇ primus fi. iaphet a q̇ galathij ꝉ bz. z. filios.   Prim⁹ aſtanes a q̇ ſarmacia. hij
ſcithaz hoies ſunt i paludis meothidis ꝓfundo hitātes q̇ exilis regio ē inſeliciaꝭ arborib⁹ referta. Scōs
Riphath al᷑raphaa a q̇ paphlagones. ꝉ paphlagonia nomē accepit. h̄ ē minoris aſie regio. Tera⁹ The
gozma a q̇ friges emerſere. ꝉ a q̇b⁹ frigia mioris aſie ꝓuicia cog̈miata fuit: q̇ poſtea dardania.vnde troia
cog̈miata ē. Scōs fi. iaphet magog a q̇ ſcithe ꝉ a q̇bus ſcithia ꝉ gothia nomen bũere. Terci⁹ Medar ſiue
made⁹ a q̇ medi a q̇b⁹ media regio nomē ſortita ē q̇ ē aſſyrie ꝉ pſie vicina. Quart⁹ fi. iaphet iauan a q̇ gre

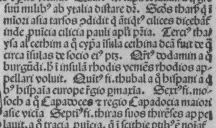

ci. hic. iiij. genuit filios   **Iaphet**   **Funda vxoꝛ**   ſui milib⁹ ab ytalia diſtare dr̄. Scōs tharb q̇ i
iſte ꝓdidit iones grecos   mioꝛi aſia tarſos ꝓdidit q̇ ātiq̇t᷑ cilices dicebāt
et a q̇b⁹ mare ioniū no| inde ꝓuicia cilicia pauli apli̇ pāa. Terci⁹ thaꝛ
mē accepit.ionia.ei gre| yſa al᷑ cethim a q̇ cypa iſſula cethina dc̄a fuit de q̇
coꝛ regio fuit.iter cariā   circa iſulas de ſocio ei᷑ ptz. Qr̄t⁹ v̇damin a q̇
ꝉ eolia q̇ nunc Turchia   burgūdi. h̄ i inſulā rhodis venienſ rhodios appel
dr̄.   Prim⁹ beliſſan a q̇   pellari voluit. Quit⁹ fi. thubal a q̇ hiſpani a q̇
heliſey. q̇ poſtea eoliꝫ a   b⁹ hiſpania europe ꝉgio pmaria. Sext⁹ fi. mo|
grecꝭ nūcupati ſunt. a q̇| ſoch a q̇ Capadoces ꝉ regio Capadocia maioꝛi
bus eolia iſula in ſiculo   aſie vicia Septi⁹ fi. thiras ſuos thiréſes appe|
mari vigitiq̇z q̇nq̇ paſ| lauit. a q̇ tracia ꝓuicia. q̇ i ſcithie ꝓtib⁹ ē noiat

Medar ſiue mare⁹   Magug   Gomer

Moſoch   Thubal   Iauan   Aſtanes

Thyras   Eliſan   Tharſis   Riphat

Dodanij   Thapſia   Thogoꝛma

Cvm ergo marem ad similitudíné suã primũ finxisset: tũ etíã feíam configurauit ad ipsius hõis effigiem. ut duo ínter se permixti sexus: propagare sobolem possent. et oẽm terrã multitudíne opplere. In ipsius aũt hois fictione: illarũ duarũ materiarũ: quas ínter se diximus eẽ cõtrarias: ignis & aqua conclusit perfecitq; rõem. Ficto eni corpe spirauit ei aíam de uitali fonte spũs sui. qui est pennis. ut ipsius mundi ex contrariis constantis elemẽtis similitudíne gereret. Constat eni ex aía & corpe. idest. qi ex cẹlo et terra. qñ quidem aía qua uíuimus uelud e cẹlo oritur a deo. corpus e terra: cuius e limo diximus esse formatum. Empedocles quẽ nescias utrũ ne ínter poetas an ínter philosophos numeres. quia de rerũ natura uersibus scpsit. ut apud romanos Lucretius. et Varro quatuor elementa constituit. idest · ignem aerem aquã & terrã. fortasse Trimegistũ sequutus. q nr̃a corpa ex his qtuor elemẽtis constituta eẽ dixit a deo. Habere nãq; ín se aliqd ignis: aliquid aeris: aliqd aquẹ: aliqd terrẹ. et neq; ignẽ esse. neq; aerẽ. neq; aquã. neq; terrã. quẹ qdem falsa non sunt. Nam terrẹ rõ ín carne est. humoris ín sanguíne. aeris ín spũ. ignis ín calore uitali. sed neq; sanguis a corpe secerni potest: sicut humor a terra. neq; calor uitalis a spũ. sicut ignis ab aere. adeo rerũ oim duo sola repíũtur elemẽta. quoỹ ois rõ ín nr̃i corpis fictione conclusa est. Ex rebus igit̃ díuersis ac repugnantibus homo factus est sicut ipe mundus ex luce ac tenebris. ex uíta ac morte. quẹ duo ínter se pugnare ín hoíe precepit. ut si aía supauerit: quẹ ex deo orítur sit ímortalis: et ín ppe tua luce uersetur. Si autem corpus uícerit aíam dictioniq; subiecerit: sit ín tenebris sempiternís & ín morte. cuius non ea uís est: ut ínuístas animas extínguat oío: sed ut puníat i ẹternũ. Eam pẹnã secũdam mortẽ noíamus: quẹ est & ipa ppetua: sicut et ímortalitas. Primã sic diffinimus. Mors est naturẹ aíantiũ dissolutio. uel ita. Mors est corpis aiẹq; seductio. Secũdam uero sic. Mors est ẹterní doloris ppessio. uel ita. Mors est aíarũ pro merítis ad ẹterna supplicia damnatio. Hẹc mutas pecudes non attíngit: quarũ aíẹ non ex deo constãtes: sed ex cõi aere morte soluunt̃. In hac igit̃ societate cẹli atq; terre: quarũ effigies ín hoíe expressa est: supioré pté tenent ea quẹ sunt dei. aía scilicet quẹ dñíum corpis habet. ínferiorem aũt ea quẹ sunt diaboli. Corpus itaq; quod qa terrenũ est: aíẹ debet esse subiectũ: sicut terra cẹlo. Est eni terra qi uasculũ quo tanq̃ domicilio tẽporali hic spiritus cẹlestis utatur. Vtriusq; officia sunt: ut hoc quod est ex cẹlo & deo iperet. Illud uero quod ex terra est: diabolo seruiat. Quod qdem non fugit hoíem: neq̃ Salustiũ q ait. Sed ois nostra uís ín aío & corpe sita est: animi imperio: corpis seruitio

ITALY

Italy, the intellectual and artistic center of the western world, was quick to avail herself of printing. Two Germans, Conrad Sweynheym of Mainz and Arnold Pannartz, set up the first press outside Germany towards the end of 1464 in the Benedictine monastery at Subiaco, in the hills near Rome. The abbot of the monastery, Cardinal Turrecremata, was a man of letters, interested in the production of Latin classics and of his own writings.

Sweynheym and Pannartz first printed a little Donatus grammar to show their type, and then Cicero's *De oratore* (undated) and Lactantius' *De divinibus institutionibus*, dated 1465. Significantly, Italy's first printed books were not religious but classical. The text of these and the two other books printed at Subiaco was set in a type that had some of the characteristics of the gothic letter and some of the round roman letter used in Italian humanistic manuscripts. Headings, paragraph marks, initials, and folios were left to be filled in by hand. The Greek occurring in the Lactantius volume, however, was cut and set in type—the first complete Greek alphabet in printing's short history.

Lactantius, De divinibus institutionibus page 108

Within three years Sweynheym and Pannartz moved to Rome, where they installed their press in the palace of a Roman nobleman. Here they immediately began to use a fully roman type suited to the Italian taste. It was the first true roman type in Italy, but a few months earlier a roman type had been cut in Strassburg (where it was not taken up) by the printer Adolf Rusch. In 1467, the year that Sweynheym and Pannartz brought out their first book in Rome, another printer began to work there, Ulrich Han of Vienna. He had been commissioned by Turrecremata to print his *Meditationes de vita Christi* and to illustrate the book with woodcuts drawn after murals in the church of Santa Maria sopra Minerva. Han's book was a quarto of thirty leaves with the text set in a good-sized semi-roman letter and thirty-three coarsely cut but handsome illustrations, some of which possessed an Italianate harmony.

Turrecremata, Meditationes de vita Christi page 110

By 1473, six years after they had come to Rome, Sweynheym and Pannartz had printed fifty-six editions, mostly of 275 copies each, and they found themselves suddenly overstocked with books. Printing had in these few years been introduced into at least ten Italian cities, and all

LACTANTIUS, *De divinibus institutionibus*. Subiaco, Sweynheym and Pannartz, 1465. Pierpont Morgan Library. 12 x 8½ in.

Dis det oculis meis fontem lacrimarum ut fleam tam misera
bilem prothoparentis nostri casum. O qp lugubzis ruina · fuerat
nempe tali legis conditione inuestigabili sapientia conditozis prothop
parens noster conditus ut si in ea rectitudinis arce qua plasmatus est
optimo suo conditozi immobiliter mansisset innexus·tāte ualitudinis
robore beatus esset · tantacp soliditate firmatus · ut nullo unquam
norie mutabilitatis impulsu.nulla infirmitate aut imbecillitate etatis
ab integritate innate ualitudinis defluxisset · Sane hac conditōe in pa
radiso locatus fuerat · teste gregozio ut si se ad conditozis obedientiā
uinculis caritatis astringeret ad celestē patriam angelozum absc̈p sue
carnis mozte transiret · Sed prochdoloz quia legē a celesti maiestate
decretam irritans conditozis sui amozē uerā stationis sue arcē destruit
lubzice mutabilitatis impulsu ab igenita soliditate perflatus a sui sta
tus glozia ꝯ splendoze cecidit dignitatis · Ita ut his cui ante uiolati
onem federis datū erat in paradiso nihil molestie·nihil indigentie sen
tire · odoriferis stipari malis · fulciri flozibus · glozia ꝯ honoze cōoz
natū cōuiuare plebibus angelozū · Illico p diuersa miseriarum gene

the new printers had been busily turning out Latin classics. In the financial crisis the partnership of Sweynheym and Pannartz dissolved. Han survived by taking a wealthy partner, and went on to print over eighty editions. But after 1480 printing in Rome was of small importance in the total output of Italian books.

The interest of a churchman had introduced printing to Subiaco and Rome. Venice, the leading commercial city of Europe, was not slow to take it up. Johannes de Spira, a goldsmith from Mainz, persuaded the authorities to grant him a five-year exclusive patent to print in Venice. He produced his first book there in 1469, but died the following year. His brother Vindelinus inherited the press but not the patent, and a rush of competitive printing immediately began. The brothers De Spira had begun work with a particularly handsome roman type, much improved over that of Sweynheym and Pannartz. In 1470 a Frenchman named Nicholaus Jenson, reported to have been sent by the king of France to Mainz to study printing, set up the second Venetian press. He immediately gained notice for his type, which was based on the De Spiras' but even finer. Some of his fame can perhaps be attributed to a flair for self-advertising; a catalog of books offered by his firm states that "the quality and value of his types is another marvel to relate for it ought to be ascribed rather to divine inspiration than to human wit." But his partners do not exaggerate when they state that "the letters are neither smaller, larger nor thicker than reason or pleasure demand." When at the end of the nineteenth century early type-forms were revived, Jenson's roman was the most admired and copied.

Aretinus,
De bello Italico
page 114

Venice had one printer at work in 1469, two in 1470, five in 1471, and twelve (half of them Germans) in 1472—all producing the same classics. The result was a crisis such as Rome experienced; some printers went out of business, others reduced their output sharply. The surviving printers turned their sights to new markets among the Venetian population and abroad. Venetian presses printed books in many tongues, including Greek, Balkan, and Armenian. Before long Venice became the printing center of all Europe; by the end of the fifteenth century 150 printers had worked there and had turned out four thousand editions.

As in Germany, the early books published in Italy remained close to the manuscript in style. Of the many processes involved in the production of a manuscript, the printers took over at first only the printing of the text. Woodcut illustrations were rare in Italian books before the last decade of the century.

One of the earliest notable illustrated books was *De re militari,* a treatise on war written by Valturius for Sigismondo Malatesta and printed in Verona in 1472. The book had many outline cuts of complicated and largely imaginary machines of war—devices for scaling castle walls, for fortification, for destruction and torture. The woodcuts were obviously printed separately from the text, perhaps because of the amount of space they took on the page. In any

Valturius,
De re militari
pages 112 and 113

TURRECREMATA, *Meditationes de vita Christi.* Rome, Ulrich Han, edition of 1478. Pierpont Morgan Library
VALTURIUS, *De re militari.* Verona, Joannes de Verona, 1472. Pierpont Morgan Library. 12 ¾ x 18 ¼ in. →

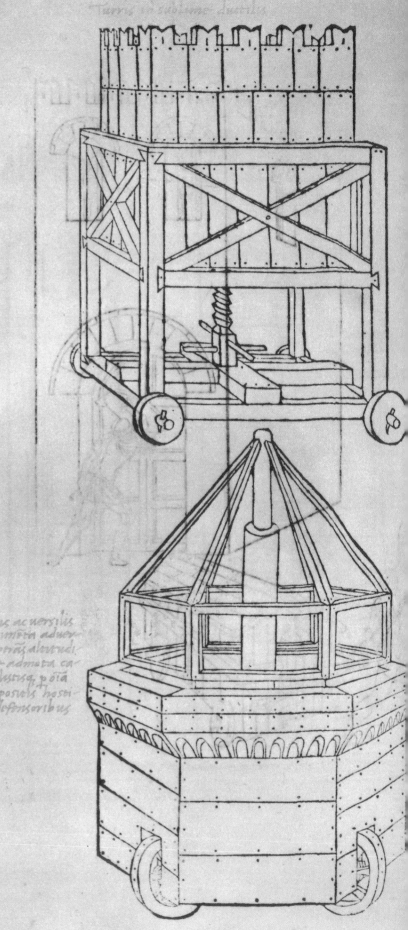

Turris mobilis ac uersilis
omnia munimenta aduer-
sa urbis supradi altitudi-
ne sunt: quae admota ca-
thapultis balistisque, p̄ōta
tabulata dispositis hosti-
um muros defensoribus
nudat.

HALAE turres sunt lignee : que apud ueteres propter specta-

se lignis erigebatur cp si ex materie larigna fiant : atcp uersiles

issime sunt : flammã enim missilem & ictus qualitate materie ac

igine sua non admittunt : Turres aũt a tornis dicte : teste uar-

uelut alii cp terretes sint : & recte lhe enĩ tam & si quãdocp qua-

re sint procul tame uidentibus rotunde existimãt . ideo quia ois

usq anguli simulachrum per longũ aeris spacium euanescit atcp

sumitur & rotũdum uidetur : Rotunde itacp aut poligonee sũt

ende quadratas enim machinę celerius dissipant : in rotunditat

usq ad centrum adigendo ledere non possunt

CVM IN HOC STATV RES essent:
bellumque cessaret ob indutias factas
Belisarius tamen romam:gotthi castra:
munitoesq̃ custodirét:querelæ & alter
catões ortæ sũt p̃ idutiis cõtra fidé uio
latis ex huiusmodi causa.Præsidiũ got
thoᵷ erat apud urbé portuensé ut supra ostédimus.Mi
lites q erãt i præsidio cũ deficerét sibi necessaria ad uictũ:
urbé illã deseruert:desertam uero Paulus Isauroᵷ præfe
ctus q hostiæ cũ classe remãserat occupauit . Nec multo
post Centũcellas urbé maritimã in tuscis desertas eodem
modo a gotthis Belisarii milites suscepert.Albã quoq̃ ur
bé quæ est i marsis eodé mõ deseruert gotthi :& Belisarii
milites occupart.Vitigis cũ has urbes captas ab hostibus
cognouisset:oratores romã misit:q ruptas contra fidem
idutias quererét.Portũ ení ac Cétũcellas & albã gotthoᵷ
oppida cõtra fas & æquũ ablata fuisse:nec deseruisse got
thos eas urbes sed uocatu suo uenisse ad se q erãt in præ
sidiis mox i eadé oppida reuersuros liberiusq̃ id fiducia
idutiaᵷ factũ esse a gotthis.Nec licuisse Belisario eas ur
bes p idutias capere.Itaq̃ restitutoém facere debere.His
legatis Belisarius i hũc modũ respõdit.Redite iqt ad regé
uestrũ:eiq̃ dicite quæ de uocatu redituq̃ præsidioᵷ alle
gãt ab eo cõponi:cæterũ oïbus patere qbus de causis got
thi eas urbes pro derelictis habuert: indutiis qdé eripere
auferreq̃ uetari.Occupare uero quæ a nullo possidentur
nequaq̃ phiberi.Ex hoc suspiciões isurrexert quærétibus
gotthis paria Belisario referre.At ení tres illæ urbes a Be
lisario susceptæ pmagnas sibi opportunitates ad bellum
afferebãt.Iã aduétabat hiems.Belisarius uero copiis abũ
dãs mittere i hiberna eqtes cõstituit. Misit igit̃ & in alia
loca & i agrũ picenũ eqtum duo milia.Præfecit autem his

APOLOGVS.

Ncomenzo contra la formica una terribile lite la mosca dandole parole
assai piene de inimicicia & cussi ornandose & fandose de assai & la formi
ca facendo uile & dicendole. o formica tu stai nascosta socte le caue della

← LEONARDUS ARETINUS, *De bello Italico*. Venice, Nicholaus Jenson, 1471. Pierpont Morgan Library.

AESOP, *Vita et fabulae*. Naples, Francesco del Tuppo, 1485. Pierpont Morgan Library

115

case, they were placed irregularly, overflowing into the margins in a free manner that gives them, unintentionally, a very modern appearance. The printer, Joannes de Verona, may be the same Giovanni Alvise who, with his brother Alberto, printed the first Italian Aesop in 1479, illustrated with lively woodcuts of quite a different nature.

The Verona Aesop shows cognizance of Zainer's Ulm edition, but is highly original in its illustrations, which became the source for a number of subsequent Italian editions. One of its features is the use of small separate floral motifs within the linear frames of the woodcuts. This is the first known use of the type ornaments known as "printers' flowers."

Aesop,
Vita et fabulae
page 115

Francesco del Tuppo, a jurist and humanist, was responsible for the publication in 1485 of the most interesting illustrated book in Naples, an edition of Aesop which he translated in paraphrase himself. Tuppo owned his own press and, as publisher, hired various printers to operate it for him. Three Germans, known as the "Germani fidelissimi" printed the Aesop in this way. The woodcut illustrations, based to some extent on those of the Verona Aesop, have a strong and curious Eastern flavor, enhanced by their patterned architectural frames. Naples was under Spanish rule at the time, and the decorative oriental quality could have been the product of a Spanish woodcutter. It may, however, simply reflect the Islamic style that had reached Naples through Sicily. The book is completed by a text set in small, firm black roman type, with square black-ground initials.

Other instances of Islamic influence occur in books produced in Naples and nearby Soncino by Hebrew printers. Joshua Solomon used a large border from Tuppo's Aesop in the Hebrew Bible he printed at Soncino in 1488, and another fine border made up of intensive scrollwork with putti, a peacock, and stags for the Hebrew Bible and the Pentateuch he printed shortly thereafter in Naples.

Regiomontanus,
Calendarium
page 117

A citizen of Augsburg, Erhard Ratdolt, working with partners, introduced the first printed decoration in Venetian books. The *Calendarium* of Regiomontanus, printed in 1476, also has the first complete title page, with the name of the book, the author, and the printer, as well as the date of issue. To these are added a description of the excellence of the book in verse and a classical border. The calendar, which contains sixty diagrams of eclipses, startlingly modern-looking in a two-color print of black and yellow, is said to have been taken by Columbus on his voyage of discovery.

Ratdolt and his partners produced seven different borders and ten sets of initials to go with them, all cut more skillfully than any woodcut seen in Italy till then. The later borders were cut in white on a black ground (which was sometimes printed in a color) and they were patterned with branchwork and foliage which grew increasingly bold. This decorative work remains unsurpassed, but, like the title page, was apparently ahead of its time; it was not copied by contemporary Venetian printers.

REGIOMONTANUS, *Calendarium*. Venice, Ratdolt, Maler, and Löslein, 1476. Yale Medical Historical Library

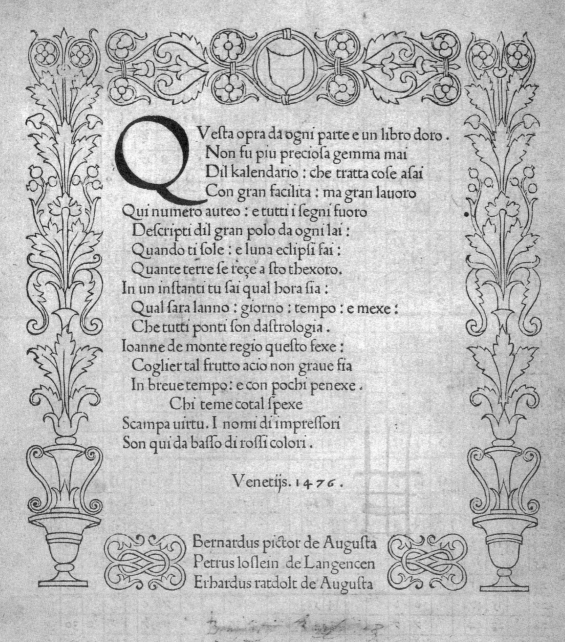

Questa opra da ogni parte e un libro doro .
  Non fu piu preciofa gemma mai
  Dil kalendario : che tratta cofe afai
  Con gran facilita : ma gran lauoro
Qui numero aureo : e tutti i fegni fuoro
  Defcripti dil gran polo da ogni lai :
  Quando ti fole : e luna eclipfi fai :
  Quante terre fe rece a fto thexoro.
In un inftanti tu fai qual hora fia :
  Qual fara lanno : giorno : tempo : e mexe :
  Che tutti ponti fon daftrologia .
Ioanne de monte regio quefto fexe :
  Coglier tal frutto acio non graue fia
  In breue tempo : e con pochi penexe .
    Chi teme cotal fpexe
Scampa uirtu . I nomi di impreffori
Son qui da baffo di roffi colori .

      Venetijs. 1476 .

Bernardus pictor de Augufta
Petrus loflein de Langencen
Erhardus ratdolt de Augufta

Euclid,
Geometriae elementa
page 119

After three years in partnership, Ratdolt began printing alone, producing mostly books of mathematics and astronomy. In the Euclid *Geometriae elementa* of 1482, Ratdolt shows both his decorative sense and his flair for technical innovation. The first page of the text has a handsome three-sided border and initial in white on a black ground. The text has been set in a close black-letter type in one column, leaving a wide outer margin for the necessary geometric figures. By some ingenious means Ratdolt constructed precise little line-cuts of the geometric figures which occur marginally throughout the book.

The first important literary classic to catch the imagination of the Venetian printers and whet their desire to publish an illustrated edition was the *Trionfi* of Petrarch. The Triumph of Love, Chastity, Fame, Time, and Divinity provided a perfect opportunity for the Renaissance illustrator, who represented each as a triumphal car in which the victor rides. Three different editions were published, beginning in 1488. By 1490 there was an outpouring of illustrated books in Venice. The finest period of Venetian illustration emerged in the last decade of the century, its typical features the very small column cut or vignette and the elaborately bordered first page derived from manuscript illumination and translated into pure line. Two distinct styles exist side by side: one lively and freely expressive, the other formal and classical. It has been assumed that there were two woodcutters' shops supplying the various printers.

The important new era of illustration was launched by the publication in 1490 of an illustrated edition of the Bible, translated into Italian by Niccolò Malermi. The first edition of the Italian Bible had been printed in 1471 by De Spira. The new edition, a handsome folio set in double columns, adorned with rich borders, and illustrated with 384 tiny lively woodcuts, was an immense success. At least ten editions of it were printed in the fifteenth century and twenty more in the sixteenth.

Malermi Bible
page 121

The Malermi Bible of 1490 had been published in Venice by Lucantonio Giunta, an enterprising Florentine, and printed by Giovanni Ragazzo. Three years later a printer known as Anima Mia brought out a copy of the Bible so close as to amount to piracy. But though the format of the book and the size (and often the subject) of the vignettes is identical, the new version is illustrated in the second or classical style of Venice. In the minute pictures, which show the hands of several woodcutters, the dignity and monumental quality of Renaissance art are often surprisingly present.

Boccaccio,
Il Decamerone
page 120

A number of literary editions came out in the styles of the two Malermi Bibles. The brothers De Gregoriis, the most varied and prolific printers of the time, brought out an edition of Boccaccio's *Decamerone* in 1492, illustrated with tiny lively cuts which were not only unclassical but often bawdy in their storytelling efforts. Small as they were, the cuts were sometimes further divided into compartments to show a sequence of action. Architectural elements were cleverly used to effect the division.

EUCLID, *Geometriae elementa*. Venice, Erhard Ratdolt, 1482. Yale Beinecke Rare Book Library. 12 x 8¼ in.
BOCCACCIO, *Il Decamerone*. Venice, De Gregoriis, 1492. Yale Beinecke Rare Book Library. 12 x 8¼ in. →
Bible in Italian (Malermi Bible). Venice, Anima Mia, 1493. New York Public Library →

Preclariſſimus liber elementorum Euclidis perſpi/
caciſſimi:in artem Geometrie incipit quāſoeliciſſime:

Unctus eſt cuius ps nō eſt. ꝃLinea eſt
lōgitudo ſine latitudine cui⁹ quidē ex/
tremitates ſt duo pūcta. ꝃLinea recta
ē ab vno pūcto ad aliū breuiſſima extē/
ſio ī extremitates ſuas vtrūq3 eoꝛ reci
piens. ꝃSupficies ē q̄ lōgitudinē ꝛ lati
tudinē tm̄ b3:cui⁹termi q̄uidē ſūt linee.
ꝃSupficies plana ē ab vna linea ad a/
liā extēſio ī extremitates ſuas recipiēs
ꝃAngulus planus ē duarū linearū al/
ternus ꝑtactus:quaꝛ expāſio ē ſup ſup/
ficiē applicatioq3 nō directa. ꝃQuādo aūt angulum ꝛtinēt due
linee recte rectiline⁹ angulus noiaꝛ. ꝃ Wn̄ recta linea ſup rectā
ſteterit duoq3 anguli ytrobiq3 fuerit eq̄les:eoꝛ vterq3 rect⁹erit
ꝃLineaq3 linee ſupſtās ei cui ſupſtat ꝑpendicularis vocaꝛ. ꝃAn
gulus vo qui recto maioꝛ ē obtuſus diciꝛ. ꝃAngul⁹vo minoꝛ re
cto acut⁹appellaꝛ. ꝃTerminⁱ ē q̄ ynilcuiulq3 finis ē. ꝃFigura
ē q̄ tmino vl termis ꝛtinet. ꝃCirculⁱē figura plana vna q̄dem li
nea ꝛtēta: q̄ circūferentia noiaꝛ:in cui⁹medio pūctⁱē: a quo⁹oēs
linee recte ad circūferētiā exeūtes ſibiinicez ſut equales. Et hic
quidē pūctⁱcētꝛ circuli dꝝ. ꝃDiameter circuli ē linea recta que
ſup ei⁹centꝛ trāſiens extremitateſq3 ſuas circūferētie applicans
circulū ī duo media diuidit. ꝃSemicirculus ē figura plana dia/
metro circuli ꝛ medietate circūferentie ꝛtenta. ꝃPoꝛtio circu/
li ē figura plana recta linea ꝛ parte circūferētie ꝛtēta: ſemicircu/
lo quidē aut maioꝛ aut minoꝛ. ꝃRectilinee figure ſūt q̄ rectis li/
neis cōtinēt quarū q̄dā trilatere q̄ trib⁹rectis lineis: q̄edā
quadrilatere q̄ q̄tuoꝛ rectis lineis. q̄dā mltilatere que pluribus
q̄3 quatuoꝛ rectis lineis continēt. ꝃFigurarū trilaterarū:alia
eſt triangulus bn̄s tria latera equalia. Alia triangulus duo bn̄s
eq̄lia latera. Alia triangulus truū inequalium laterū. Waꝛ iterū
alia eſt oꝛthogoniū:vnū.ſ.rectum angulum babens.Alia ē am/
bligonum aliquem obtuſum angulum babens. Alia eſt oꝛigoni
um:in qua tres anguli ſunt acuti. ꝃFigurarū autē quadrilateraꝛ
Alia eſt q̄dratum quod eſt equilaterū atq3 rectangulū. Alia eſt
tetragon⁹long⁹:q̄ eſt figura rectangula : ſed equilatera non eſt.
Alia eſt belmuaym: que eſt equilatera : ſed rectangula non eſt.

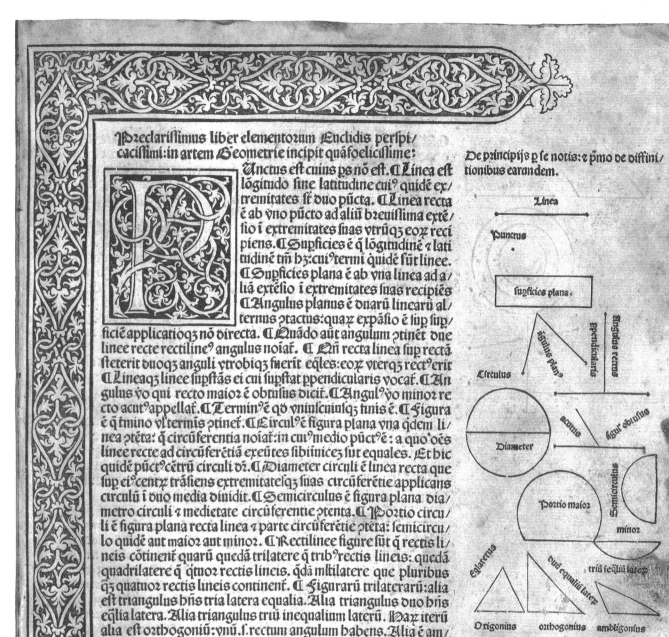

g la nella fúmita de piu alti monti appa
riuan la domenica matina iraggi del
la feguente luce ogni umbra partitafi
& manifeftaméte le cofe fe cognofcie
uano:quando la Reina leuatafi colla fua compa
gnia iprimieramente alquanto fuper le rugiado
fe herbette andarono & puoi infu la meza terza
una chiefetta loro uicina uifitata in quella il diui
no officio afcoltarono & a cafa tornatofi : puoi
che hebbono con letitia & fefta mangiato. Can
tarono & danzarono alquanto & appreffo licen
tiati dalla Reina chi uoleffe ádarfi a ripoffare po
te:ma hauendo il fole gia paffato il cierchio del
merigio.Come alla Reia piacq; al nouellare ufa
to tutti appreffo alla bella fontana a federe pofti
fi per comandamento della reina cofi Neiphile
comincio

f E cofi ha difpofto dio chio debba alla
prefente giornata dare con la mia no
uella cominciamento a me piace &po
amorofe dóne conciofia cofa che mol
to detto fia delle beffe facte da le dóne agli huo
mini una factane da úo homo a una dóna mi pia
ce da racontare non gia perche io intenda di bia
fimar i quella cio che lhomo fecie.O di dire che
alla dóna non foffe bene inueftito anzi per com
mendare lhomo & biafimare la donna &p mon
ftrare che anchefglihomini fanno beffare chi cre
de loro come effi da cui egli credono fonno bef
fati.auenga che chi uoleffe piu propriamente par
lare quello chio dire debbo non fi direbbe beffa
Anzi merito concio fia cofa che ciafcuna donna

de effere honeftiffima &la fua caftita come la fua
uita guardare.ne per alcuna cagione acontami
narla conducierfi : & quefto non poffendofi co
fi apieno tutta uia fare come fi conuerebbe per
la fragilita noftra . Affermo colei effere degna
del fuocho laquale acio per prezo fi conducie.
doue chi per amore cognofcendo le fue forze
grandiffime peruiene da giudice nó troppo rig
gido meriti perdono come pochi di paffati mó
ftro Philoftrato in madonna Philippa obferua
re imparato.

Nouella de Guilfardo.

f V adúq; gia in Millano uno todefco
al foldo: il cui nome fu Guilfardo pro
de della perfona : affai leale a coloro
nél cui feruigio fi metteua: ilché rade

EL PRINCIPIO DIO CREOE EL
cielo:& la terra. Et la terra era isructuosa:et
uacua & le tenebre erano sopra la facia de
labisso: Et el spirito del signore era menato
sopra le aque. Disse dio: Sia facta la luce. Et
facta e la luce. Et uide dio la luce esser bona
Et diuise la luce da le tenebre:& appello la
luce di:& le tenebre nocte. Et facto e la sera
& matina un di etiam disse dio:Sia facto el
firmaméto in mezo dele aque:el ql diuida
le aque dale aque. Et sece dio el firmaméto
Et diuise le aque cherano sotto el firmamé
to. Et facto e cosi: Et chiamo Dio el firmaméto cielo. Et facto e sera & matina el secó
do di. Etiã disse dio. Le aque che sono sotto
el cielo siano cógregate in uno loco & apar
ga la arida: Et facto e cosi. Et chiamo dio la
rida terra:& le congregatione dele aque ap
pello mare. Et uide dio esser bono: & disse.
Germine la terra herba uirente:& facia el se
me:& el legno pomifero che facia el fructo

secódo la sua generatione. La seméza del
quale sia in se medesimo sopra la terra:&
cosi facto e. Et la terra pdusse la herba uirente:& faciéte il seme secódo la sua gene
ratióe. Et el legno faciente el fructo & hã
uente ciaschaduno el seméte secódo la sua
specie:& uide dio essere bono:& facta e se
ra & matina el terzo di. Etiam disse Dio.
Siano facte le luminarie nel firmamento
del cielo:& separino el di & la nocte & sia
no in segni:& tépi:& di:& anni:pche Re
splendano nel firmaméto del cielo:& illu
miano la terra. Et cosi facto e. Et sece dio
duoi grãdi luminarii el luminare magio
re che soprastesse al di:& el lumiare mino
re che soprastesse ala nocte. Et etiam sece
Dio le stelle: Et puose quelle nel firmamé
to del cielo: pche lucessino sopra la terra:
& signorizasseno al di & ala nocte:& di-
uidesseno la luce & le tenebre. Et uide dio
eér bono:& facto e sera & matina:el quar
to di. Etiã disse Dio: Producano le aque
el reptile de lanime uiuente & uolatile so
pra la terra:sotto el firmaméto del cielo.
Et creo Dio le balene grande:& ogni aia
uiuéte & mutabile:lequal le aque haueua
no pducte nele sue specie:& ogni uolatile
secódo la sua generatióe. Et uide Dio esser bono:& benedisse essi dicédo. Crescet
te & multiplicate:& rempiete le aque del
mare. Et multiplichino gli uccielli sopra
la terra. Et facto e sera & matina el quinto
di. Disse etiã Dio pduca la terra lanima ui
uente nela sua generatióe:& iuméti:& gli
reptili:& le bestie dela terra secódo le sue
qualitade. Et facto e cosi. Et sece dio le be
stie dela terra secódo le sue specie li iumé
ti & ogni reptile dela terra nella sua gene-

to optatissime carne sentendo, nelle quale lalma sua uigendo, se nutri-
ua se euigiloe suspirulante, & reaperte le occlute palpebre. Et io repente
auidissima anhellando alla sua insperata reiteratione riceuute le debilita-
te & abandonate bracce, piamente, & cum dulcissime & amorose lachry-
mule cum singultato pertractantilo, & man uagendulo, & souente bassian
tilo, præsentandogli, gli monstraua il mio, Immo suo albente & pomige-
ro pecto palesemente, cum humanissimo aspecto, & cum illici ochii esso
sécia uario di hora, riuéne nelle mie caste & delicate bracce, Quale si læsio
ne patito non hauesse, & alquantulo reassumete il contaminato uigore,
Como alhora ello ualeua, cum tremula uoce, & suspiritti, mansuetamen
te disse, Polia Signora mia dolce, perche cusi atorto me fai? Di subito, O
me Nymphe celeberrime, me sentiui quasi de dolcecia amorosa, & pieto-
sa, & excessiua alacritate il core p medio piu molto dilacerare, per che quel
sangue che per dolore, & nimia formidine in se era constricto p troppo &
inusitata læticia, laxare le uene il sentiua exhausto, & tuta absorta, & attoni
ta ignoraua che me dire, Si non che io agli ancora pallidati labri, cum so-
luta audacia, gli offersi blandicula uno lasciuo & mustulento basio, Am-
bi dui serati, & constrecti in amorosi amplexi, Quali nel Hermetico Ca-
duceo gli intrichatamente conuoluti serpi, & quale il baculo inuoluto
del diuino Medico.

The vignettes are amusing, but the glory of the *Decamerone* lies in its two large double-column cuts, used in repetition to head the tales of each of the ten days, and in the charming border around the first page.

The De Gregoriis brothers printed over a hundred books in the fifteenth and sixteenth centuries, but none is more famous than the *Decamerone* and the *Fasciculo di medicina*, printed in 1493. The *Fasciculo* was a medical book with a practical intent. It contained charts of the male and female figures, the diagnosis of urines, the indications or contra-indications of treatment according to the signs of the zodiac, and similar material. The printers, however, saw fit to embellish it with four full-page cuts of a purely artistic nature, showing the author at his professor's pulpit, a professor with students, a doctor's visit to his patient, and a lesson in dissection. The figures in these illustrations, despite some inexpertness in cutting, have the masterly stance of Renaissance painting, and Hind suggests that they may have been designed by Mantegna or Bellini.

The large illustrated editions produced by Giunta and the De Gregoriis were intended for the merchants of Venice who had acquired wealth but not aristocratic tastes. The most discriminating book buyers still preferred a fine manuscript. They valued printed books only for their contents and preferred them in the simplest of styles, to which any decoration desired could be applied by hand.

Aldus Manutius was the first great scholar-printer. He was interested in printing the unpublished classics of Greek and Latin literature, and for this purpose he assembled a group of learned humanists and technical assistants to form a publishing office. By 1498 the press had published its first work of great importance, a large five-volume Aristotle.

The following year Aldus printed a book commissioned by a wealthy merchant: the *Hypnertomachia Poliphili (The Dream of Poliphilus)*, a fanciful love story written by the Dominican friar Colonna. The story of the lover's search for his beloved in a classical landscape led to a series of illustrations by an unknown artist in which, for the first time in a printed book, classical architecture and objects were pictured in the greatest detail. Some of the illustrations are in a delicate shaded style, like fine pen sketches, and have a Botticelli spirit. Others, especially the architectural ones, are in pure, exact line. The book presents a great variety of impressions: full-page architectural structures of startling shape, classical processions and rites, intimate scenes of Poliphilus alone or with his beloved. Throughout the roman text, cut by Francesco Griffo, are scattered classical objects and fragments, making an ingenious variety of page arrangements. Simple chapter headings in capitals the same size as the text give full value to the large floriated capitals. Paper, margins, and presswork are the finest imaginable. It is small wonder that the *Poliphilus* took Europe by storm. It is said that in France this one

Hypnertomachia Poliphili pages 122, 124 and 125

producesse, quali sono questi nel diuo fronte affixi, di questo cælico fig-
mento præfulgidi & amorosi, Et percio per tanti iurgii obsesso el tristo co
re & da tanta discrepante controuersia de appetiscentia sustiniua, Quale
si tra essi una fronde del astante lauro del tumulo del R e de Bibria in medio collocata fusse, Ne unque la rixa cessare, si non reiecta, Et cusi pensita
ua non cessabondo tanto litigio, si non da esso core tanto piacere de costei
(non factibile) fusse ablato. Et per tale ragione non se potea firmaméte có
uenire el uoluptico & inexplebile desio de luno ne de laltro, Quale homo
da fame exarcebato & tra multiplici & uarii eduli fremente, de tutti cupi-
do di niuno integramente rimane di lardente appetito contento, Ma de
Bulimia infecto.

LA BELLISSIMA NYMPHA AD POLIPHILO PER-
VENTA, CVM VNA FACOLA NELLA SINISTRA MA
NV GERVLA, ET CVM LA SOLVTA PRESOLO, LO IN
VITA CVM ESSA ANDARE, ET QVIVI POLIPHI-
LO INCOMINCIA PIV DA DOLCE AMORE
DELLA ELEGANTE DAMIGEL
LA CONCALEFACTO, GLI
SENTIMENTI INFLAM
MARSENE.

ESPECTANDO PRAESENTIALMENTE EL
reale & intelligibile obiecto duna præstantissima repræ-
sentatione de tanta uenustissima præsentia & diuo aspecto, & de uno copioso aceruo & uniuersale aggregatione
de inuisa bellecia & inhumana formositate, Exiguo &
exile per questo & impare reputaua tutte anteuidute iex-
timabile delitie, & opulentie & elate magnificentie, ad tanto ualore quan
to e costei. O fœlice dunque colui che tale & tanto thesoro di amore quie
to possiderae. Ma non solamente possessore fœlice, ueramente beatissimo
dico colui che ad tutti sui desii & imperio humile succumbendo dallei sa
ra per qualunche modo posseduto & obtento, O altissimo Ioue, Ecco lo
ipresso uestigio della tua diuina imagine, relicto in qsta nobilissima crea-
tura, Onde si Zeusis essa sola hauesse hauuto ad cótemplatione, laudatissi
ma sopra tutte le Agrigétine puelle & dello orbissimo mondo di súma &
absoluta pfectione, cógruamente per singulare exéplario harebbe oppor
tunissimo electo. Laquale formosa & cælicola Nympha, hora ad me feste

book was responsible for the changeover, in the first quarter of the sixteenth century, from the gothic to the roman letter.

Having produced the one masterpiece, Aldus never again printed a fully illustrated book. He turned his attention again to scholarly printing, which he revolutionized in the first year of the sixteenth century.

Florence, essentially aristocratic, took to printing with less enthusiasm than Venice. Her wealthy citizens who wanted books could have them copied on vellum in the finest school of calligraphy in Italy. But scholars welcomed the German invention which spared them expense or labor in obtaining copies for study. The books printed in fifteenth-century Florence were classics for scholars or small booklets of religious or popular nature for the lower classes.

The first known printers in Florence were Bernardo Cennini, a goldsmith, and Johann Petri of Mainz. Cennini produced a handsome Virgil with commentary; Petri, an edition of Boccaccio's *Filocolo* in 1471 and of Petrarch's *Trionfi* in 1472. With the crisis in publishing felt all over Italy in 1472, printing ceased altogether for a few years.

When printing was resumed, the first illustrated books appeared in Florence—not with woodcuts but with copperplate engravings. Florence was, then as now, the city of Italian goldsmiths. Metal engraving as a means of making prints had been practiced there since shortly before the middle of the fifteenth century. A number of Florentine painters, among them Pollaiuolo, worked in copperplate engraving. It is not surprising, then, that in 1477 when Nicolas Laurentii published Bettini's *Monte sancto di Dio*, he illustrated it with three copperplate engravings which he printed directly on the type page. With this success behind him, he understook four years later a far more ambitious venture. It was an edition of Dante's *Divine*

Dante,
La divina commedia
page 127

Comedy, probably commissioned by Lorenzo de' Medici, illustrated with copperplate engravings after designs by Botticelli—one for each of the hundred cantos. The first nineteen engravings were made, but the difficulty of printing them in position—a process requiring two separate impressions—was apparently too great. Only the first two or three plates were printed on the text page; sixteen or seventeen others were printed separately and pasted in. The rest were never engraved. The completed engravings are extraordinarily graceful, expressive and complex, but their printing is poor and gray. Laurentii was more successful in his printing of Berlinghieri's *Geographia* in 1480-82, mainly because its engraved fold-out maps called for separate printing in any case. Copperplate engraving for book illustration was not taken up again seriously until the second half of the sixteenth century.

The first woodcut-illustrated books began to appear in Florence around 1490. Florentine woodcuts quickly exhibited a special character which set them apart from all other Italian woodcuts. Their small, complex compositions reflect the influence of the Florentine school of

DANTE, *La divina commedia*. Florence, Laurentii, 1481. Pierpont Morgan Library. 16 x 10½ in.

certi nobili dintorno cefforono infino a tempi di Carlo magno. Carlo imperadore de romani : et ep fo
popolo romano moffo da prieghi de fiorentini preftorono aiuto a rifarla : et da Roma uennono molti
gentili huomini adhabitarla infieme con quegli che erono reftati. Fu reedificata ne glianni di chrifto.
octocento due al principio daprile. Altri dicono a di. xxx. di marzo. Allhora fu trouata in arno la fta
tua di Marte benche ropta : et per quella medefima oppinione che haueuono depfa la pofono in fu un
pilaftro al ponte uecchio. Et quiui ftecte infino allanno di chrifto. M. ccc. xxxiii. helquale anno uenne
tal diluuio che Arno ne meno el ponte uecchio et glaltri due ponti difobto : et in quefto modo rouino
dinuouo la ftatua. Adunque in quefto luogho Danthe pone loppinione che hebbeno enoftri antichi di
quefta ftatua : laquale molti dicono effere heretica oppinione. Ma non fono quefte fue parole : ne fua
oppinione : ma dello fpirito che parla : Elquale lui induce a dire quefto per manifeftare una uulgare op
pinione di molti. Credo anchora faluo fempre el piu uero iudicio che non fia contro a noftra religione
che fecondo aftrologia fi fabrichi una ftatua con tale conftellatione che habbi qualche momento : et for
za in fe. Onde Paolo fiorentino mathematicho ne fuoi tempi excellentiffimo colloco la ftatua delleone
in fu la ringhiera : che cigne el fiorentino palazo : la cui tefta ragguarda Melano : che molti credono che
nō poco giouaffi contro alla potētia de uifconti in quegli tēpi formidabile alla noftra republica. Legge
fi anchora che Zoroaftre perfa fabbrico in Tebe ecatompyle citta degypto la ftatua di Memnone chon
la cythara : laquale fonaua. Quanto allo excidio et diftructione di firenze non ofo dire contro alloppini
one di tanto poeta. Ma non fo chome Atylla poteffi far quefto : Conciofia che Paolo diacono : et glaltri
che fcripfono la hiftoria datylla affermino che lui non ueniffi mai in tofcana : ne paffaffi mai apennino.
Preterea Alchindo elquale diligentemente fcripfe le chofe facte da Carlo magno Neffuna mentione fa
che lui reftauraffi Firenze : Ma folamente narra che due pafque domenicali fi trouo in firenze. ET SE
NON Fuffi chen ful paffo darno. Quafi concluda che fe decta ftatua non fuffi ftata honoreuolmente
ripofta in ful pilaftro del ponte uecchio/quefta feconda reedificatione farebbe ftata indarno : perche di
nuouo farebbe perita la citta. ALCHVNA VISTA : perche non era intera ma ropta : et quella che
reftaua era rofa dalla ingiuria de tempi : et dalla uetufta. IO FE IVBETTO. Conchiude quefto fpi
rito che fimpicco in cafa fua. Iubetto nella citta di Parigi e/ elluogho doue fono le forche : et doue fim
piccono econdennati a tale fupplicio. Adunque fece iubetto delle fue cafe : cioe ne fece luogo di forche
Ne expreffamente pone chi choftui fuffi. Ma alchuni uogliono che intenda di meffer Rocco de mozzi :
elquale confumate le fue riccheze molte et uarie per fuggir gli ftenti della pouerta fimpicco. Altri in
tendono meffer Lotto de gliagli : elquale per pentimento dhauer dato una fententia falfa chon la pro
pria fua dorata cintola fappicco. Meffer Giouanni boccaccio dice : che in quegli tempi molti fiorentini
fimpiccorono : Et per quefto Danthe lafcia in ambiguo chi coftui fuffi.

.f. iiii

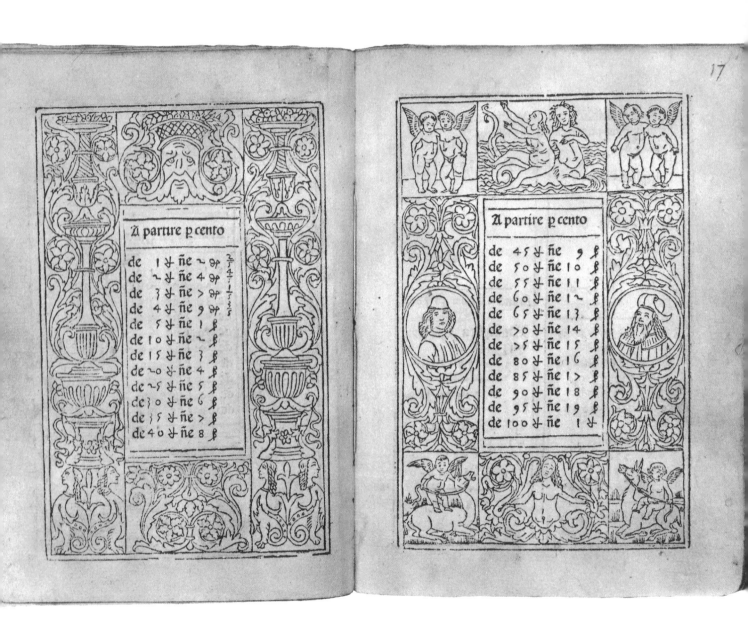

Ã partire p cento

de 1 ⅟ ñe ~ ⅘
de ~ ⅟ ñe 4 ⅘
de 3 ⅟ ñe > ⅘
de 4 ⅟ ñe 9 ⅘
de 5 ⅟ ñe 1 ⅛
de 10 ⅟ ñe ~ ⅛
de 15 ⅟ ñe 3 ⅛
de ~0 ⅟ ñe 4 ⅛
de ~5 ⅟ ñe 5 ⅛
de 30 ⅟ ñe 6 ⅛
de 35 ⅟ ñe > ⅛
de 40 ⅟ ñe 8 ⅛

A partire p cento

de 45 ⅟ ñe 9 ⅛
de 50 ⅟ ñe 10 ⅛
de 55 ⅟ ñe 11 ⅛
de 60 ⅟ ñe 1~ ⅛
de 65 ⅟ ñe 13 ⅛
de >0 ⅟ ñe 14 ⅛
de >5 ⅟ ñe 15 ⅛
de 80 ⅟ ñe 16 ⅛
de 85 ⅟ ñe 1> ⅛
de 90 ⅟ ñe 18 ⅛
de 95 ⅟ ñe 19 ⅛
de 100 ⅟ ñe 1 ⅟

17

CALANDRI, *Arithmetica*. Florence, Morgiani and Petri, 1491. Pierpont Morgan Library

painters—especially Botticelli and Ghirlandaio. The woodcuts were often shaded in various planes of depth, and they were characteristically framed in strongly patterned borders.

One of the earliest woodcut-illustrated books in Florence was the *Arithmetica* of Calandri, printed in 1491-2 by Morgiani and Petri. This very small, thick book was one of the first illustrated popular textbooks. Its pages of small black-letter text and of arithmetic tables are surrounded by light, fanciful borders in pure line, more in the Venetian than the later Florentine tradition. The problems in arithmetic, set in two little columns, have tiny woodcuts at their base. *Calandri, Arithmetica page 128*

The year after the *Arithmetica* appeared, Miscomini printed De Cessolis' *Libro di giuoco di scacchi (Book of the Game of Chess)*, illustrating it with fourteen woodcuts that showed a more typically Florentine style, with areas of shading and of pure black giving warmth and richness. The book presented, in the guise of a game of chess, the various stations and occupations of men. The frontispiece, which shows chess players watched by a king and others, is a particularly fine composition, suggestive of Botticelli's influence. The strong black-and-whites of the chess board are echoed in the patterned black-ground border.

Most of the illustrated books printed in Florence were far from ambitious. They were little booklets hawked in the streets to the populace—religious tracts, mystery plays, romances or ballads. These booklets were usually illustrated with a woodcut accompanying the title; sometimes there was another at the end of the booklet. The same woodcuts often served various booklets. The cut which represents St. Augustine in his *Soloquii*, printed in 1491 by Morgiani, appears as St. Antoninus in his *Confessionale*, printed in 1493.

In 1492 Savonarola came to Florence at the request of Lorenzo de' Medici and began the six fiery years of preaching there that ended in his death at the stake. A series of his tracts and sermons was printed in booklet form, mostly by the priest Libri. Savonarola was apparently aware of the persuasive value of illustration. The booklets were illustrated with title woodcuts, some of which contained imaginary depictions of Savonarola. The *Dyalogo della verità prophetica* shows the black-robed monk talking with seven Florentines under a tree. The Duomo of Florence is visible in the distance, and in mid-air appear a dove and tongues of flame.

Savonarola's *Epistole*, a typical fourteen-page booklet which Libri printed, has on its first page a woodcut of a man kneeling at an altar. The architectural lines of the chapel give great strength and depth to the illustration, enhanced by the areas of hatching and pure black. The patterned black-ground border sets off the whole noble little composition. *Savonarola, Epistole page 131*

Libri seems to have printed a great many Florentine booklets of all kinds, including both sacred and profane popular plays. The mystery plays known as *sacre rappresentazioni* remained a Florentine diversion through the sixteenth century. They were usually in rhyme, and many

Florentines, including Lorenzo de' Medici, took a hand at writing them. Their most prolific author was a woman named Antonia Pulci. The booklets in which they were published had a traditional form of title decoration: a framed woodcut of a herald angel above a woodcut showing a scene from the play. These woodcuts were reused through the following century. Popular romances or *novelle* in prose or verse were published in the typical Florentine format, at once unpretentious and full of the downward-reflected grace of a high artistic culture. Lorenzo and his scholar-companion Politiano wrote a number of *novelle* and ballads. The *Story of Two Lovers* was written by Pope Pius II, a Piccolomini.

Piccolomini,
Story of Two Lovers
page 132

One of the little booklets of the time was a translation into rhyme of the letter from Columbus —*Lettera dell'isole che ha trouato nuouamente il re dispagna*—printed in 1493. Its title cut shows the King of Spain, enthroned, looking across a very small ocean with ships to the shores of the New World, crowded with shapely Indians, buildings and a palm tree.

Few large or fully illustrated books were printed in Florence. An ambitious Florentine publisher like Lucantonio Giunta found it more practical to move to Venice. However Piero Pacini commissioned several fully illustrated books from Florentine printers in the last five years of the fifteenth century and the early part of the sixteenth. The *Epistole e evangeli*, a large quarto (large for a Florentine book), was printed for him by Morgiani and Petri in 1495, with 144 framed woodcuts besides other decorations inserted in the text. An Aesop was printed for Pacini by Bonaccorsi in 1496, illustrated with woodcuts which made much use of white line cut into the black ground. Pulci's *Morgante maggiore* was printed for Pacini in 1500–01, with 149 woodcuts. These books, especially the *Epistole e evangeli*, rank among the best Italian books of the time. In general, however, Florentine printing was not to be considered in the same class as Venetian printing. The typography and printing were by no means as fine, and Florence's total output of the last ten years of the century was less than a single year of Venice's output. The distinction of Florentine printing lay in the particular beauty of its woodcut illustrations, mostly in humble booklets for the populace. Noble patrons still preferred to have their finer printed books illuminated to the end of the century.

Milan, Bologna, Ferrara all had printers at work in 1471. Milan produced a good number of incunabula—more than eight hundred; Bologna, about three hundred. Ferrara seems to have had only one press working at a time, but towards the end of the century Lorenzo Rossi printed two of the finest Italian illustrated books there, with characteristics of both Florentine and Venetian style. The *De claris mulieribus (Of Famous Women)* by Foresti, which Rossi printed as a folio in 1497, has Venetian-style borders surrounding two full-page cuts and the first page of text that faces one of them. One of the large cuts shows the author presenting his book to the Queen of Hungary. The intensely black ground of the cut contrasts brilliantly

Foresti,
De claris mulieribus
page 133

℃ Frate Hieronymo da Ferrara seruo iutile di
Iesu Xp̄o a tutti li electi di Dio & figluoli del
padre eterno desidera gratia pace & consola,
tione del spirito sancto.

Olendo noi dilectissimi imitare el nostro
saluator̄:Elquale molte uolte cedette al
la grande ira & acceso furore delli scribi & pha
risei habbiamo lassato il predicare isino a tanto
che allui piacera : Ma sapendo che il demonio
non si cura de corpi:ma desidera leanime & ch

a

❡ PROEMIO DI SER ALEXANDRO BRACCIO AL
preftantiffimo & excellentiffimo giouane Lorẽzo di Pier frã
cefco de Medici fopra la traductione duna hyftoria di due a,
manti compofta dalla felice memoria di Papa Pio .ii.

 Enche molti fieno li exempli Lorẽzo mio excel
lentiffimo : pequali facilmente in altri ho potu
to comprehendere quanto fieno ualide & gran
di leforze damore & molte carte habbi riuolte:
doue lincendii fuoi fitractano & fannofi mani,
fefti : niente dimãco alchuna cofa non ha potuto
piu ueramente monftrarmi lafua potentia: che lo experimento
che ho facto in me fteffo: conciofia cofa che nella mia florida eta

a

PICCOLOMINI, *Storia di due Amanti (Story of Two Lovers).* Florence, c. 1495. Metropolitan Museum
FORESTI, *De claris mulieribus.* Ferrara, Lorenzo Rossi, 1497. Yale Beinecke Rare Book Library. 12 x 8 in.

·DEO·
INVISIBILI·ET·
IMMORTALI·

℃ De Maria virgine ppetua: deiq̃ genitrice glorioſiſſima:
celozum atq̃ angelozum regina.　.Capitulum ·Pzimum

Arie beatiſſime ⁊ immaculate ſem
per virginis: genitricis dei ac dn̄i
noſtri ieſu chriſti vitam conſuma
tiſſimam: oium q̃ perfectiſſimam:
boc in exozdio ſcripturus: que.ſ.
omni genere mirificozuz exemplo
rum totum terrarum ozbem reple
uerat. Uereoz ne pondē laudis quã
meruit obzutus: magis imbecillitatez ingenij mei detegã
q̃ ſuas inennarabiles diuinaſq̃ virtutes ſicut par eſt rep̃
ſentem. Cum ſit ipſa angelozum Regina: ſacrarium ſpiri
tus ſancti. ⁊ totius ſanctiſſime trinitatis domicilium: poz
taq̃ per quam celeſte regnuz ingredi licet. Sitq̃ pzeterea
⁊ virtutum omnium ſpecimen/errantium ſemita/honeſta
tis totius nozma:atq̃ deſtitutis ſolatiuz/afflictis refugiũ
demuin quoq̃ nauigantium ſalutis poztus. Plane hēc ta
lis ⁊ tãta/ante omnia ſecula:atq̃ anteq̃ ſuſpicari quis au
deret/creata fuit. Et q̃q̃ apud nos poſtmodum in carne
fuerit fabzicata/apud deum nibilominus ante ſecula erat:
etſi non ſubſtantia carnali/tamen plena diſpoſitione. Di
uina etenim illa pzouidentia/cui omnia pzozſus cognita ⁊
pzeſentia ſunt: quuz ⁊ angelozum ⁊ bominuz deffectionē:
ante conditam condendamue/buius mundi molē ab eter
no(luce omni clarius)pzeuidiſſet ⁊ angelozum quidem in
ſtaurationem per bomines:bominum vo p filium ſibi na

with the playful border in pure line. A similar contrast is found in the text page of dense, black gothic type surrounded by its own light linear border.

The small portraits of famous women distributed through the text actually number only fifty-six, but they are repeated many times. Sometimes the same cut even appears on two facing pages to represent two different women. Nevertheless these portraits have a great deal of charm, with their backgrounds of floral motifs against a dark ground. Towards the end of the book the style changes from a generalized to a specific one, and the portraits of contemporary women seem to have been copied from actual paintings.

Rossi's other remarkable book, the *Epistles of St. Jerome*, also printed in 1497, uses one of the borders of the *De claris mulieribus*. The principles of contrast are different in this book. The type is set in a somewhat heavy roman in two columns, with black-ground initials. These dark elements contrast with the crisply airy Venetian borders and with the many small, light-line cuts set into the columns. The cuts are in the popular style of the early Malermi Bible; they have a delightful naive humor which is to be found also in Rossi's borders, made by the same artist.

Verona has been mentioned for its important early illustrated books, Naples for its Aesop. Milan, the most productive city after Florence, published a number of books worthy of notice, among them several editions of the works of the Lombard musician Gafurius. His *Theorica musicae* of 1492 is illustrated with primitive but attractive woodcuts of an organist and a compartmented page of musical experiments. Gafurius' *Practica musicae* was printed in 1496 in a semi-roman type with a fine border of angelic and human musicians—Gafurius and his choirboys among them. The border and matching initial exhibit the firmness that characterizes Lombard art.

FRANCE

Printing was brought to France at the initiative of two officials at the Sorbonne, the Prior Heynlin and the Librarian Fichet, who in 1470 invited three German printers to set up a press at the university. For a period of three years the foreign printers had turned out sober, well-printed editions of Cicero, Virgil, and Terence in a roman type based on Italian models, when a political change of wind suddenly deprived them of official support. Left on their own, the three printers—Friburger, Gering, and Crantz—moved to private quarters and set up an independent press. They hoped to attract a more general readership, and to this end they set their new books in gothic letters more familiar to the French eye. Their new editions, like those they had produced at the Sorbonne, had only the text printed and depended on the rubricator for initials and other touches of red and blue, or on the illuminator for greater elaboration.

Before long competitive printers were at work in Paris. The first of them was Jean Dupré, who, in 1481, immediately produced the first illustrated book in that city, a Paris Missal with the usual illustrated subjects: full-page pictures of God the Father enthroned and of the Crucifixion. Two months later he printed a much finer Missal for Verdun, with an added cut of the Mass of St. Gregory. The illustrations and the delicate scrolled borders that surround both cut and upright gothic text are in the fine, elaborate style of French illumination. *Paris Missal page 137*

By 1485 illustrated books were established in popularity. The designers, working in a city where manuscripts, church decoration, and even daily dress were colorful to the highest degree, wisely chose in their printed illustrations to depend on the quality of line and the play of black and white for effect. From the beginning their illustrations were in this sense self-sufficient. But in their style of drawing, their choice and interpretation of subject matter and particularly in their borders they remained extremely close to illumination, just as French type hewed closely to the manuscript letter.

Jean Dupré was in touch with several provincial printers and cooperated with them in the production of books outside of Paris. In 1486 with Pierre Gérard of Abbeville he produced one of France's printed masterpieces, St. Augustine's *Cité de Dieu*. Dupré sent up from Paris *St. Augustine, La Cité de Dieu page 136*

ST. AUGUSTINE, *La Cité de Dieu*. Abbeville, Jean Dupré and Pierre Gérard, 1486-87. Pierpont Morgan Library 15 x 10¼ in. →

Paris Missal. Paris, Jean Dupré, edition of 1489-90. Pierpont Morgan Library. 13 x 9½ in. →

Cy cõmence le pViii. liure/ des cho=
ses qui sont deputees es pVii. liures pre=
cedens/ iusqs au tẽps nr̃seigñr iesucrist

I ay promis a es=
crire de la naissan
sãce du cours a sin
deues des deup ci
tez/ desñlles lune
est de dieu/ a lau
tre de ce siecle/ en lañlle ceste est peserine/
en tant cõme il appartiẽt a la lignee des
hões/ Aprez ce que iap premierement de

boute a layde de dieu/les ennemys de la
cite de dieu/qui mettoient leurs dieux
uant ihesucrist createur de celle cite/a q
par seur tresmauuaise enuie/ ont enui
sur les crestiens: laquelle chose iap fai
es dip Bolumes precedens/mais de ce
moiẽne pmesse que iap recordee main
nant/laquelle est partie en trois/ Jap
mene la naissãce de ces deup citez/ ou
liure/a es quatre subsequens/ Aprez i
demene le cours dicelles/a pñdre du
mier homme iusques au deluge en B
liure lequel est le pB. liure/a de la iusq

Incipit missale scdm vsum ecclesie pa/
risien. Dnica pria aduentus. Introitus
D te leuaui aiam me
am deus meus in te cō
fido non erubescam ne
qʒ irrideant me inimi
ci mei etenim vniuersi
qui te expectāt non cō
fundentur. ps. Vias tuas dñe demonstra
michi et semitas tuas edoce me . Gloria

patri. Sicut erat. Lyrieleison.iii. Christe
eleison.iii. Lyri el.iii . Non dicitur Glia
i excelsis vsqʒ ad natiuitatē dñi qñ fit de
tempore. Dñs vobiscum. Et cum spiritu
tuo. Oremus.   Oratio
Excita quesumus dñe potenti
am tuam et veni. vt ab imi
nentibus peccatorū nostroꝝ pe
riculis: te mereamur protegēte eri
pi.te liberante saluari. Qui viuis

the materials, the type and the woodcuts for the two-volume work, as well as his best crafts-men. The illustrations, twenty-three large woodcuts, used one at the beginning of each "book," were taken directly from an illuminated manuscript, but they are translated into pure line with a little open shading. Elements of architecture or construction are drawn stone by stone to produce a decorative overall pattern. The views outside windows are detailed. The effect of this clear detailed line is light within a very black border of broad line, and the gothic type used in one size strikes a tone somewhere between the light picture and the black border. Expansive margins frame the neat double columns of type, and the general effect is very hand-some.

At this time a new printer came on the scene. Guy Marchant produced some of the most effec-tive and popular books in fifteenth-century France. His *Danse Macabre* of 1485 shows the skeleton Death claiming his partners from all walks of society. The strongly designed cuts were taken from manuscript illustrations which were in turn based on the murals in the Cemetery of the Innocents, a favorite strolling place in medieval Paris.

Compost et kalendrier des Bergiers page 139

The *Compost et kalendrier des Bergiers* which Marchant printed in 1491 was a sort of Farmer's Almanac of its day, with weather forecasts, rules for health, and moral precepts. The calendar pages are headed with small cuts of the occupation of the month—sheepshearing, sowing, wine-pressing—and bordered at the sides with tiny representations of the religious holidays and the zodiac. A few bucolic scenes appear in larger cuts, and the moral teachings are underlined with a tree of vices and a tree of virtues, and a wonderfully brutal series of tortures of the damned copied from Vérard's *Art de bien Vivre et bien Mourir*. The popularity of the book took it to the farthest provinces of France. Editions appeared in Germany and in England, where it was reprinted into the seventeenth century. Marchant issued a single edition of a *Compost et kalen-drier des Bergères*, with much material derived from its companion volume, but with new full-page illustrations of the shepherdesses at their occupations of the month.

Pierre le Rouge in 1488-89 produced one of the great editions of Paris, the two-volume large folio *Mer des Hystoires*. The book is a universal chronicle translated from an edition printed in Lübeck in 1475, and extended to include Charles VIII, then King of France. It is decorated with hundreds of woodcuts—a great many of them repeated stock cuts—and with particularly beautiful illuminated-style borders executed in fine line. The illustrations include maps of the world and of the Holy Land, and innumerable genealogical tables derived from Rolewinck's *Fasciculus temporum* and the *Nuremberg Chronicle*.

The dominant figure in French publishing from 1485 until 1512 was Antoine Vérard, book-seller to the King. His ample means made it possible for him to employ several printers at once, and his connections gave him access to a large group of purchasers in and around the court. As a result he published at least three hundred editions, most of them in the vernacular.

Compost et kalendrier des Bergiers. Paris, Guy Marchant, edition of 1493. Pierpont Morgan Library
BOCCACCIO, *De la généologie des Dieux*. Paris, Antoine Vérard, 1498. Pierpont Morgan Library. 13 x 9¼ in. →

Septembre.
fructus maturi septembris sunt valituri.
Et pira cum vino panis cum lacte caprino
Aqua de vrtica tibi potio fertur amica.
Tunc venam pandas species cum semine mandas.

Mil iiii.c.iiii.py.viii.			Mil v.c.et vii.				
ti	iii	xxvii	f	ti	ii	viiii	S.leu s.gille	z
			g	v	vi	v	s.iuste confesseur	(t
v	v	vv	A				s.godegran martir	z
			b				s.marcel martir	a
vviii	i	vviii	c	vviii	iiii	vii	s.victorin martir	b
vii	v	vlvi	d	vii	vi	l	s.zacharie prophete	c
vv	v	vl	e				s.iehan martir	d
iiii	iii	vliv	f	vv	vi	vvvi	Natiuite nostre dame	e
			g	iiii	i	v	s.queran abbe	f
vii	viii	vvii	A	vii	v	vvvvi	s.hylaire pape	g
			B	i	v	vliii	s.prothe.s.iacin	h
i	iii	v	c				s.sir confesseur	i
			d	iv	v	vvvii	s.phi lippe euesque	lz
iv	vii	li	e				Exaltacion scte croix	
vvii	vi	vvii	f	vvii	iv	vii	s.valerian martir	m
			g				s.eufemie vierge	n
vi	vi	vv	A	vi	vi	lii	s.lamber euesque	o
viiii	vi	vviii	b	viiii	i	vliii	s.ferrue martir	p
							s.ianuier martir	q
iiii	iv	vvviiii	d	iii	vi	vvviv	s.euloge martir	r
vi	vii	vvviv	e				s.mathieu apostre	s
			f	vi	iii	vli	s.maurice martir	t
viv	vi	viii	g	viv	v	vviv	s.tecle vierge	u
viii	v	vlvi	A				s.solemne euesque	v
			B	viiii	iii	vviv	s.frimin euesque	u
vvi	vi	vvvvii	c	vvi	vii	vvviiii	s.cyprian martir	v
v	ii	liii	d	v	ii	vvviiii	s.cosme et damien	z
			e				s.eupere confesseur	
viii	ii	v	f	viii	ii	iv	s.michiel de gargan	(t
			g	ii	v	iv	s.hierome	

Septembre a xxx.iours.Et la lune xxx.

Leod:

HEbes comme theodonce efcript fut fille de iuno qui delle recite vne telle fable. Que apollo appareilla vng conuy a iuno merastre en la maifó de son pere iupiter. et entre autres chofes lui mit deuant des letues sauuages Quant iuno qui iufques a lors sterile auoit este les eut mengees par desir et appetit incontinant elle fut enceinte et enfanta vne fille nommee Hebes. Et pource quelle estoit belle elle fut prinse par Jupiter a loffice de bouteilliere / et fut faicte deesse de iouuence. Quant icellui Jupiter auecques les autres dieux estoit alle deuers les ethiopienspor menger z banqueter aduint que quant icelle Hebes leur ministroit les breuua ges et quelle en alant moins copement quelle ne deuoit les ditz breuuages chey oyent / parquoy elle leua tous ses habil lemens vng peu plus hault et monstra aux dieux par cas de fortune ses cho ses honteuses / et pource aduint que Ju piter la osta dudit office de bouteilliere z substitua en son lieu Ganymedes fre re de Laomedon roy de troye. Fina blement les oetes la baillerent en ma

homerus riage a Hercules qui estoit ia receu ou nombre des dieux. Homere en son o dissee dit quelle fut conceue de Jupiter Certes ie ne lay point escripte ne don

nee a Jupiter pource que ie la trouue e stre mise fille par les latins poetes tant seulement de iuno sans aucun pere.

Sensuit ce que ie iuge estre prinse de ce ste fiction. Le venerable andalo disoit Andalo deux choses attribuees entre les signes du zodiaque a iupiter lequel ilz dient e stre pere dapollo / lesquelles deux choses les astrologiens ont dit maisons / cestas sauoir le sagitaire z les poissons. Car quât le soleil / cestadire apollo est au sa gitaire z que la maison de iupiter est p chaine de lyuer les letues sauuages sôt mises deuât iuno / cest adire la terre cest a entendre le grant froit. Car ainsi que les phisiciens dient les letues agrestes z sauuages sont tresfroides / z le froit fait son operation sur le bort de la terre z fait condenser z sarrer les pores z ou uertures de la terre / affin que la chaleur meslee auec la terre besoigne enuiron les choses quit sont dedens la terre Et quant ladicte chaleur a reschauffe lu midite de la terre elle fait ouurir les ra cines des grains et des plantes et les ramplist de humeur par laquelle il se enflent z sont faictes grosses. Et ainsi quant le soleil entre au signe du sagitai re la terre est faicte grosse et enflee pour le froit intêsif / laquelle terre semble en autonne estre sterile. Finablemêt quât le temps aduient de son enfantement / cest adire a la prime vere elle enfanta he bes / cest a entendre ieunesse Et la est la renouation de toutes choses branches fleurs / grains. Et en ce temps toutes choses elle gette   Et ainsi quant le printemps vient lequel est chault et humide / les dieux Cest a entendre les corps celestielz baillent z ministrêt bru uages / cest a dire humectations / lesqlz corps celestielz ainsi quil est ailleurs dit selon lopinion daucus sont peuz des humiditez des vapeurs qui de terre se elieuent. Finablement quât le têps de

Qui a este premierement dieu appel
le enuers les gentilz/zpayens

AE qui dois la grandeur aux
natures non acoustumee en
trer/nouueau chemin tenir
ay propose le plus prudente
ment que pourray/De loing regarder

des quelz haulte criuage ie pourray mõ
nauire desancrer. Affin que plus droite
ment par la faueur du bon ẽt ie puis
se estre porte ou moncourage desire Le
que ie pense facilemẽt faire maiʃq iaye
ẟnefois trouue celuyʃ les anciens ont
pmierement sainct estre dieu. Affin ʃie
a ij

Dmine ne in furoze tuo arguas me:
neqz in ira tua corripias me Misere
re mei domine quoniam infirmus sū

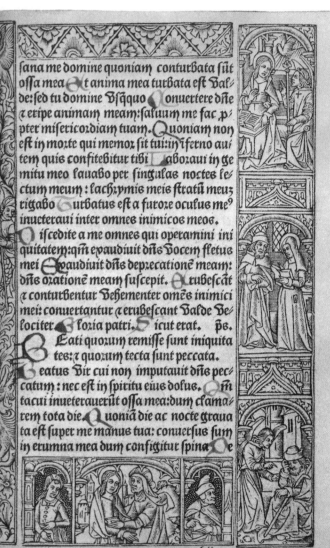

sana me domine quoniam conturbata sūt
ossa mea Et anima mea turbata est Bal-
de: sed tu domine Vsqquo Conuertere dūe
ɤ eripe animam meam: saluum me fac pp-
pter misericordiam tuam. Quoniam non
est in morte qui memor sit tui: in inferno autem quis confitebitur tibi Laboraui in ge-
mitu meo lauabo per singulas noctes le-
ctum meum : lachrymis meis stratū meū
rigabo Turbatus est a furore oculus me9
inueteraui inter omnes inimicos meos.
Discedite a me omnes qui operamini ini
quitatem: qm exaudiuit dūs Vocem fletus
mei Exaudiuit dūs deprecationē meam:
dūs orationē meam suscepit. Erubescāt
ɤ conturbentur Behementer omēs inimici
mei: conuertantur ɤ erubescant Valde Be-
lociter Gloria patri. Sicut erat. ps.
Eati quorum remisse sunt iniquita
tes: ɤ quorum tecta sunt peccata.
Beatus Vir cui non imputauit dūs peccatum : nec est in spiritu eius dolus. Qm
tacui inueterauerūt ossa mea: dum clama-
rem tota die Quoniā die ac nocte graua
ta est super me manus tua: conuersus sum
in erumna mea dum configitur spina De

foii.

Horae in the Angers use. Paris, Philippe Pigouchet, 1496-97. Pierpont Morgan Library

Vérard had been an illuminator, which may explain his taste for illustrated and decorated books. He was, however, a shrewd businessman, and sometimes his business instincts led him to betray his otherwise fine taste. He avidly acquired the blocks of other printers and used them sometimes well, sometimes inappropriately. He made repeated use of the same cuts, occasionally altering them to suit the new situation a little better.

Nevertheless, Vérard was responsible for a great many of the attractive printed books of Paris. His earlier books were eclectic, reflecting the styles of various French printers, but from 1492 till the end of the century he published books in a consistent style, with woodcuts in a piquant, sharply drawn line. His edition of Boccaccio's *De la généologie des Dieux* published in 1498, is illustrated with thirteen large cuts in this lively style, accompanying a crisp calligraphic text. Vérard was addicted to a curious manuscript usage popular for a while among French printers: the use of an exaggeratedly large and flourishing letter "L" on title pages, which usually began with the article *le*. These "L's" were often extremely grotesque, blossoming into faces, animals, or bizarre combinations thereof, such as a nude woman, a monkey, and a bird.

Boccaccio, De la généologie des Dieux pages 140 and 141

Despite his importance as a publisher of printed books, when Vérard prepared a volume for a noble patron such as Charles VIII of France, Henry VII of England or the Count of Angoulême, he did all he could to make it like an illuminated manuscript. He printed these books on vellum and had the cuts painted over by an illuminator, often quite regardless of the picture beneath. The richly produced manuscript was still clearly the ideal in France, and it remained so into the sixteenth century.

The most important books produced by the presses of fifteenth-century France were the Books of Hours which began to be printed in 1486 and from then on were turned out in hundreds of editions for use all over the Christian world. The models for these books were established by Dupré and Vérard, and were very much influenced by the exquisite manuscript Books of Hours of the time.

The printed Books of Hours were illustrated at first comparatively simply, but soon with a richness rivalling their manuscript models. Each page, whether it contained text or illustration, was surrounded by a border, and these borders grew more and more densely elaborate and detailed. As in the manuscript Books of Hours, the facing pages were designed as related units. The first two printed Horae, published by Vérard, were modest efforts. Dupré's first Horae, prepared in 1489-90, inaugurated the beautiful series. The book itself was small enough to hold comfortably in one hand, the illustrations of a gentle simplicity, in pure line. This small size of Book of Hours was known as *Petites heures;* Vérard began to publish a larger series of *Grandes heures* or *Heures royales*, and added areas of pure black to the linear borders.

For three years Dupré and Vérard were the only producers of Horae, until the printer Philippe

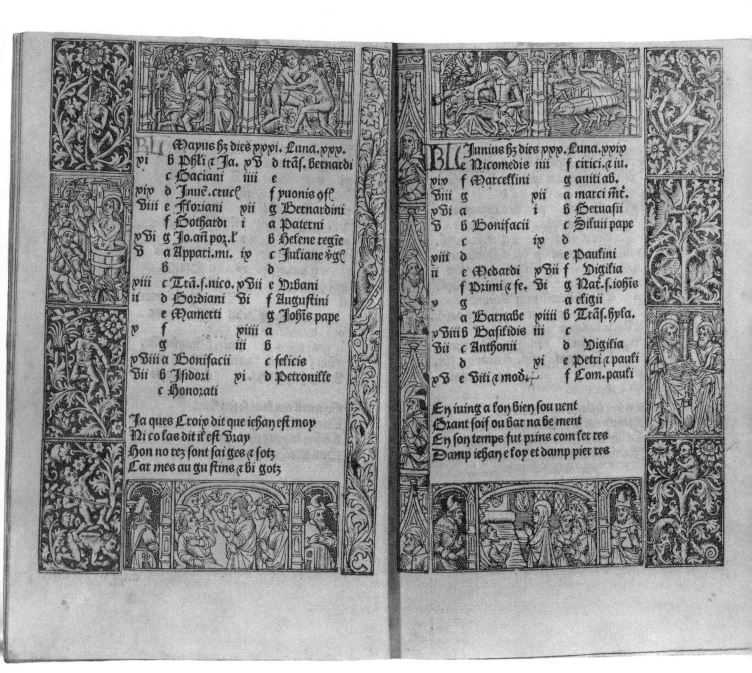

Pigouchet entered the field. Pigouchet, with his publisher Simon Vostre, produced both the most numerous and the most typical of the fifteenth-century Horae. They were dense with decoration, the line enriched with what is known as a *criblé* effect: areas of black punched with tiny dots or stars. In the typically Gothic way, they mixed religious subjects with scenes from ordinary life. Some of Pigouchet's most charming borders are those showing children's games, the stag hunt, or scenes from the Dance of Death.

As more printers began producing Horae, influences from Italy, reflected through Basel, crept in. Renaissance architectural borders of increasing elaboration surrounded cut and text. By the end of the century, the classical influence was dominant.

At Lyons, the only French town that rivalled Paris in printing, conditions were entirely different. Lyons was a robust commercial center, on the trade routes into Germany, Italy, and Spain. As opposed to the scholarly and aristocratic character of printing at Paris, book production at Lyons was from the start a popular and commercial enterprise. In 1473 a citizen named Barthélémy Buyer engaged a Netherlands printer, Guillaume Le Roy, to print a book of popular religious treatises. German printers followed as a matter of course, and one of them, Martin Huss, printed the first illustrated book there in 1478 (three years earlier than at Paris), using cuts from Basel. Cuts from Augsburg, Ulm, and Strassburg also supplied the earliest Lyons book illustrations; when they were not available, they were copied in workshops set up for this purpose. An Aesop appeared, based directly on the Ulm Aesop but with stiffer cutting. Cuts from the original Augsburg *Spiegel des menschlichen Lebens* appeared in a Lyons edition and then moved on to Spain, where they were used again a decade later.

But before long, by about 1480, a distinctive Lyonese school of illustration became discernible, in which the earthy story-telling quality of the German woodcuts was tempered by a French decorative sense. Le Roy's books became important exponents of this school: the *Abuzé en court*, the *Doctrinal du temps présent* and the *Fierabras*—the first two satires, the last a romance. These were printed in a dashing black letter apparently modeled on that of Colard Mansion at Bruges, derived from the manuscript of the Burgundian romances of chivalry. Lyons became the place to buy romantic literature; at its commercial fairs a merchant could provide himself with a tale of chivalry such as *Les quatre fils Aymon* or a poetic volume such as the *Roman de la Rose*, as well as an illustrated moralistic work.

After 1490 there were more scholarly books printed at Lyons, and printing became more general. The high point of Lyons' book production of the century is the *Comedies* of Terence, printed in 1493 by Johannes Trechsel of Mainz. The book is set in two sizes of type, one for the text and the other, very small, for the commentary. A full-page cut near the front of the

Horae
in the Angers use
pages 142 and 144

L'Abuzé en court
page 146

Les quatre fils Aymon
page 147

Terence,
Comoediae
pages 148 and 149

L'Abuzé en court. Lyons, Guillaume Le Roy, c. 1485. Library of Congress →
Les quatre fils Aymon. Lyons, Jean de Vingle?, 1493. Pierpont Morgan Library →
TERENCE, *Comoediae*. Lyons, Johannes Trechsel, 1493. Pierpont Morgan Library →   145

MAdame Je viens deuers vous.
Comme singuliere maistresse.
Et supplie a deux genoulz.
Quepar vostre noble largesse.
Acquites vers moy la promesse.
Soubz laquelle auec vous me tiens.
Et ay tenu par Jeunesse.
Affin dauoir de vous des biens.

Les quatre filz aymon

Cherea.   Thais.   Pythias.

a Pud antiphonem uterꝗ pater & mater/
quaſi dedita opera domi erāt:ut nullo mo
do introire poſſē: ꝗn uiderēt me. Interim
dū añ oſtiū ſto: notus mihi quidā obuiā uenit. ubi
uidi:egomet in pedes (quātū queo) in angiportū

a Pud &c.Hic chē
rea reddit cauſā
cur etiā rediēs ī
uiciniā ſuā nō mutaue/
rit ueſtē. Che. apud an
tiphonē.i.in domo an
tiphonis uterꝗ parens
ſ. mī & pr̄. & uterꝗ di/
xit. nā maſculinū prae/
pōderat fœminio erāt

domi quaſi dedita opera.i.conſulto de induſtria ut nullo modo poſſem introire.
quín.i.ꝗ nō uiderent me.interim.i.dū haec agunt dū ſto ante oſtiū quidam notus
uenit obuiā.i.in occurſum mihi.ubi.i.poſtꝗ uidi eū ſcilicet egomet dedi ī pedes.i.
cōuerti cōieci ſeu cōtuli me q̄tū queo ī quoddā angiportū.i.uicū anguſtū nec puiū
deſertū.i.nō frequētatū. Angiportū ti neutrū.uel angiportus ti maſculinū Currūꝗ
eni diciť ꝗuic⁹ ē anguſtus nō paruiⁱ ut Donatus & Seruius ſentiūt. uel iter cōpēdia
riū ait Feſtus ī oppido. eo ꝗ ſit anguſtrs portus.i. additus ad portū. Vel ſcdm Var
ronem diciť angiportum ꝗ ſit anguſtū & p quod nihil agi pōt prae nimia anguſtia

n

book shows in great detail a theater and playgoers. Throughout the book the plays are copi-ously illustrated with larger-than-half-page cuts which show the actors on stage; these are full of detail and convey a strong sense of theater.

Other towns had printers, some transiently, others, such as Poitiers and Rouen, continuously. But by far the most important French printing was done at Paris and Lyons in the fifteenth century. Despite the infiltration of classical influences, the French book remained modeled after the manuscript. It was not till the end of the first quarter of the sixteenth century, when the full force of the Renaissance had been felt in France, that she began to produce the more conscious and architectonic books that made her the world's leader in typography.

THE NETHERLANDS

The Netherlands played a leading role in the production of block books, and there are suggestions of primitive experiments in printing there. Nevertheless, the number and quality of early printed books in the Netherlands is not remarkable. The first known date of presses at work is 1473, nearly two decades after the production of the Gutenberg Bible. Utrecht had one; another was at Alost, in what is now Belgium, in the hands of John of Paderborn, who had learned printing in Italy. Printers appeared for longer or shorter periods in other towns. The town of Deventer had a sustained output of books, but they were commercially produced ecclesiastical or educational works of no particular merit.

At Brussels, the monastic order of the Brothers of the Common Life was active in the dissemination of books of all sorts, manuscripts and block books as well as printed books. It was their belief that a spread of learning would bring about an increase of faith. They operated a press of their own from 1476 until 1487, turning out popular books in Latin.

Woodcuts from block books quite naturally found their way into a number of Netherlands printed books. But there were a few Netherlands printers of an enterprising nature who commissioned series of original cuts. Gerard Leeu of Gouda printed in 1480 one of the most delightful books of the fifteenth century, the *Dialogus creaturarum*. It was a version of the old manuscript bestiaries—a collection of fables in which animals, inanimate objects, and fabulous beasts speak together. The many small woodcut illustrations of Leeu's book have a joyous, innocent humor. They are set into a close, upright gothic type, adorned with rubrics and printed in wide margins of excellent paper. The first page of the text has a large cut of the sun and the moon and a striking black-ground initial, all surrounded by a vigorous floral border. The book achieved international popularity in its own day; Leeu himself reprinted it seven times, in Latin, Dutch, and French.

Gerard Leeu was in close contact with a printer in Haarlem named Jacob Bellaert; they shared the same woodcutter, and often the same type and cuts. This woodcutter made the illustrations for one of Leeu's most successful books, the *Histoire de Paris et Vienne*, issued in 1487

Dialogus creaturarum pages 152 and 153

set Qui cum rocham veniſſet ſupra dicta fieri ꝺ iſſualit eo ꝗ ſe=
nex eſſet et parum viuere poſſet·illi autem iuuenes multa p̄e=
lia romanis adhuc poſſent mouere Et cum rogaretur ut ſaltē
remaneret nullatenus acquieuit Rediens ergo crudeli mozte
iteriji Otile quidē remanere ſibi fuiſſet Sed ꝓpter iuſiurandū
non fuiſſet honeſtum et ꝓpter vtilitatem romanozū nō fuiſſet
vtile ᛜDe carſlācho qui voluit ſe regulari ꝺyalogus quiqua=
geſimuſoctauus

Carſlanchus eſt auis ſimilis falconi potens et virtuoſus
hic in iuuentute voluit ſe regulari dum virtutibus p̄e=
fulgeret Sed timoze auſteritatis regule diſtulit dicens
Credo ꝗ nō potero ieiunare·ſurgere ad matutinum·caſtitatē
tenere et voluntatem ꝓpriā abnegare Et quia bonum non in=
choauit timoze penitentie non bene mediauit ymmo male fini
uit dicens Qui non bonum p̄e timoze facit perit cū mero=
re ᛜSic enim multi cupiunt cōuolare ad graciam dei ſed ti=
met carere delicijs mundi Pzouocat quidem amoz xp̄i eos ſȝ
reuocat cupiditas ſeculi Tales enim ſolent dicere ſeruirem li=
benter deo·libenter intrarem religionē·ſed timeo ꝗ non poſſē
auſteritatem regule ſuſtinere Iſti nō attendunt illud a pk̄i ad
philippeū·iiij°·ōnia poſſū in eo qui me confoztat Id eſt xp̄s
Ot dicit bern·in ſe ſperantibus de9 eſt theſaur9·i pauptate ſo
lacium·in ſolitudine glozia·in ambicione honoz·in contemp=
tu vmbzaculum in pzotectione a pluuia et ab eſtu ᛜFabu

¶ Dyalogus creaturarū optime mozalizatus·omni materie mozali io-
cūdo mō applicabiꝰ: ad laudē dei ⁊ edificacioūe hoīm Incipit feliciter

¶ De sole ⁊ luna Dyalogus pzimus

Sol est secundum philosophum oculꝰ
mundi · iocunditas dei · pulchzitudo
celi · mensura tempozum · virtus et
ozigo omnium nascencium · dominꝰ
planetarum · doctoz et perfectoz omnium stellarum ⸝⸝ luna vero ut dicit
Ambzosius in exameron est decoz noc-
tis · mater totius humozis et mini-
stra · mensura tempozum · domina-
trix maris · immutatrix aeris et emu

after Leeu had moved his press to Antwerp. For Bellaert he illustrated a Dutch version of *Belial* called *Der Sonderen Troest (The Sinner's Trust)*, an allegory of the redemption of man presented as an action in a court of law, with Christ, as Moses, and Belial disputing for man's soul. There is an intensely Gothic Netherlandish quality to the illustrations, many of which are made up of separate cuts fitted together variously to provide different groupings of persons or background. The same quality is in the narrow, angular type.

The Burgundian city of Bruges had an odd distinction in the history of printing: The first book in the English language was printed there, by the Englishman William Caxton. Caxton, who had been apprenticed in the textile industry in England, went to the cloth-making center of Bruges in pursuit of his trade and prospered there. He had been Governor of the Merchant Adventurers from 1463 till 1469 — a post roughly corresponding to that of English consul at Bruges — when he entered the service of Margaret of York, English-born Duchess of Burgundy. For her he translated the *Recuyell of the Histories of Troy*, and having learned something of the art of printing on a sojourn in Cologne in 1471, he thought it practical to print his own translation. In Caxton's own words: "for as moche as the wrytyng of the same my penne is worn, myn hande wery and not stedfast, myn eyen dimmed with ouermoche lokyng on whit paper . . . and also because I haue promysid to dyuerce gentilmen and to my frendes to adresse to hem as hastily as I myght this sayd book. Therfore I haue practysed & lerned at my grete charge and dispence to ordeyne this saide book in prynte after the maner & forme as ye may here see."

In setting up his press, Caxton took Colard Mansion, a calligrapher and illuminator in the library of the Duke of Burgundy, to work with him. Between 1474 and 1476 they printed three books together: the *Recuyell; The Game and Pleye of the Chess*, a translation of De Cessolis' moralization of the game of chess; and a book in French, *Les quatre derniers choses* (*The Four Last Things* — Death, Judgement, Hell, and Heaven). The first two books were set in a moderate-sized calligraphic gothic type, based on the Burgundian writing of the time, the *lettre bâtarde*. The French book was in a new type — smaller, more condensed and at the same time more elaborate and angular — altogether much less harmonious and readable.

In 1476 Caxton left Burgundy for his native England. He took the newer, more idiosyncratic type with him and set up, in the precincts of Westminster Abbey, the first press in England. Mansion retained the earlier type in Bruges and printed with it and a new larger type he cut until in 1484 he fled his creditors. Before that happened, he printed alone twenty-seven books, one of which is very possibly the first book illustrated with copper engravings. Boccaccio's *De la ruine des nobles Hommes et Femmes*, printed in 1476, had nine engravings made for it in the contemporary Burgundian style of illumination. They were printed separately, pasted in

willich wt nijt vandē iuedē is pplato den president geuangē doer valsche
lijtkelicke getuygeniſſe gecruyſt handē en voetē doer nagelt uptē vijfthiē
ſtē dach in maerte veroerdelt en indē cruce gehangē voir ons ſondarē mit
luyder ſtemmē help help ſijnē geeſt geuēde en achterliet ſijn doode lichaē
der aerden te begrauen ghelijc hij in ſijn leuen voirſeit hadde ende als de
waerheyt der ewangelien dat volcomelic tuyghen

Nde is mit groter gloriē als bwinder der tijttelicker doot mit dē
vaē der victoriē iu ſijn hant houdēde ter ſtont neď gedaelt ter hel
lē die hij mit ſijnre godlicker ſchijnſel omſchenē heeft roupēde tot dē prin
cē der hellē nit ſijnre ſoeter ſtēme ſeggēde o ghi princē ondoet v poertē en
daer ſal ingaē de coninc der gloriē Tot welcke roepige de princē der hellē
mit bwonderige buaert ſijnēde antwoirdē wt ď hellē ſeggende wie is deſe
conic der gloriē. hij anttwoirde conic heer ſtarc en mogēde idē ſtrijde waer
bij deſe princē der hellē onderlinge ſprakē wie deſe conic der gloriē weſen
mocht dus ſtarc en machtich. en bwonderdē hē ſeer wāt ſij nye ſoe ſtarckē
dode en vreſelic mit ſoe groter tracht en mogentheit ter hellē gecomē en
was en ſlotē de poertē nnerē en torrē vaſter dā ſij gewoē warē. dit deheer
ſiende ſeyde anderwerf tot dē princē der hellen ondoet v poertē zi. En ſij
dat weygerēde mair meer haer poertē ſlotē. ſeidē wie is deſe coninck der

and colored, to make them as close as possible to illuminations. In 1483 these illustrations became the model for Jean Dupré's edition of the book—the first secular illustrated book in Paris. Mansion's only other illustrated book was a moralized version of Ovid's *Metamorphoses*, set in Mansion's large, bold type and illustrated with woodcuts based on manuscript illuminations but cut with a crisp distinction of their own. Vérard's chief woodcutter after 1490 was obviously much influenced by these illustrations.

Printing at Bruges, though it lasted little more than a decade, had thrown off important spores.

ENGLAND

Caxton's move from Bruges to Westminster in 1476 brought printing for the first time to English soil. The earliest dated book to come from the new press was *The Dictes or Sayengis of the Philosophers*, printed in 1477 in the elaborate and ungainly type that Caxton had brought with him from Bruges. It was very likely preceded by the undated *History of Jason*, and it was followed the next year by the *Canterbury Tales*, still in the large *lettre bâtarde* type. A series of popular books ensued: Malory's *Morte d'Arthur*, a number of French romances which Caxton translated himself, Aesop, and various devotional works.

In 1481 Caxton's first illustrated book appeared: the *Myrrour of the World*, with little cuts made by the awkward hand of a novice woodcutter. About two years later (c. 1483) Caxton printed his second edition of *The Playe of the Chesse*, this time illustrated with cuts in which the playing pieces represent the various classes and conditions of man. The woodcuts are all repeated, and they are inexpertly drawn and cut, but two of them are especially effective—one showing a man at the chess board, the other a king (Nebuchadnezzar's son) and his partner at chess.

De Cessolis, The Playe of the Chesse page 158

In 1484–5 Caxton produced three of his most important illustrated books: an Aesop, an edition of the *Canterbury Tales*, and a *Golden Legend*. Of the many fifteenth-century copies of the Ulm Aesop Caxton's is perhaps the farthest astray, but for all its grossness it has some primitive charm. The *Canterbury Tales* are illustrated with a large cut of the pilgrims at a round table (very crowded and jolly) and individual cuts of each of the tellers of the tales, mounted on their horses. The horses are stumpy and ungainly, but the characterizations of the pilgrims are of real interest.

Chaucer, Canterbury Tales page 159

The *Golden Legend* was the most extensively illustrated of Caxton's books, but its cuts were so poor that he was apparently persuaded to look for a new woodcutter for his next illustrated books, the *Speculum vita Christi* and the *Fifteen Oes*. Both of these books have cuts with a fine Netherlandish touch, far superior to anything seen in English books till then. The *Fifteen Oes* (a book of fifteen prayers beginning with "O") has a cut of Calvary strongly reminiscent of

DE CESSOLIS, *The Playe of the Chesse*. Westminster, Caxton, c. 1483. Pierpont Morgan Library →
CHAUCER, *Canterbury Tales*. Westminster, Caxton, 1484. Pierpont Morgan Library →

157

He causes Wherfore this playe was founden ben iij
The first was for to correcte and repreue the kyng
for whan this kyng enylmerdach sawe this playe / And
the barons knyghtes and gentilmen of his court playe
wyth the phylosopher / he merueylled gretly of the beaulte
and noueltee of the playe . And desired to playe agaynst
the philosopher / The philosopher ansewerd and sayd to hym
that hit myght not be don / but yf he first lernyd the play
The kyng sayd hit was reson and that he wold put hym
to the payn to lerne hit /   Than the phylosopher began to

¶ The Tale of The Nonnys preest

¶ And here begynnyth his tale

A Poure Wydow som dele y stept in age
Was somtyme dwellyng in a cotage
Beside a groue stondyng in a dale
This wydow of whiche I telle you my tale
Syn that day that she was last a wyf
In pacience leede a ful sympyl lyf
For lytil was her catel and her rent
By husbondry of suche as god her sent
She fonde her self and eke her doughtryn two
Thre large solvys had she and nomo
Thre kyne & eek a sheep that hight malle
Wel soty was her bour and eek her halle
In whyche she eet many a slender meel
Of poynaunt salwe ne knewe she neuer adeel
Ne deynte morcel passyd thorough her throte
                                                    E iii

Alamon in his parablys sayth that a good spyryte makyth a flouryng aege that is a fayre aege ⁊ a longe. And syth it is soo: I aske this quēstyon. Whiche ben the meanes ⁊ the causes that enduce a man in to a mery spyryte.: Truly to my beste dyscrecōn it semeth good dysportes ⁊ honest gamys in whom a man Joyeth wythout ony repentannce after. Thenne folowyth it ꝑ gode dysportes ⁊ honest games ben cause of mannys fayr aege ⁊ longe life. And therfore now woll I chose of foure good dysportes ⁊ honeste gamys that is to wyte:of huntynge:hawkynge: fysshynge:⁊ foulynge. The beste to my symple dyscrecōn why che is fysshynge:callyd Anglynge wyth a rodde: and a lyne

Flemish painting in its spirited movement. Handsome leaf and flower initials accompany the text in one of Caxton's strange, wayward types, and medieval borders, crudely printed, surround the pages.

Despite his interest in illustrated editions, Caxton was not a printer of fine books; in appearance, his books fell considerably short of the standards set by French, Italian, and German printing. He was essentially a man of letters who translated twenty of the eighty-some books he printed, and who wrote prefaces and epilogues to many of his editions which bear the mark of his delightful wit.

During Caxton's lifetime other printers set up shop in England. Oxford University had a German printer, Theodoric Rood, from 1478 till 1486 or –87, printing scholarly books in Latin. The Oxford press was killed off when Richard III issued a law permitting free import of books to England. The competition of fine foreign editions was too much for a struggling new English academic press.

John Lettou, a Lithuanian who learned to print at Rome, appeared in 1480 as a printer in England and was joined a little later by a Belgian, William Machlinia, who went on to print on his own. These men produced mostly law books and a few popular religious books. Machlinia printed the first of the English Books of Hours, known as Primers, as early as 1485 at the same time as—perhaps even slightly before—the first French ones. He used woodcut borders similar to those of Jean Dupré, but they were much more crudely cut, and the illustrations they enclosed were stiffly Germanic.

The only other English-born printer of Caxton's time was an anonymous schoolmaster at St. Alban's who produced eight books between 1480 and 1486, apparently using Caxton's type. Six of the books were scholastic; two were popular, with some attempt at illustration. The more ambitious of the two was *The Book of St. Albans* by Juliana Berners, entitled *Of Huntyng and Hawkyng and also of Coats Armour*, which contained a number of crude little cuts, some of them small coats of arms printed in several colors.

Wynken de Worde, an Alsatian, seems to have come to England with Caxton in 1476 and to have worked as his foreman. When Caxton died in 1491, De Worde took over the press, and became the most prolific of England's early printers. Before the end of the fifteenth century he had turned out 110 books that we know of; at the end of his long career of printing, which lasted until 1534, the number was close to 800. Throughout his career De Worde acknowledged the mastership of William Caxton by printing Caxton's characteristic device at the end of his books or by making the initials WC an important part of his own numerous and fanciful devices.

Many of De Worde's books were reprints of Caxton's editions or those of other printers. In 1495 he reprinted Caxton's *Polychronicon* in a good upright type, using some of Caxton's leaf and flower initials. Its woodcut music example was the first printed in England.

The Book of St. Albans
page 160

The following year he brought out an edition of *The Book of St. Albans* with new cuts apparently obtained from different sources, very different in their style and competence. A good-sized illustration of a gentleman and his retainers out for sport is sophisticated in design and rather well cut. The treatise on *Fishing with an Angle*, added to the new edition, is illustrated with a naive cut. However, its black border, combined with a heavy black initial, nicely complements the straight black-letter type.

De Worde printed translations of Pigouchet's *Chasteau de Labour*, Marchant's *Kalendrier des Bergiers*, Vérard's *Art de bien Vivre et bien Mourir*, and the Basel *Narrenschiff* with successful copies of the illustrations. His most original book was *All the Proprytees of Thynges*, a translation of Bartholomeus' *De proprietatibus rerum* which he printed in 1495.

Wynken de Worde was not a great innovator, but he did much to develop English type into the pointed black letter that remained in use through the seventeenth century. In general, he was content with a stock solution to the decorative problems of printing. He liked to use some kind of title cut in his books, and the same schoolmaster with birch rod served for many a grammar, the same mounted knight graced many a romance. A man of enduring tradition, it is fitting that he began the tradition of Fleet Street as the printers' and publishers' locale when he moved his press there from Caxton's old quarters in 1500.

Richard Pynson, a Norman, began printing at about the time Wynken de Worde did and printed roughly half as many books as his competitor, many of them the same foreign works. He relied heavily on foreign cuts (either bought or copied), but what his books lacked in originality they made up for in workmanship. His decorative initials and woodcut borders in the style of Dupré made the *Morton Missal*, which he printed at the turn of the century, the finest English service book of the time.

England had been slow to start in printing, and it was even slower in making its own contribution to the art. The tradition of fine manuscript had died out too soon to furnish models for the early presses, which were forced to find them in foreign styles. In printing, Caxton remained the personality of the century, giving at least the stamp of his own taste to the first English books.

SPAIN

The first printers in Spain were three Germans, sent to the commercial town of Valencia in 1473 by the leading German European export-import firm of the time, which had a factory there. Of the three, Lambert Palmart stayed on in Valencia, but the other two printers, John of Salzburg and Paul Hurus, went to Barcelona in 1475. From that time on printing offices cropped up all over Spain, especially in commercial centers and university towns. By the end of the century printing had been practiced in twenty-five or thirty Spanish towns; in at least fourteen of them the first printers had been Germans.

Printing did not become centralized in one or two important Spanish cities for the reason that Spain was not a unified country until the sixteenth century. It consisted of five separate kingdoms, four of them Catholic: Aragon, Castile, Navarre, and Portugal. The fifth, Granada, was in Moorish hands until 1492. The political independence of these states as well as the isolating nature of the Spanish terrain made for a number of local centers of diverse character.

In one respect early Spanish printing was like that of France: the first few books produced by the newly arrived foreign printers were in roman type, which was quickly replaced, except in humanistic works, with a round gothic type more to the Spanish liking. On Spanish soil these types, even in German and French hands, took on a typically Spanish appearance. Whatever force it is which establishes a local character in design acted strongly on the early printers in Spain. A Spanish book is unmistakably that, even when its woodcuts have been copied from German originals. The special decorative sense of Spain prevails: heavy mass in a limited area played against decorative detail. The dark mass may be provided by black-ground initials or borders, by a few words of heavy type, by sharp areas of pure black in a woodcut. The detail may be supplied by the type itself, often beautifully decorative. A special characteristic of early Spanish books is the large woodcut title page, often an armorial design—again, in a sense, the large effect played against the balance of the book. The Gothic qualities of early Spanish printing, together with the high level of craftsmanship and materials, lasted well into the sixteenth century—at least until 1530—much later than in the rest of Europe. The patronage and

echar del lugar donde estaua. Boluiendo despues dela sepultura: lle=
go se a el aquel que lo hauia echado de alli/z dixo le con malenconia. di
me maluado.no te mãde yo q̃ no te assentasses ay: z tu en verguéça del
rey z de todos nosotros te tornaste donde estauas primero. Asio del con
mucho rigor: z leuo le ala carcel. A poco rato ayuntaron se los caualle=
ros z hombres de pro de toda la tierra/por ordenar rey z señor: z leuan=
to se entre ellos aq̃l q̃ lo hauia puesto enla carcel. z dixo les como aquel
mancebo q̃ hauian hallado ala puerta dela ciudad/ jamas hauia queri=
do apartar de vn lugar por mucho que gelo hauia mandado: ni hauia
hecho honrra alguna al cuerpo del rey/ z que no deuiera ser aquello sin
algun gran misterio/o era loco del todo. Todos mãdaron luego traher
lo: z desque fue ante ellos: preguntaron le quié era z de donde venia. El
qual les respõdio. hijo soy de tal rey: el qual vos conoçistes triunphante
z magnifico: z muerto el/mi hermano vsurpando se todo el reyno: abun
trabajaua por me matar z perder. z con este miedo vine aqui a vuestra
ciudad. Oyendo aq̃sto los que hauian conoçido a su padre: a grãdes bo
zes llamaron. viua el rey. viua el rey. lo que a todos plugo mucho/ z to=
maron le por su rey z señor. z luego con muchas cerimonias lleuaron le
como rey por toda la tierra. z quãdo llego ala puerta donde estauã los
scriptos de sus cõpañeros: mando ende escriuir: que la discrecion/ la di

influence of the church were particularly important; almost half of the Spanish incunabula were of a religious nature. Nevertheless, most of these early books were in the Spanish vernacular, and romances figured heavily among them.

A number of Spain's early printers kept the nomadic habits which had brought them there in the first place. Paul Hurus, one of the first three printers at Valencia, moved on from Barcelona to Saragossa, where he established a firm that was unrivaled in that city for three-quarters of a century. Hurus had translations made of a variety of foreign favorites—Breidenbach's *Peregrinationes*, Aesop's *Fables*, Boccaccio's *De mulieribus claris*, the block book *Ars moriendi*, Ketham's *Fasciculus di medicina*—using copies of the original woodcuts and sometimes the original blocks themselves. He often used large woodcut title pages, such as that in the romance *Cronica de Aragon:* a strong, simple image of an angel holding a heraldic shield. The most lavish of his publications was the *Officia quotidiana* which he printed in 1500, with fifty woodcut illustrations and over a thousand initials.

Friedrich Biel of Basel (or Fadrique Aleman de Basilea, as his Spanish mark reads) beginning in 1485, printed for over thirty years at Burgos, turning out religious and legal books and romances. He was a fine craftsman, as his Spanish edition of the *Directorium humanae vitae* shows. Biel illustrated the text with 125 cuts the width of the type page and with little figures of men and women pointing from the margins to the morals in the text. (The same use of little pointing figures had been made in the second illustrated book printed in Germany, Boner's *Edelstein*.) Biel's larger cuts, copied from Prüss's edition printed at Strassburg ten years earlier, have become rather Spanish in the process, especially in their borders.

Bidpai,
Exemplario contra
los engaños y peligros
del mundo
page 164

One of the very few sets of original Spanish illustrations of the century is in Villena's *Doze trabajos de Hércules (The Twelve Labors of Hercules)* printed by Antonio de Centenara at Zamora in 1483. These awkward cuts of the Herculean exploits have a characteristic Spanish wildness. Despite their primitive cutting, they are not carved into wood but are actually metal cuts.

Also printed from metal cuts are the black-ground borders in Martorell's quixotic romance *Tirant lo Blanch,* printed in 1491 at Valencia by Spindeler. The borders, with motifs of men and beasts scrambling through tight scrolls, are set close to the round gothic type, and even fill in the space between the two columns. The effect is dense, heavy, and very decorative.

The university town of Salamanca acquired printers relatively early, thanks to the scholar Antonio de Lebrija (or Nebrissensis) who brought the first printers there in 1481. They worked with an anonymity that has not since been pierced, printing mostly the writings of Nebrissensis and other humanist scholars. However, the same printer who produced Nebressensis' *Gramatica castellana* also printed, in 1496, an edition of Boccaccio's *La Fiametta* with a charm-

Boccaccio,
La Fiametta
page 167

ing woodcut title page. The Salamanca printers used both gothic and roman types, and embellished them with fine arabesque black-ground initials.

Alcalá, also a university seat, became early in the sixteenth century the center of activity of the printer Arnald Guillen de Brocar, famous for his Polyglot Bible. Brocar began his career, which blossomed fully in the sixteenth century, at Pamplona in 1489.

Seville made a slow start with Spanish printers, who produced only a few books in the ten years in which they held sway. Real activity began with four Germans commissioned by Queen Isabella in 1490, who sometimes signed their books *cuatro compagñeros alemanes*. A year or so later a second German printing office was established by Meinhard Ungut, who soon took a Polish partner known as Polonus. The two printed a great many fine and varied books. By the early sixteenth century, Seville, center of the burgeoning relations with the New World, was the leading Spanish city in printing activity.

Portugal had a unique beginning in printing: for the first four years its printed books were all in Hebrew. The Rabbi Eliesar was the only printer in Lisbon from 1489 until 1493. His books are remarkable for their black-ground initials and borders of Islamic appearance, with delicate white scrollwork and rhythmic beasts. Another Hebrew printer, Abraham ben Samuel d'Ortas began printing in 1495 at Leiria, using metal-cut borders of a similarly Moorish influence. In 1493 Valentin Fernandez of Moravia set up a press in Lisbon which he operated until 1516. In 1495 he was joined by Nicolaus de Saxonia, and together, at the order of the King and Queen of Portugal, they printed one large, splendid book in Portuguese—the *Vita Christi* of Ludolphus de Saxonia. They adorned it with a scrollwork border, fine initials, and with a large woodcut of Christ on the Cross and a smaller one of the King and Queen at prayer. Then, having produced Portugal's finest early book, the printers parted company.

BOCCACCIO, *La Fiametta*. Salamanca, 1496. Pierpont Morgan Library

IVNII IVVENALIS AQVINA
TIS SATYRA PRIMA.

SEMPER EGO AVDITOR
tantum? nunquám ne reponam
Vexatus toties rauci theseide
Codri?
Impune ergo mihi recitauerit ille
togatus?
Hic elegos? impune diem consumpserit ingens
Telephus? aut summi plena iam margine libri
Scriptus, et in tergo nec dum finitus, Orestes?
Nota magis nulli domus est sua, quam mihi lucus
Martis, et æoliis uicinum rupibus antrum
Vulcani. Quid agant uenti, quas torqueat umbras
Aeacus, unde alius furtiuæ deuehat aurum
Pelliculæ, quantas iaculetur Monychus ornos,
Frontonis platani, conuulsáq; marmora clamant
Semper, et assiduo ruptæ lectore columnæ.
Expectes eadem a summo, minimóq; poeta.
Et nos ergo manum ferulæ subduximus, et nos
Consilium dedimus Syllæ, priuatus ut altum
Dormiret. stulta est clementia, cum tot ubique
Vatibus occurras, perituræ parcere chartæ.
Cur tamen hoc libeat potius decurrere campo,
Per quem magnus equos Auruncæ flexit alumnus,
Si uacat, et placidi rationem admittitis, edam.
Cum tener uxorem ducat spado, Meuia thuscum
Figat aprum, et nuda teneat uenabula mamma,
Patricios omnes opibus cum prouocet unus,

A ii

THE
SIXTEENTH
CENTURY

ITALY

The new century brought remarkable changes in books. In Italy, Aldus Manutius, intent on making the classics readily available, produced in the year 1501 a revolutionary new edition: an octavo Virgil, light, inexpensive, compact, and set in the first italic type. The type, designed by Francesco Griffo, was based on a cursive version of the humanistic script. The Virgil was a book to be carried about, slipped into the pocket or saddlebag. Later that year Aldus printed the works of Juvenal and Persius in the same style. Before long this new kind of book was being *Juvenal and Persius,* printed everywhere, and italic became the type of the century. *Opera* *page 168*

If Aldus' name is one of the best known in the history of printing, it is with ample reason. The intrinsic beauty and wide influence of his classical *Poliphilus* alone would have brought him credit. The creation of the octavo editions with their close-setting, economical cursive type made him the inventor of the modern book and the leader of the printing world of his time. Aside from this, his central purpose had been from the start the publication of unavailable Greek classics. All that had appeared in print in Greek was a grammar, the *Idylls* of Theocritus, a poem of Hesiod, and a Greek Psalter, published at Milan; at Florence, the first Greek edition of Homer. Aldus added to this list in quick succession Lascaris' *Erotemata*, the great five-volume Aristotle, and, in small format, Aristophanes, Thucydides, Sophocles, Herodotus, Xenophon, Euripides, and Demosthenes—all before 1504. The Greek type he used in these editions was specially cut and followed the vagaries of a contemporary Greek hand rather than more ancient models—not the most fortunate choice, but one which influenced Greek types for some time to come.

After Aldus' death his press was carried on throughout the sixteenth century, first by his father-in-law and then by his youngest son Paul. The firm continued to turn out, in Aldus' style, the neatest possible little editions, with modest unaccented pages given only to the Aldine *Viaggi fatti* embellishment of occasional geometrically shaped type-page endings known as pendentives. *page 170* Their title pages bore Aldus' mark, the anchor and dolphin, along with the name of the book and sometimes a description of its contents. The later Aldine press kept also the tradition of

VIAGGI FATTI DA

VINETIA, ALLA TANA, IN PER=
SIA, IN INDIA, ET IN COSTANTI
NOPOLI: con la descrittione particolare di Città,
Luoghi, Siti, Costumi, et della PORTA del
gran TVRCO: & di tutte le Intra=
te, spese, & modo di gouerno
suo, & della ultima Im=
presa contra Por=
toghesi.

AL   DVS

IN VINEGIA M. D. XLIII.

QVIVI COMINCIA LA SECONDA

PARTE CHE APPARTIENE AL

VIAGGIO CHE IO IOSA=

PHAT BARBARO FE

CI IN PERSIA

COME AMBA

SCIATORE.

SSENDO la nostra Illustrissima
Signoria in guerra con l'Ottomanno
del. 1471. Io come huomo uso à sten=
tar, & prattico tra gente Barbara,
& uolonteroso di tutto il bene di essa
Illustrissima Signoria, fui mandato insieme con uno am
basciator de Assambei signor della Persia, ilqual era
uenuto à Venetia à confortar la Illustrissima Signoria
che uolesse proseguir la guerra contra il detto Ottomá
no; conciosiache anchora lui con le sue forze gli uenì
ua incontra. Partimmo adunque da Venetia con due
galee sottili & drieto di noi uennero due galee grosse
cariche di artiglierie, & gente da fatti, & presenti
che mandaua detta Illustrissima Signoria al detto As=
sambei, con commissione che io mi apresentassi al pae
se del Caramano, & à quelle marine; & uenendo o=
uer mandando li Assambei gli donassi tutte dette cose.
Le arteglierie furono bombarde, spingarde, schioppet

handsome folio volumes in roman letters with fine initials. Paul was in turn succeeded in the last quarter of the century by a son, but by this time the glories of Italian printing had passed away.

A family of publishers and printers that approached the fame of the Aldii were the Giunta, branches of which were working simultaneously in Florence and Venice. Lucantonio Giunta in Venice had made a name for himself with his illustrated editions, which included the Malermi Bible, in the last decade of the fifteenth century. In the sixteenth century his firm specialized in large, splendid missals and other service books of the church for which Venice was world-famed, as she had been for manuscript service books. The illustrations in these books were no longer in the pure, delicate line of the past century; they were richly and darkly shaded.

*Missal
page 172*

Filippo Giunta in Florence produced small classical editions in close imitation of the style of Aldus. Giacomo Giunta, also of Florence, was the publisher of a fantastic volume which he had printed in Venice in 1527—the *Triompho di Fortuna*, a heavy folio devoted to the science of astrology. It was crammed with illustrations ranging from full-page to less than an inch in size, most of them devices for forecasting and controlling one's fate. The larger illustrations were in the currently popular densely shaded style, but the very small ones, perhaps because of their size, had the economical expressiveness of earlier woodcuts.

*Fanti,
Triompho di Fortuna
page 173*

Rappresentazioni, popular poems, and the sermons of Savonarola continued to be produced in Florence in the style which had crystallized in the last decade of the fifteenth century. Some new cuts were made for them, but the original group continued to be used and remained the best. Also in continuation of the Florentine tradition of the late fifteenth century was Frezzi's allegorical poem, the *Quatriregio*, published in 1508 by Pacini and printed, at least in part, by Filippo Giunta, with innumerable woodcuts in the best Florentine style.

Of the many printers who began to print small italic books in Italy, Antonio Blado of Rome was by far the best. Blado was the papal printer from 1516 till 1557. In his nontheological books he worked in an intensely individual style, often using a beautiful italic type designed by the calligrapher Arrighi. Arrighi was the author of a writing book that helped spread the cursive style used in the Papal Chancery. His fluent italic types followed the same forms, and had a great influence on sixteenth-century type design, in France as well as Italy.

Aside from the types, the charm of Blado's pages comes from his use of *piccoli ferri*, the small ornaments cast in metal which we know as "printers' flowers" or "fleurons." He had a unique sense for disposing the type and these dark little accents on the page, as evidenced by his edition of Sannazaro's *Sonetti e canzoni*, printed in 1530.

*Sannazaro,
Sonetti e canzoni
page 175*

Blado used comparatively little illustration, but one of his most interesting books is the *Trattato di scientia d'arme* of Camillo Agrippa which he printed in 1553 in Arrighi's italic. It is illustrated with copperplate engravings showing the positions of dueling, handsomely drawn (they

*Agrippa,
Trattato di
scientia d'arme
pages 176 and 177*

Missal in the use of Monte Cassino. Venice, Lucantonio Giunta, 1515. Pierpont Morgan Library

SIGISMONDO FANTI, *Triompho di Fortuna.* Florence, Giacomo Giunta, 1527. Pierpont Morgan Library. 13 x 9 in.

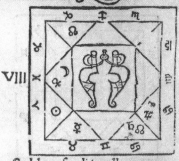

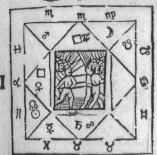

Di Faraone le Antiche memorie
Ben dimostrato si ha la legge hebrea
Quanto sia Crudelta persida e rea
E di Nerone le Romane historie.

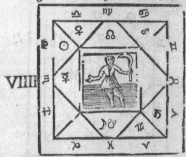

Se del morso e di te nulla non cura
Il sboccato corsier de furor pregno
Puoneli vn fren come questo disegno
De guarda barbuzal e imboccatura.

Certo dubbioso e tal Habbatimento
Chio veggio vn dal Caual alontanare
Laltro alla staffa cadendo restare
Tal che niun sia ne vincitor ne vento.

De l'ascendente in gradi maschi essendo
Il Signo e Diana in Tauro anchora
Che in casa de fratelli ancho dimora
Maschio sera se la ragion comprendo.

Fia questo anno penuria fermamente
Se Saturno signor sia dannato
In gradi puteal in sesto lato
Ouer casat prouedi diligente.

Anchor che i te Ragion lustrate veggia
Se con la parte auersa hauer poi patto
Per me io te consiglio chel sia fatto
Ancho che alquato di dannarti creggia.

Che non sia rotta certamente creggio
La fe da la quale dal conubio hai presa
Che in casa vener di fiducia veggio
Tutta del fuoco del suo figlio accesa

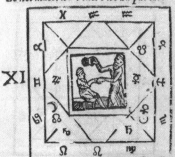

Se per Vener e Cintia in alto stato
Et la figura ben disposta a ponto
Mostrano il ben nudrir a buo fine gioto
Se nel materno ventre no ha parlato

Altri mali Altre pene Altri tormenti
Io veggio apparechiar nel basso inferno
Per quei che guerra ingiustamete ferno
Piu che a ragion al apetito intenti.

Il sommo Ioue in meggio il ciel locato
E di Oroscopo il sir dimostra aperto
Quando vn signor la man ti pora certo
Sopra la spalla a grandirai tuo stato.

La vrina che spiumamente in color rosso
Febre dinota con dolor di testa
Pur se la cura sia subita e presta
Fia cotal mal da l'infermo rimosso.

have been hazarded as the work of Michelangelo and any number of other artists of the time) but badly placed on the page because of separate printing. Another edition of Blado's illustrated in copperplate, a large folio of architectural drawings by Labacco printed in 1552, has an engraved title page in which airy pillars flanked by figures act as a portal to the book. It is one of the earliest engraved title pages (the first being an isolated example at Florence in 1512) —a forerunner of the style that was to flourish in the late sixteenth and the seventeenth centuries.

In Venice after 1534 Francesco Marcolini printed some attractive books, using italic types and simple formats. He was a friend of Pietro Aretino's, and printed many of his books. His *Petrarcha spirituale* of 1536 is in italics based on Arrighi's, and has a fine woodcut portrait of Petrarch. By far the most prolific and influential printer around the middle of the century was Gabriel Giolito, active in Venice from 1539 till 1578. His richly imaginative publications with their elaborate classical headpieces, their fleurons and their historiated initials attracted the emulation of the printers of the day, Marcolini among them. The initials, a strange fad, were illustrated with personalities or activities whose names began with the letter of the initial—a conceit that was taken up avidly.

Giolito printed a large number of illustrated books with finely cut blocks to balance with the finer italic type and smaller format of the books of the day. Ovid's *Le trasformationi (Metamorphoses)*, printed in 1553, with its lightly hatched woodcuts and flanking ornaments, is *Il Petrarcha* among his most successful books. *Il Petrarcha*, the poems of Petrarch which he printed in 1545, *page 179* shows the tasteful imagination that informed his earlier books, allowing him to combine many elements into a pleasing whole.

Giolito's early title pages bore only his mark, a phoenix, for decoration, but he soon began to produce more active ones. He advanced to such designs as putti lifting a curtain, and further to architectural forms swelling with human figures and ornament. The architectural title page with flanking columns had originated at Basel in Johann Froben's publications. Giolito launched the series of elaborations on this motif that progressed into the Baroque book. Most of Giolito's title pages were woodcuts, but one was a copperplate engraving; the rich hatchings of the style were actually more suited to copperplate technique.

The first half of the sixteenth century had seen a large increase in book production, in spite of which the quality of printing had remained remarkably high. There was a great concern for letter-forms, evidenced by Paccioli's *Divina proportione* of 1509 and later books that dealt with the philosophical and technical bases of the shapes of letters. But political forces became increasingly adverse; after Charles V sacked Rome in 1527, the subjugated Italian city-states lost much of their individual style.

The changes which occurred in Gabriel Giolito's books illustrate well the conditions that

SANNAZARO, *Sonetti e canzoni*. Rome, Blado, 1530. Yale Beinecke Rare Book Library. 8 x 5 in.

SONETTI, E CANZONI

DI. M. IACOBO SANNAZARO

GENTILHVOMO NA

POLITANO.

Staua com' huom, che ferma gliocchi al sole,
E riguardar no'l puo, ne muoue il uifo.
Senno, beltà, ualor la terra mai
Simil non uidde, ne fi dolci accenti
Sonaro in detti fi le ggiadri, e gai.
Onde se i miei grauofi afpri tormenti
Hebber breue conforto, hor che farai
Tu fignor mio che ogn' hor le uedi, e senti?

PARTE SECONDA DE, SO

NETTI, E CANZONI DI

. M. IACOBO SANNAZARO

GENTILHVOMO NA-

 ## POLITANO,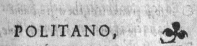

Spente eran nel mio cor l'antiche fiamme,
Ed à fi lunga, e fi continua guerra,
Dal mio nemico homai speraua pace.
Quando all' ufcir delle dilette selue,
Mi sentii ritener da un forte laccio,
Per cui cangiar conuiemmi e uita, e ftile.

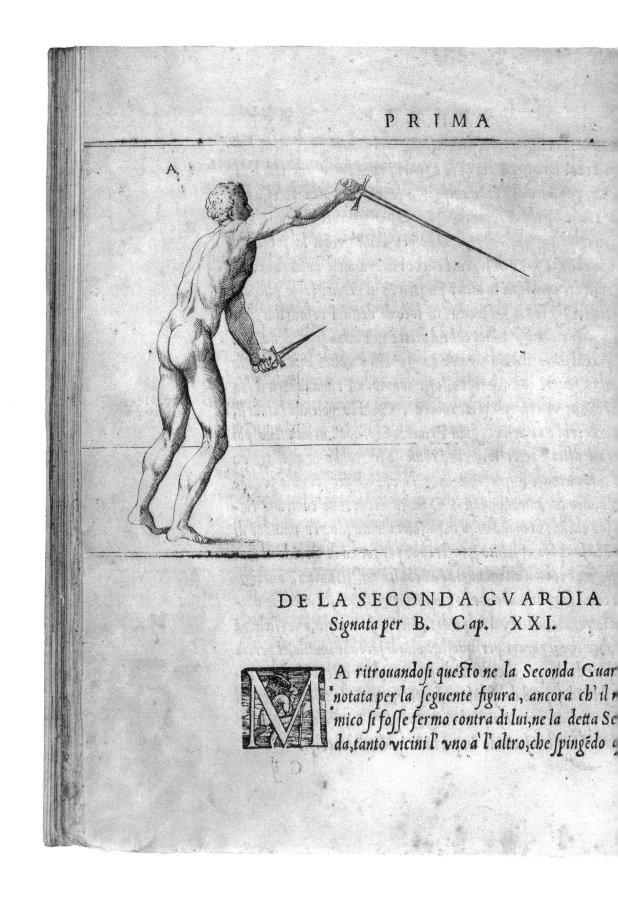

DE LA SECONDA GVARDIA
Signata per B. Cap. XXI.

MA ritrouandosi questo ne la Seconda Guarnotata per la seguente figura, ancora ch'il n
mico si fosse fermo contra di lui, ne la detta Se
da, tanto vicini l'vno à l'altro, che spingēdo q

si voglia di loro potessero giungersi con l'arme, dico che mouendosi il nemico per ferire, Questo subito schifarebbe la persona,
trapassando verso la parte sinistra de l'auerssario, & spinge-
rebbe contra di esso a l'auantaggio, mentre si ritrouasse co'l piè
destro in aria, doue la sua spada restarebbe nel uoto, per la cir-
cunferēza, & moto, che farebbono tutti doi li corpi, perche Questo potrebbe mettere la punta sua nel medesimo loco, nel quale te-
neua l'altro il pugno dritto : considerando ch'il nemico volendo
venir' innanzi darebbe da se ne la spada, & questo fatto li suc-
cederebbe, tenendo la mano bassa, con la quale se bisognasse, potrebbe parar' alzandola in suso co'l fugir' di vita, si come dissi,
si che offendendolo restarebbe in Quarta alta verso, la sua parte sinistra, ciò è del nemico. Et se tutti doi si ritrouassero anco
in detta Guardia di Seconda, vicini come di sopra, & non
mouendosi il nemico, Questo per tentarlo, abbassarebbe la
spada ponendola in croce di dentro contra la sua, tāto che si toc-
cassero, Ma pche forse altri m'imputarebbono, dicēdo che con
quella occasione, il nemico li potrebbe dare d'vna punta
determinata nel petto, schifando la spada contraria,
dico che studiosamente douerebbe far'tal' atto, solo per farlo mouere, perche nel medesimo tēpo
che esso spingesse di fore sopra la spada di questo, Questo gli andarebbe
sotto di Quarta contra il suo col
po, et cedendo con la persona lo ferirebbe.

affected printers and publishers as the sixteenth century wore on. Giolito's earlier books were Italian classics—Petrarch, Boccaccio—and contemporary authors such as Aretino. But the Inquisition and the Counter-Reformation were at work, and around 1560 it became dangerous to produce any book which could be construed as inimical to church or state. The gay, licentious literature of the Renaissance was listed in the Index of prohibited books along with many early pagan writings. Giolito himself was summoned before the Inquisition because of prohibited books found on his premises. It is not surprising that his later publications were mostly translations of Greek and Latin histories and devotional books, and far less attractive than his earlier books.

One of the worst influences on Italian printers was the fact that about 1557 Venice began to supply most of Italy with standardized type-faces that replaced the individually cut faces. Excessive mixing of these mediocre types accompanied other excesses in style. Illustration declined as ornament prospered. Paper quality and printing techniques became increasingly poor. Toward the end of the century the repressive social atmosphere, mass-production techniques, and an overripe taste had driven Italian printing to its depths.

TRIOMPHO QVARTO DI

MESSER FRANCESCO PETRARCA,
NEL QVALE SI VEDE LA FAMA DELLE
NOSTRE OPERATIONI, MAL GRADO
DELLA MORTE, RESTAR NELLA
MEMORIA DEGLI HVOMINI.

DEL TRIOMPHO DI FAMA.
CAPITOLO PRIMO.

D A P O I , *che morte
triomphò nel uol =
to,
Che di me spesso triom
phar solea;
Et fu del nostro mon
do il suo sol tolto;
Partissi quella dispie=
tata & rea*

*Pallida in uista, horribile & superba,
Che'l lume di beltate spento hauea;
Quando mirando intorno su per l'herba
Vidi da l'altra parte giunger quella,
Che trahe l'huom del sepolcro, e'n uita il serba.*

H AVENDO
noi ueduto il sen=
sitiuo appetito del
mondo, La ragio
ne de l'appetito,
Et la morte de la
ragione triomphare, Hora nel pre
sente quarto triopho, in tre cap.
distinto, uedremo, com'a principio dicemmo, la fama da infinita
moltitudine d'huomini famosi ac
compagnata, a la morte predomi
nare Onde'l Poeta dice, Che da-
poi che morte triomphò del bel
uolto di Madonna Laura per essa,
ragione intesa, quale spesse uolte
di lui soleua triomphare, e del no

GERMANY

Certain German and Swiss cities caught the Renaissance spirit next after Italy, before it burst out in France. For a few years in the first third of the sixteenth century these cities led Europe in the production of both scholarly and illustrated books.

Albrecht Dürer's book illustrations, not a side product but a major expression of that prodigious genius, could not fail to dominate the early years of the century. His *Apocalypse*, printed in 1498, had shown the measure of his mature powers. In 1511 he printed three other series of woodcuts in book form: the *Life of the Blessed Virgin*, the *Great Passion* with twenty very large woodcuts, and the *Little Passion* with thirty-seven smaller ones. In them Dürer showed his capacity for dramatic movement, for the expressive figure, for light emerging from dark.

Great as they are as works of art, and immense as their influence was on illustrators to come, these works of Dürer's are less illustrated books than series of cuts accompanied by a few lines of text. But the same is true of many of the illustrated books of the time whose smaller format may make the fact less obvious. Perhaps it was the inevitable result of major artists having turned full attention to illustration.

At the same time, Dürer was deeply concerned with letter-forms and set down rules for the construction of both roman and gothic letters in his books on proportion. He insisted on a geometric basis to all art, without which "many young men of a happy talent for the pictorial art ... have run riot like an unpruned tree, so that unhesitatingly and without compunction they turn out their works, purely according to their own judgement."

Dürer was the greatest of a generation of extraordinary professional illustrators that flourished in the first half of the century in Nuremberg and Augsburg, Frankfurt and Basel. Some of them, such as Hans Springingklee and Hans Schaüfelein, were for a time Dürer's pupils. A good number of the Nuremberg and Augsburg artists worked at some time on the many grandiose book projects of the Emperor Maximilian, designed to glorify the House of Hapsburg. Some of these projects were so ambitious that they were never completed. The *Weisskunig*, which undertook to describe the parentage, education, and exploits of Maximilian with

PFINTZING, *Teuerdank*. Nuremberg, Schönsperger the Elder, 1517. Woodcuts by Schaüfelein. Yale Beinecke Rare Book Library. 14¼ x 9½ in.

Als Neydelhart mißriet sein valschait

Die Er dem Held het zůberait

Fiell Jm in seinen valschen mut

Wie dann gwonlich ein pösen thůt

Ein Kůrriser den Er wol kannde

Freydig vnnd kůn was Er genanndt

Bald Er Jm mit seiner hande schrib

Das Er keins wegs auſſen belib   K iiii

Teuerdank
page 181

249 illustrations by Burgkmäir, was put on a press for the first time two and a half centuries later, in 1775. But the *Teuerdank*, a chivalric romance of the wooing of Mary of Burgundy by Maximilian (said to have been dictated by the Emperor to his secretary Pfintzing, who rendered it into verse), was achieved in all its intended glory. It was printed on fine vellum at Nuremberg in 1517 by Schönsperger the Elder for private distribution by the Emperor. Schäufelein made the Gothic, knightly illustrations for the large folio, and a special black-letter type was cut for it with extra pieces that extended as elaborate flourishes into the margins. The type was one of the first in the style known as "Fraktur."

Dürer himself participated, along with Hans Springingklee and Wolf Traut, in the most outrageously grand of Maximilian's printing schemes: the *Triumphal Arch and Procession*—a series of woodcuts intended, when put together, to form an immense design glorifying the Hapsburg line. The *Triumphal Arch* alone consisted of 192 woodcuts which combined covered an area of about ten by twelve feet.

While activity of the one sort went forward at Nuremberg and Augsburg, at Basel (Swiss since 1501) a quite different printing activity was taking place. The humanist scholar Erasmus formed his association with the printer Johann Froben in Basel in 1513, and the cosmopolitan university town quickly became the European center of scholarly printing. The books which Froben printed were mostly those of Erasmus and of his friends such as Sir Thomas More: translations of the Greek classics, new editions of the Latin ones, studies of the texts of the Greek and Latin Fathers of the Church, books and pamphlets critical of the contemporary Church. Froben printed in a very solid roman type instead of the generally used gothic, and the style of Basel typography which grew up—heavy and dense, with a large use of classical borders and initials, headpieces and tailpieces—was for a while the dominant influence on European printing. It was the first classical influence on French bookmaking before Renaissance Italy made itself directly felt.

The title borders that were a characteristic feature of German humanist typography were of a general nature and could be applied to almost any book or tract at hand. About a thousand borders were in circulation at home and abroad, the finest of them designed by Hans Holbein. The style had been introduced by Urs Graf, an illustrator and soldier of fortune whose military adventures in Italy sent him back to Basel full of classical motifs such as architectural portals and clambering putti. Shortly afterwards Holbein came to Basel from Augsburg and began producing a series of borders which ranged through many variations on the motifs of arch and putti. These grew more sculpturesque and complex all the while, and finally embraced a biblical or a classical scene, such as the death of Cleopatra, in an architectural framework. Holbein's headpieces and tailpieces are either classical episodes or humorous genre scenes; a

More,
Epigrammata
page 183

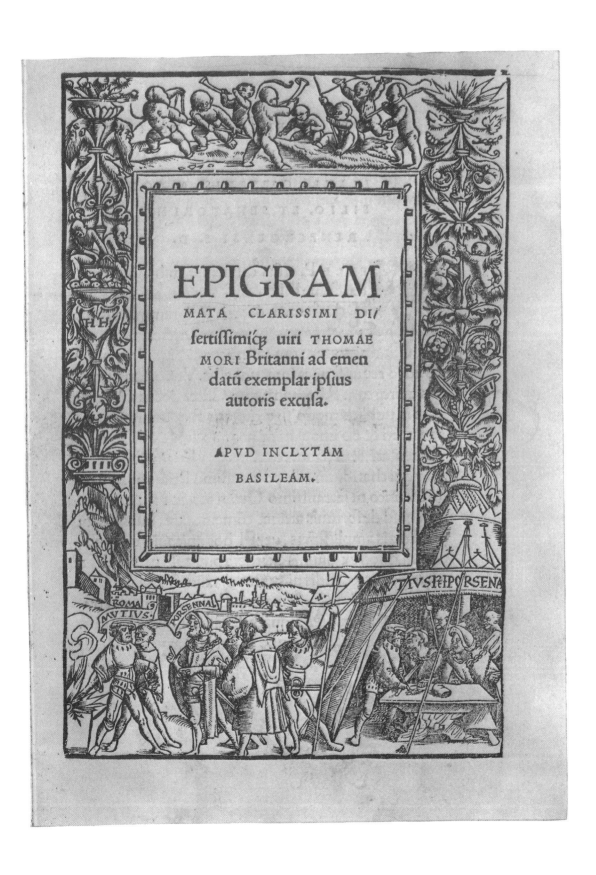

EPIGRAM
MATA CLARISSIMI DI/
sertissimiq̃ uiri THOMAE
MORI Britanni ad emen
datũ exemplar ipsius
autoris excusa.

APVD INCLYTAM
BASILEAM.

SIR THOMAS MORE, *Epigrammata*. Basel, Johann Froben, 1520. Woodcut border by Hans Holbein the Younger.
Pierpont Morgan Library

famous set shows villagers chasing a fox and then dancing homewards. Among his numerous sets of historiated initials are those with dancing peasants, children at play, and scenes from the Dance of Death.

That the greatest of Holbein's designs for printing, the illustrations for the *Dance of Death* and the Old Testament, were first printed in Lyons is not particularly surprising; relations between Lyons and Basel printers were fluent at that time. Basel types, borders and initials were on many a Lyons press, and by the same token, Lyons printers often turned out an edition for such busy Basel printers as Anton Koberger.

Printing at Wittenberg gained its importance just before 1520 from the residence there of Martin Luther, lecturing on the Bible at the university. Like Savonarola, Luther appreciated the persuasive value of the pictorial image. His tracts were given further impact by the woodcuts of his friend Lucas Cranach and Cranach's son Hans. The *Passional Christi und Antichristi*, illustrated by the elder Cranach and printed by Grunenberg in 1521, was presumably initiated by Luther. Its illustrations show on facing pages scenes from the Life of Christ parodied sharply by scenes from the papacy.

Passional Christi und Antichristi page 185

The high period of German book illustration declined about 1535 except in Nuremberg and Frankfurt. In the latter city the artist Hans Beham produced his best work, the *Biblische Historien*, a series of small illustrations to the Bible, in 1533, and an *Apocalypse* in 1539 with brief text and minute illustrations full of fine detail: whole cities tumbling, the heavenly host above a vast landscape, all enclosed in a small rectangle.

For a while, around the thirties, German type itself had some interesting additions. A good italic appeared in Basel, cut with sloping capitals to go with it. France, England and Italy imported it between 1540 and 1550. But Basel's leadership as a center of book production had suffered reverses, beginning around 1524, when the Protestant reformers, like their Catholic adversaries elsewhere, imposed a censorship of books. The initiative passed to France, where it remained despite the eventual recovery of the Basel industry.

After Froben's death a new printer rose to prominence from among Basel's many good printers: Johann Oporinus distinguished himself with his excellent editions of the Greek and Latin classics and the writings of Luther. His most important book was Vesalius' great contemporary anatomy, *De humani corporis fabrica*, printed in 1543—an immense volume of 667 pages set in even roman type, with neat running heads and page numbers, and marginal notes in a small, fluent italic. The deep pages of unparagraphed text he punctuated with rather playful square initials showing putti in such activity as dissecting a boar or performing a circumcision on one of their fellows. Throughout the book are innumerable anatomical illustrations of the greatest clarity, precision, and—strange for the subject—grace. The Belgian

Vesalius, De humani corporis fabrica page 186

Antichristi.

Hie sitzt der Antichrist ym tempell gots vñ ertzeygt sich alß got
wie Paul⁹ vorkundet 2. Thessal 2. vorandert alle gotlich ord=
nung wie Daniel sagt vnnd vntherdruckt die heylig schrifft /
vorkeufft dispensacion / Ablas pallia Bisthumb lehen / erhebt
die schetz der erden / Lost vff die ehe / beschwerdt die gewissenn
mit seynen gesetzen / Macht recht vnd vmß gelt zureyst er das /
Erhebt heyligen / Benedeyet vñ maledeyet yns vierde geschlecht
vñ gebewt ßeyn stym zuhoren gleych wie gots stym c. sic ois
dis .19' vnd nûnants sall ym eynreden. 17 q. 4. c. nemini.

Passional Christi und Antichristi. Wittenberg, Grunenberg, 1521. Woodcuts by Lucas Cranach. Pierpont Morgan
Library

185

A, A1,3 Quicquid costarum hucusque à uertebris fertur, osseum omnino est: hícq; primùm costæ in car
tilaginem degenerant. Reliquarum notarum index figuris subijcietur.

PRIMA DECIMINONI CAPITIS FIGV-
RA, QVA THORACIS OSSIVM INTEGRA COMPAGO
anteriori facie exprimitur, duodecim nimirum thoracis uertebræ, et duodecim
utrinque costæ, unà cum pectoris osse pluribus efformato ossibus.

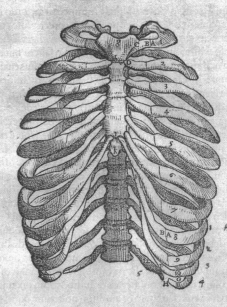

SECVNDA PRAESENTIS CAPITIS FIGV-
RA, POSTERIOREM INTEGRAE THORACIS OS-
sium compagis faciem proponens. Iuuerit modò obiter tres figuras contueri, quibus
in huius libri calce totus ossium contextus triplici facie delineatur.

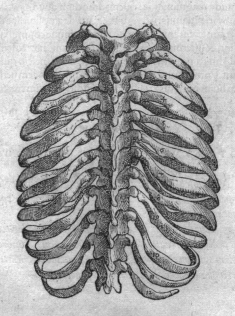

TER

artist Calcar, who worked in Italy under the supervision of the anatomist Vesalius, did not stop short of providing landscape backgrounds for the full-page skeletal figures or those showing the layers of muscle.

The scientific interest of the time brought a flow of descriptive texts and illustrations. The first of the great flower books, Fuch's *De historia stirpium,* appeared in Basel in 1542 with hundreds of large naturalistic illustrations in fine outline. Conrad Gessner's *Historia animalium,* the beginning of modern zoology, was printed at Zurich between 1551 and 1587, with detailed descriptions of all animals then known and splendid, remarkably accurate illustrations. By the second half of the century German black-letter types, both the pointed Fraktur and the rounded Schwabacher, had evolved to almost the forms they have today. Roman type was seen less and less as the century neared its end. There was a steady decline in both typographic taste and quality of printing; grossly indiscriminate mixtures of types were badly printed on cheap paper.

Illustrators first strove to attain through woodcuts the rich or realistic effects more appropriate to copper engraving. Toward the end of the century (later than in Italy and the Netherlands) they abandoned woodcut for engraving in all but the cheapest books. Jost Amman was the leading illustrator of the latter half of the century; he is known best for his pictures of the printing crafts in the *Eygentliche Beschreibung aller Stände auf Erde (Original Description of all Stations on Earth).*

Despite the generally debased book production of the end of the century, isolated examples of fine or attractive books appeared, always of a scientific or technical nature. In 1590 the De Bry family began printing their long series of travel books that ran far into the seventeenth century —well-printed volumes with fascinating illustrations that gave a glimpse into the farthest corners of the opening world.

VESALIUS, *De humani corporis fabrica.* Basel, Johann Oporinus, 1543. Woodcuts by Calcar. Yale Medical Historical Library. 17 x 11 in.

HORAE, in laudem beatiss. semper virginis
MARIAE, secundum consuetudinem ec‐
clesiæ Romanæ.

AVE GRATIA PLENA, DOMI‐
NVS TECVM. BENEDICTA
TV IN MVLIERIBVS.

Ad matutinum Versus.

Omine labia mea aperies. ℞.Et
os meum annunciabit laudē tuā.
℣.Deus in adiutoriũ meũ intēde
℞.Dñe ad adiuuādũ me festina.
Gloria patri,& filio,& spiritui sā
cto. Sicut erat in principio,& nunc,& semper,

D.iiij.

FRANCE

France invaded Italy by force of arms in the late fifteenth and early sixteenth centuries and was in turn captured by force of spirit. French soldiers came back with strong new impressions of the Italian Renaissance, and the court of Francis I gave favor to the new trend. On a rising tide of political power, the French aristocrary patronized the arts. There was enthusiasm for all things Italian. Francis I imported Italian artists and craftsmen—Leonardo not the least among them—and French scholars and artists in turn went to Italy to study. The imported style, at first purely imitative, was quickly tempered by local influences; by the end of the first quarter of the century France had a Renaissance style of her own.

In printing, a break with the gothic book of the past was initiated early by such scholar-printers as Josse Bade and Henri Estienne, who, struck with the beauty of Aldus' *Poliphilus*, began to print their classical editions in roman type, with initials and title pages in the Venetian style. Estienne was the first in an illustrious line of scholar-printers; after his death in 1520 his foreman, Simon de Colines, married his widow and maintained the press until a son, Robert Estienne, was old enough to take it over. De Colines opened his own press then, and the two men dedicated themselves to the formal and architectonic ideals of Renaissance typography, concerned with the pure beauty of the text. Together, by the end of the first half-century, they transformed French printing and made French typography the most sought-after in all Europe —the standard of excellence for the next two centuries. In this they were aided considerably by Geoffroy Tory, illustrator, decorator, and typographic theorist, and Claude Garamond, type-founder. Tory, a near-legendary figure with a background in philosophy and the editing of Latin texts, opened a shop for illustrating, publishing, binding, and, for a time, printing. His illustrated Books of Hours were a deliberate revolt against the current richly shaded style, much influenced by Basel. The first of Tory's Horae, printed for him in 1525 by Simon de Colines, is the antithesis of these: its delicate Renaissance borders and illustrations are executed in cool, pure line which perfectly matches the weight of the roman type. Tory had modeled his drawings after the classic Venetians, but they achieved an elegant grace that is peculiarly

Horae
page 188

French. The almost incredibly fine borders were cut by Tory himself.

Estienne and De Colines had begun to print scholarly books in the Aldine tradition—inexpensive octavos and sextodecimes in a neat italic, as well as larger volumes. Title pages were a regular feature of these books; they carried only the device of the press as decoration, or a simple classical border, often in the form of an arch. The hallmark of the new typography was a mixture of types—roman and italic, capitals and lower case types of various sizes—put together with consummate taste. Tory contributed handsome roman initials on a square *criblé* background, based on the principals which he set forth in his *Champ fleury*. The *Arithmetica practica* of Oronce Fine, produced in 1542, is a fine example of De Colines' printing.

Van Hutten,
Ars versificatoria
page 192
Tory,
Aediloquium
page 192

Fine,
Arithmetica practica
page 191

The *Champ fleury*, which Tory published himself in 1529, dealt with the "true proportions" of roman letters according to the human face and body, and was to some extent indebted to the theories of Paccioli and Fanti. The several sets of initials which Tory designed, and the headpieces and printers' flowers that accompanied them, were the perfect complement to the new lighter roman type faces coming into use. They found an enthusiastic reception in Paris and elsewhere, and Francis I showed his appreciation of Tory's talents by creating for him the office of *Imprimeur du roy*.

Tory's connection with the types cut by Claude Garamond is not entirely clear; Garamond is reputed to have been in some sense a pupil of his. The new roman types that Garamond cut were based strongly on those of the *Poliphilus*, but with refinements that induced Aldus' own son to import them just after midcentury. Estienne and De Colines began using the new fonts in 1531 and 1532 respectively, and from that time through the next two centuries France's dominance in type design was established.

Robert Estienne was not only a printer of typographically fine books; he was a scholar who compiled dictionaries in Latin, Greek, and Hebrew which became the standard works at universities all over Europe. With the death of his patron, the liberal-minded Francis I, it was no longer prudent for Robert to remain in France. Bigots had begun, as in Italy, to be suspicious of the pagan languages and of the critical approach to the Bible which scholars like Estienne, influenced by Erasmus, had adopted. He removed himself to Geneva, where he set up a new press, leaving the Paris press to his brother Charles, a doctor of medicine at the Sorbonne. Later his son and grandsons carried on the tradition of scholarly printing.

Although scholarly books had gone over entirely to the roman letter, certain types of books continued to be printed in the French black letter, especially popular romances and liturgical books. About 1540 Denys Janot began the vogue for printing romances in roman type, with Renaissance ornament and illustration. Italics were also coming more and more into use in France. Janot used them in 1539 to print the verses in *Le Théâtre de bons Engins (The Theater of Good Machines)*, a little book of pictures accompanied by morals of the type known as an "emblem book."

De la Perrière,
Le Théâtre
de bons Engins
page 193

Chriſtianiſſimo Galloru̅ Regi,

FRANCISCO, EIVS NOMI-
nis primo, Orontius Finæus Delphinas,   S. D.

IVINA PROVIDENTIA
factum eſſe puto, FRANCISCE Rex
Chriſtianiſſime, vt quæ præclara ſunt & dif
ficilia, quantò magis ab ipſis deſiderantur &
perquiruntur hominibus: tantò tardiùs à pau
cis plurimùm inueniantur, & in ſua diffe-
rantur tempora, illiſque deſtinentur inuento=
ribus, quos ſolus Deus ad hæc nouit eſſe dele-
ctos. Cùm ob multa, tum vt igneus & planè
cæleſtis ille diuini ſplendoris vigor, mentibus
noſtris inſitus, magis atque magis eluceſcat : & ad perſcrutanda latentium rerum
arcana acriori nos vrgeat ſtimulo, in illorúmque aſſidua contemplatione & inda-
gatione fixam oblectet intelligḗtiam. Quod ſi tam in diuinis & naturalibus, quàm
mechanicis & ciuilibus rebus, locum habere compertum eſt: in ijs artibus, quæ ſolæ
Mathematicæ, hoc eſt, diſciplinæ nŭcupari meruerŭt, vſu maximè venire (opinor)
negabit nemo . Quanquam enim ipſæ Mathematicæ, medium inter intellectilia
ſenſiliáque locum obtinentes, cæteris artibus tum fide & ordine, tum certitudine ac
integritate (præter ſummam quæ illis ineſt vtilitatem) longè præſtare viden-
tur: rariores nihilominus ſemper habuere profeſſores, & inſigniora theoremata, ma-
iori cum difficultate , longioríque temporis ſucceſſu adinuenta atque demonſtrata.
Quemadmodum in ea diſciplina, quæ Geometria vocitatur, de Circuli licet intueri
quadratura. Quæ tametſi ab omnibus philoſophis ſciḗtia cōtineri fuerit exiſtimata,
& tāto tempore à tam doctis perquiſita viris: hactenus tamen videtur fuiſſe deſi-
derata , facta interim non modica rerum Mathematicarum acceſſione: multa enim
ſcitu digniſſima, quæ prius erant abſconſa, prodiere nota.   Cùm igitur præfatam
Circuli quadraturam, extra artem non eſſe intelligerem, & illius inuentiōe ad me
non ſine diuino numine iure quodam deuolui: qui & patre philoſopho ac Mathema=
tico inſigni Franciſco Finæo ſum natus, & ad has diſciplinas natura factus (quas

a.ij.

TORY, *Aediloquium.* Paris, Simon de Colines, 1536. Pierpont Morgan Library

VAN HUTTEN, *Ars versificatoria.* Paris, Robert Estienne, 1528. Yale Beinecke Rare Book Library

XIIII.

Pour peu de cas trebuche foy legere,
  Et pour ung rien soudain amont se lance:
Vne plumette, ung grain de cheneuiere,
Plus poisera, contre elle à la balance.
Garder nous fault que n'ayons accointance
A gens qui sont amys selon fortune.
Vraye amytié, tousiours est opportune:
Et se cognoist en temps d'aduersité.
Les bons amys (selon la uoix commune)
Ne sont cogneuz qu'a la necessité.

C iiii

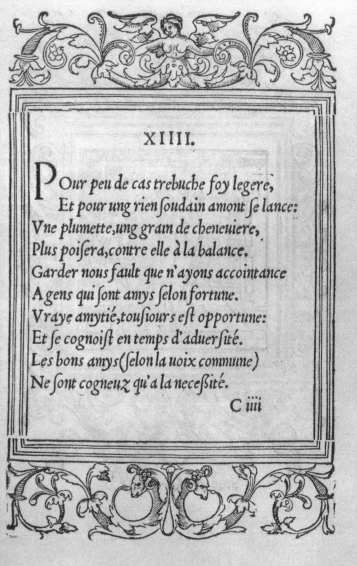

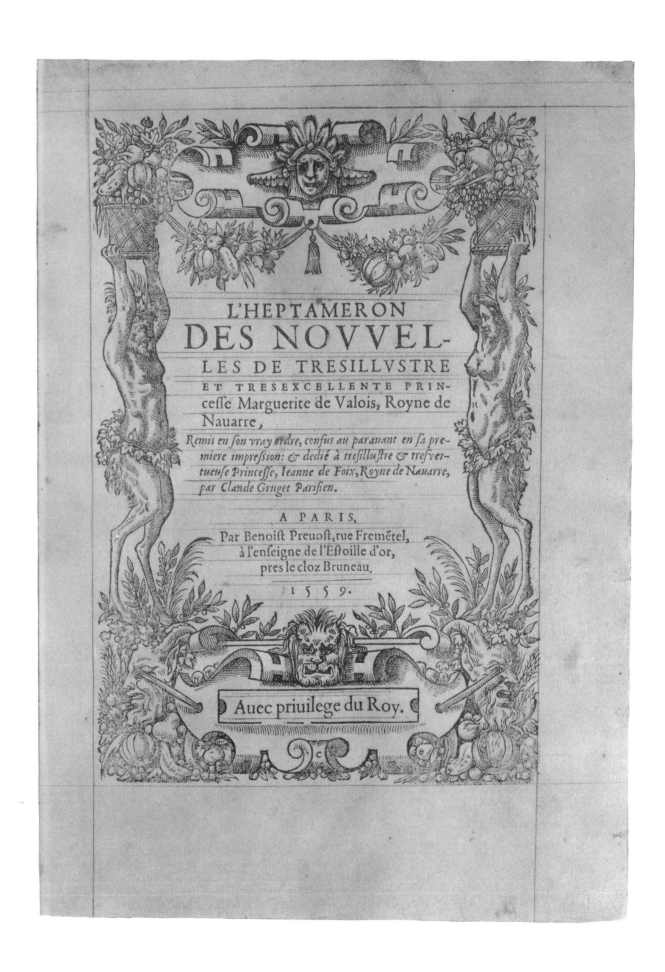

L'HEPTAMERON
DES NOVVEL-
LES DE TRESILLVSTRE
ET TRESEXCELLENTE PRIN-
cesse Marguerite de Valois, Royne de
Nauarre,

Remis en son vray ordre, confus au parauant en sa pre-
miere impression: & dedié à tresillustre & tresver-
tueuse Princesse, Ieanne de Foix, Royne de Nauarre,
par Claude Gruget Parisien.

A PARIS,
Par Benoist Preuost, rue Fremétel,
à l'enseigne de l'Estoille d'or,
pres le cloz Bruneau.

1559.

Auec priuilege du Roy.

MARGUERITE DE VALOIS, *L'Heptameron*. Paris, Benoit Prevost, 1559. Pierpont Morgan Library

LA HVICTIESME IOVRNEE DES

NOVVELLES DE LA ROYNE DE NAVARRE.

E MATIN VENV,
s'enquirent si leur pont s'a-
uancoit fort, & trouuerent
que dedans deux ou trois
iours il pourroit estre para-
cheué: ce qui despleut à quel-
ques vns de la cõpagnie: car
ils eussent bien desiré, que
l'ouurage eust duré plus lon-
guemẽt, pour faire durer le
contentement qu'ils auoient
de leur heureuse vie. Mais voyans qu'ils n'auoient plus que deux
ou trois iours de bon temps, se delibererent de ne le perdre pas. Et
prierent ma dame Oisille de leur donner la pasture spirituelle, com-
me elle auoit accoustumé: ce qu'elle feit, mais elle les tint plus
long temps, qu'auparauant. Car elle vouloit, auant que partir,
auoir mise fin à la Cronicque de sainct Iean. A quoy elle s'acquita
si tresbien, qu'il sembloit que le sainct esprit plein d'amour & de
douceur, parlast par sa bouche. Et tous enflammez de ce feu,
s'en allerent ouyr la grand messe. Et apres disner, ensemble par-
lans encores de la iournée passée, se desfioïet d'en pouuoir faire vne
aussi belle. Et pour y donner ordre, se retirerent chacun en son
logis iusques à l'heure, qu'ils allerent à leur chambre des comptes
sur le bureau de l'herbe verde, ou des-ia trouuerent les moynes

Ff iij

Around midcentury a new decorative influence arose: a more developed series of Renaissance forms associated with the school of Fontainebleau. This style shows itself in such books as Jacques Kerver's French edition of the *Poliphilus* published in 1546, in which the pure line drawings of the original have become more complex and shaded, and Aldus' simple title page with its few lines of type is replaced with a design of satyrs, fruit, and putti. The *Heptameron*, a group of novels by Marguerite de Valois, printed in 1559 by Benoit Prevost, is one of the most fortunate examples of the workings of a lusher fantasy.

De Valois,
L'Heptameron
pages 194 and 195

The large commemorative books that became popular in the seventeenth century had begun to appear. The *Entrée de Henry II*, recording the triumphal entry of the king into Paris amid processions and elaborate constructions built for the occasion, was printed in 1549 with illustrations of the event by Jean Goujon, France's leading sculptor.

In a period in which pure typography and typographic decoration were exalted, imaginative illustration did not flourish. The most interesting illustrated books of the latter half of the century were descriptive books dealing with travel, science, or architecture. Among the best of them is the *Livre de Perspective*, written by Jean Cousin and printed by Le Royer in 1560. The large folio is in roman type with initials after the floriated ones in Aldus' *Poliphilus*. It is illustrated with complex perspective drawings of more than column width. The title page is a rather gentle cartouche with figures, but the dedicatory page just after it is an early example of the violent perspective associated with Baroque art. The nondiagramatic illustrations in the book itself are in the earlier classic tradition, while the headpieces which embellish typographic pages show a fine late Renaissance fantasy.

Cousin,
Livre de Perspective
page 197

At Lyons, the only French rival to Paris in publishing, the emphasis continued to be on commercial production. Nevertheless, early in the century a series of octavos was directly plagiarized from Aldus, down to the Aldine device. Much more legitimately, Sebastian Gryphius, a scholar-printer of the same cut as the Estiennes, began in 1528 to produce small-format books, mostly in Latin, using roman and italic types which, along with border and initial material, he imported from Basel. The Trechsel brothers, Lyons printers, also had close connections with Basel; in 1538 they produced two slight octavos bearing the illustrations of Holbein the Younger for the *Dance of Death* and selections from the Old Testament.

Dance of Death
page 199
Selections from
the Old Testament
page 198

All this time Lyonese printers were continuing to turn out romances and large numbers of law books in the old French gothic type.

Lyonese printing entered its great typographic period shortly after the appearance as printer of Jean de Tournes in 1542. De Tournes had apprenticed with the Trechsels and began to print with Basel types, but very quickly took up the Parisian Garamond. He enhanced his fine pages with Tory's *criblé* initials and with new arabesque borders and fleurons of unsurpassed beauty and elaboration.

Froissart,
L'Histoire et chronique
pages 201 and 202

JEAN COUSIN, *Livre de Perspective.* Paris, Le Royer, 1560. Pierpont Morgan Library. 15½ x 11¼ in.

de Iehan Cousin.

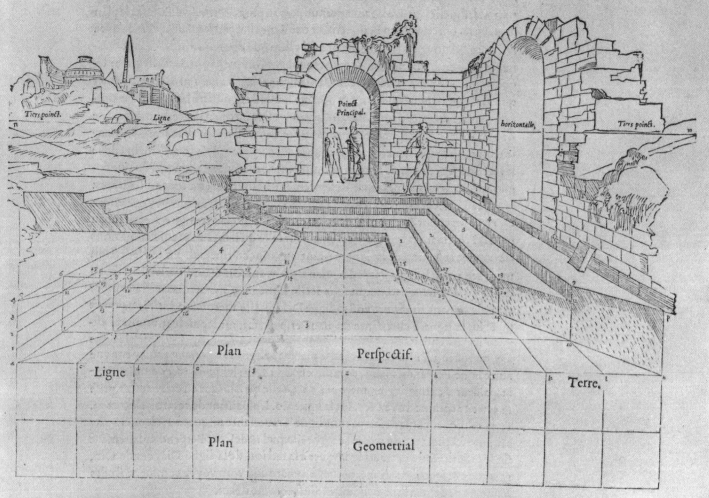

CESTE presente figure contient vne maniere de descente qua-
drangulaire, ayāt quatre faces, esquelles y a degrez pour descen
dre iusques au Cētre d'icelle quadrature. Et pource que le plan
Geometrial ne cōtiēt seullemēt que des quarreaux, ie n'ay mer-
qué la Platte forme entierement, me contentant vous presenter
lesdits quarreaux distincts de proportions egualles sus la ligne
Terre, merquee a.b: & les autres lignes merquees c.d:e.f:g.h:i.k.l:desquelles les
distinctions sont renuoyees au poinct Principal, par lignes Visualles ou Pyrami-
dalles, pour estre faite la section d'icelles lignes, par l'intersection des deux lignes
Diagonalles, tirants aux deux Tiers poincts, comme voyez icy a à m:& b à n.
Puis ay tiré vne ligne du plan Geometrial depuis la ligne Terre iusques à la hau-
teur des degrez que ie veux feindre, comme voyez icy a. à o: & b.à p: sus laditte

I iij

PHARAONIS fomnia de feptem bobus & fpicis, eductus è carcere Iofeph exponit. Super annonam Aegypti conftituitur.

GENESIS XLI.

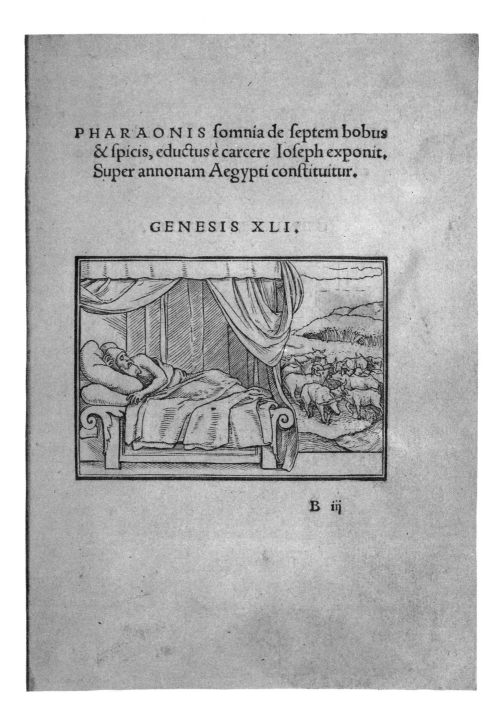

B iij

Selections from the Old Testament. Lyons, the Trechsels, 1538. Woodcuts by Hans Holbein the Younger. Yale Beinecke Rare Book Library

Gradientes in ſuperbia
poteſt Deus humilia=
re.
DANIE. IIII

Qui marchez en pompe ſuperbe
La Mort vng iour uous pliera.
Cõme ſoubz uoz piedz ployez l'herbe,
Ainſi uous humiliera.

D

Dance of Death. Lyons, the Trechsels, 1538. Woodcuts by Hans Holbein the Younger. Pierpont Morgan Library

199

The role that Tory played in Paris was taken in Lyons by Bernard Salomon, whose prolific output of illustrations, arabesque borders and fleurons all went to De Tournes. Salomon's work was influenced by the Fontainebleau school. His illustrations, mostly small-scaled compositions, were crowded with figures and full of motion, their landscape backgrounds particularly fine and vivid. The designs he made for Ovid's *Metamorphoses* which De Tournes printed in 1557 contain within the compass of each small page an illustrative cut and text surrounded by an ornate figured border. The illustrations for the New Testament are more simply set, as are those of the Aesop printed in 1570.

Aesop,
Vita et fabulae
page 203

Evidence indicates that De Tournes's publications owe much to Robert Granjon, a Parisian type designer whose influence was almost as great as that of Garamond. Granjon cut especially fine italics, which had italic capitals to go with them; these italics appear in De Tournes's books. In 1557 Granjon, who had been visiting Lyons yearly, married Bernard Salomon's daughter and settled in Lyons. He printed a few books himself, using a new typeface, *lettres de civilité*, that he had designed after the current French handwriting—a French counterpart to the italic. He also designed fleurons made up of separate pieces that could be rearranged to form different configurations. Both the fleurons and the *lettres de civilité* became popular in Belgium—the type far more so than in France, where it never really caught on. Granjon became the principal furnisher of types of all kinds to Plantin in Antwerp. Late in the century he was called to Rome, where he designed types for the Vatican press.

The middle third of the century was the high point in both taste and quality for French books. By about 1560 decoration was becoming more and more dense. Headpieces began to be filled in with convoluted lines, and title pages were more and more overloaded with a freight of mythological figures and nudes. Copperplate engraving was beginning to encroach on woodcut title pages; Lyons was especially quick to take it up. The enthusiasm spread to the Netherlands, and Flemish engravers brought their crisp technique to France. Near the end of the century two engravers, Leonard Gaultier and Thomas de Leu, were supplying printers with engraved title pages and portraits by the hundreds, presaging the seventeenth century when the woodcut would be driven from the scene entirely.

The Wars of Religion began to cut into book production in numerous ways. The Church, in its opposition to Huguenots and Freethinkers, had oppressed scholarly work and driven such scholar-printers as Robert Estienne from the country. (Etienne Dolet, printer at Lyons, met a worse fate: he was hanged as a heretic and burned with a pile of his books.) The number of books produced, which had been at a peak between 1550 and 1570, declined drastically at Paris and even more at Lyons; type and paper became poorer, and many of the products of the press were nothing more than cheap propaganda pamphlets. At the end of the sixteenth century, printing was at an ebb in France as it was throughout Europe. The Golden Age was over.

Cy commence le Prologue de meſſire Iehan Froiſſart, ſur les Croniques de France & d'Angleterre, & autres lieux voiſins.

*

AFIN que les honnorables empriſes & nobles auétures & faicts-d'armes, par les guerres de France & d'Angleterre, ſoyent notablement enregiſtrés & mis en memoire perpetuel, parquoy les preux ayent exemple d'eux encourager en bien faiſant, ie vueil traicter & recorder Hiſtoire de grand' louenge. Mais, auant que ie la commence, ie requier au Sauueur de tout le monde, qui de neant crea toutes choſes, qu'il vueille creer & mettre en moy ſens & entendement ſi vertueux, que ie puiſſe continuer & perſeuerer en telle maniere que tous ceux & celles, qui le lirõt, verront, & orront, y puiſſent prendre ebatement & exemple, & moy encheoir en leur grâce.

On dit, & il eſt vray, que tous edifices ſont maſſonnés & ouurés de pluſieurs ſortes de pierres, & toutes groſſes riuieres ſont faictes & raſſemblees de pluſieurs ſurgeons. Auſſi les ſciences ſont extraictes & compilees de pluſieurs Clercs: & ce, que l'un ſcet, l'autre l'ignore. Non pourtant rien n'eſt, qui ne ſoit ſceu, ou loing ou pres.

Donc, pour attaindre à la matiere que i'ay empriſe, ie vueil commencer premierement par la grâce de Dieu & de la benoiſte vierge Marie (dont tout confort & auancement viennent) & me vueil fonder & ordonner ſur les vrayes Croniques, iadis faictes par reuerend homme, diſcret & ſage, monſeigneur maiſtre Iehan le Bel, Chanoine de Sainct-Lambert du Liege: qui grand' cure & toute bonne diligẽce meit en ceſte matiere, & la continua tout ſon viuant au plus iuſtement qu'il peut, & moult luy couſta à la querre & à l'auoir: mais, quelques fraiz qu'il y fiſt, riens ne les plaingnit. car il eſtoit riche & puiſſant (ſi les pouuoit bien porter) & eſtoit de ſoy-meſme large, honnorable, & courtois: & voulontiers voyoit le ſien deſpendre. Auſſi il fut en ſon viuant moult aimé & ſecret à monſeigneur meſſire Iehan de Haynaut: qui bien eſt ramenteu, & de raiſon, en ce liure. car de moult belles & nobles aduenues fut il chef & cauſe, & des Roys moult prochain. parquoy le deſſuſdit meſſire Iehan le Bel peut delez luy veoir pluſieurs nobles beſongnes: leſquelles ſont contenues cy-apres. Vray eſt que ie, qui ay empris ce liure à ordonner, ay par plaiſance, qui à ce m'a touſiours encliné, frequenté pluſieurs nobles & grans Seigneurs, tant en Frãce qu'en Angleterre, en Eſcoce, & en pluſieurs autres païs: & en ay eu la congnoiſſance d'eux: & ay touſiours, à mon pouuoir, iuſtement enquis & demandé du faict des guerres & des auentures, & par eſpecial depuis la groſſe bataille de Poitiers, ou le noble Roy Iehan de France fut pris.† car deuãt i'eſtoye encores moult ieune de ſens & d'aage. Nonobſtant ſi empris ie aſſez hardiment, moy iſſu de l'eſcole, à dicter & à ordonner les guerres deſſuſdites, & porter en Angleterre le liure tout compilé: ſi-comme ie fei, & le preſentay adonc à Ma-dame Philippe de Haynaut, Royne d'Angleterre: qui liement & doucement le receut de moy, & m'en fit grand profit. Et peut eſtre que ce liure n'eſt

De qui Froiſſart a pris la preſente Hiſtoire.

†*De quel temps eſtoit Froiſſart. ſur quoy faut noter qu'il ne porta que partie de ce premier Volume à la Royne Philippe. car vous verrez qu'il racomptera la mort d'icelle, ſelon l'ordre des temps, en cedit premier & preſent Volume.*

a mie

mesler du mien à les restituer en leur naturel, pour la raison que i'ay autrefois dicte en
semblable cas, sur les Memoires du Signeur d'Argenton, & selon que verrez par
nostre annotation 33. & par quelques autres, qui vous pourront satisfaire : comme
i'espére que le reste vous contentera semblablement en ce, qui pourroit requerir
nostre diligence. Laquelle ie vous prie prendre en gré, pendant que ie
tasche, de mieux en mieux, à respondre à la bonne opinion, que
vous ont peu faire conceuoir de moy mes labeurs précedens,
&, en accomplissant mes promesses, donner fin à œuure
de plus-longue traitte : ainsi que i'espere faire de brief,
en faueur de nostre nation Françoise, moyenant
l'aide du Tout-puissant : qui nous vueille
tenir en sa saincte grace. A Lion,
ce premier iour de l'an, 1559.
commenceant à la Cir-
concision de nostre
Saueur.
*

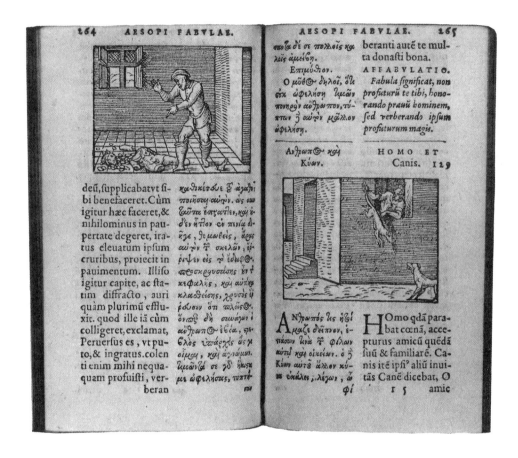

σαντα δέ σε πολλοῖς καὶ
λοῖς ἀμείβῃ.

Επιμύθιον.

Ὁ μῦθος δηλοῖ, ὅτι
ὃκ ὠφελήσῃ ἡμῶν
πονηρὸν ἄνθρωπον, τύ-
πτων ᾖ αὐτὸν μᾶλλον
ὠφελήσῃ.

beranti autē te mul-
ta donasti bona.

AFFABVLATIO.
Fabula significat, non
profuturū te tibi, hono-
rando prauū hominem,
sed verberando ipsum
profuturum magis.

Αϑρωπ@ καὶ
Κύων.

HOMO ET
Canis. 129

deū, supplicabatvt si-
bi benefaceret. Cùm
igitur hæc faceret, &
nihilominus in pau-
pertate degeret, ira-
tus eleuatùm ipsum
cruribus, proiecit in
pauimentum. Illiso
igitur capite, ac sta-
tim diffracto , auri
quàm plurimū efflu-
xit. quod ille iã cùm
colligeret, exclamat,
Peruersus es , vt pu-
to,& ingratus.colen
ti enim mihi nequa-
quam profuisti, ver-
beran

καϑικέτδυε ῷ ἀγαϑῆ
ποιῆσαι αὐτὸν, ὡς οω
ζωῆτα ἔσαγωτⁱεν, καὶ ἐ-
δὲν ἧπον ἐν πενία δι-
ῆγε , ϑυμωϑεὶς , ἄρας
αὐτὸν τῷ σκελῶν, ἐ-
ρέψεν εἰς τὸ ἐδάφ@,
σεσοκρ/γυσαζης ἐπ ῷ
κεφαλῆς , καὶ αὐτῆκα
κλασϑείσης, χρυσὸς ἠ
ρύσσεν ὅτι πλεῖσ@.
ὄνπερ δὴ συναγων ὁ
αὐϑρωπ@ ἐϛία, φη-
σλὸς ὑπάρχῃς ὡς μ
οῖμαι , καὶ ἀγνώμων.
ἡμῶντά σε γὸ ἥκιςα
με ὠφελήσας, τύπτο
σαι

Ανϑρωπός τις ἠϑέ-
λα ζι δεῖπνον, ἑ-
σιάσων ἱνὰ ῷ φίλων
αὐτῷ καὶ οἰκείων. ὁ ᾗ
Κύων αὐτᾶ ἄλλον κύ-
να ἐκάλει ,λέγων , ὦ
φί

HOmo qdā para-
bat cœnā, acce-
pturus amicū quedā
suū & familiarē. Ca-
nis itē ipsⁱ aliū inui-
tās Canē dicebat, O
amic

r 5

AESOP, *Vita et fabulae.* Lyons, Jean de Tournes, 1570. Woodcuts by Bernard Salomon. Pierpont Morgan Library
← FROISSART, *L'Histoire et chronique.* Lyons, Jean de Tournes, 1559-61. Pierpont Morgan Library. 13¼ x 8 in.

203

THE NETHERLANDS

The great event of sixteenth-century Netherlands printing was the establishment of the Plantin Press. Antwerp had become the center of trade in the Spanish Netherlands, and it was already liberally supplied with good printers when Cristophe Plantin arrived there from France in 1555. An energetic businessman, Plantin built up, in thirty-four years of printing, a publishing house second to none in Europe. By 1575 the style of his books set the standard from England to Italy. The firm had branch offices in Paris, Leyden, and Salamanca and sold books as far away as Africa and America.

Plantin's style of printing was essentially French, but it was a heavier and more ornamented version of French typography which became more so with the years. Some of his types were cut in the Netherlands, but he imported Garamond's roman type and made constant use of Granjon's fonts of italics, *civilité*, and Greek type. A specimen book of his types published in 1567 showed forty-two different fonts. He was one of the first printers in Antwerp to take up with enthusiasm the use of elaborate fleurons, many of which were made by Granjon.

Despite rather humble origins, Plantin was not far from the tradition of the scholar-printer: the leading intellectual figures of his day were both known at his house and published at his press. His output was enormous and embraced the fields of theology, law, science, botany, philology, and the classics. He was a publisher of dictionaries, of atlases, of herbals, of emblem books, and of great numbers of liturgical books for the Spanish church, for which his press had a special privilege which lasted into succeeding generations. The formats of these books ranged from the smallest 32 mo. to huge folios.

Printing was a dangerous craft at the time of the Catholic-Calvinist controversy, and Plantin suffered from accusations of heresy. In 1561 he was forced to flee to Paris for almost two years, and his property was confiscated. It was perhaps partly from the desire to convince the authorities of his orthodoxy that he undertook the ambitious Polyglot Bible for Phillip II of Spain, the second of the great printed Polyglot Bibles. The plan, which was to print side by side the Bible in Greek, Hebrew, Syriac, Aramaic, and Chaldean, involved great difficulties in editor-

Biuium virtutis & vitij.

Hinc luxu compta, inde situ horrida femina pu-
     gnant
Alcidem in partes flectere quæque suas.
Nititur inculta hinc iuga scādere se duce Virtus,
Hinc Vitium pronos mergere deliciis.
                            Deum

Deum odisse impudentiam.

Pernix accipiter, piscis, Nili incola dirus
     Equus, quid ordine hærent?
Symbolon hoc loquitur Phariæ tria verbula gēti,
     Deus odit impudentes.

                     D 2   Iræ

ship and a vast outlay of money. Plantin ordered the Hebrew characters from Le Bé in Paris and the Greek and Syriac from Granjon. He almost foundered under Phillip's dilatoriness in payment, but in 1573, after five years' work, he managed to bring the huge eight-volume Bible to successful and handsome conclusion. It became the cornerstone of his reputation.

Plantin revived an interest in illustrated books in the Netherlands. His earliest books contained woodcuts, but he soon began to use the Antwerp print engravers for engraved title pages and illustrations. He commissioned the foremost Netherlands artists, who worked in a style close to that of Salomon in Lyons, but his editions failed to reach the level of taste of the best French books. Nevertheless, they achieved immense popularity. The series of little emblem books that he published, for example, ran into some fifty editions. The *Emblemata* of Hadrianus Junius, printed in 1565, is the most attractive of the series.

Junius, Emblemata page 205

Heavier and grander are the *Psalterium* of 1571 and the *Antiphoner* of 1573, set in large gothic type with massive music notes. The great atlas of Ortelius, the *Theatrum orbis terrarum* of 1584, has an engraved title page and maps, and a fine prefatory dedication to Phillip II in spaced capitals.

After the death of Plantin in 1589 the press was carried on by a son-in-law, Jan Moretus, and his heirs. It continued to operate for almost three centuries, but the decline of the humanist tradition changed the nature of its output which, thanks to the Spanish monopoly, became mainly liturgical. Between 1608 and 1645 Rubens, a friend of the family, designed many title pages and ornaments for the editions of the Plantin press.

The Musée Plantin in Antwerp preserves to this day, in the splendid house occupied by Plantin and his heirs, the equipment of the Officina Plantin—seven presses (two of them from Plantin's time), types, and meticulously kept records, which transmit a clear image of the press in its great time.

SPAIN

The Gothic style persisted in Spanish books until the middle of the sixteenth century—far later than in any other country. Book production remained scattered in a number of local centers. Spain was unified in 1516, but the five separate kingdoms of Aragon, Castile, Navarre, Portugal, and Granada maintained separate governments for a long time after they were under one king. The Emperor Charles V had far wider horizons than those of Spain; by 1519 he ruled the entire Austrian dominion including the Netherlands, as well as Naples, Sicily, and other parts of Italy. Not the least of his interests were the Spanish holdings in the New World. The far-reaching domain of this monarch centered his activity outside of Spain, and it was not until well into the reign of his successor Philip II that a central court was set up at Madrid, in 1560.

The Spanish books printed in the first quarter of the century were designed and produced at the height of the style set by the Spanish incunabula. They were large books, either folios or quartos, set in the rather heavy round gothic type used throughout Spain. Roman types were used very little, and only in humanistic books. Heavy black woodcut initials were characteristic, differentiated somewhat by regional flavor. Borders were often used, either as one-piece frames or made up of separate pieces that could be fitted together in a variety of ways.

The vigorous woodcut illustrations, finer than those in fifteenth-century books, were often surrounded by decorative border pieces. Title pages remained a strong center of interest, with their large woodcuts surrounded by borders. The woodcut on a title page might represent the author or the hero of the book, a scene from a romance, or a coat of arms—royal, regional or ecclesiastical. As the century progressed more information was added to the title page—including the name of the publisher, who was no longer necessarily the printer—and the woodcut took correspondingly less of the page.

The most notable product of the sixteenth-century Spanish presses is the Polyglot Bible printed by Arnald Guillen de Brocar between 1514 and 1517 at the University of Alcalá. It was the first of the great printed Bibles that set side by side for comparative study the text of

¶ Carta tercera de relació: embiada po₂ Fernã
do co₂tes capitan ⁊ justicia mayo₂ del yucatan llamado la nueua españa
del mar oceano: al muy alto y potentissimo cesar ⁊ iuictissimo seño₂ dõ
Carlos empe₂ado₂ semper augusto y rey de españa nuestro seño₂: delas
cosas sucedidas ⁊ muy dignas de admiracion enla conquista y recupe₂
racion dela muy grande ⁊ marauillosa ciudad de Temi₂titan: y delas
otras p₂ouincias a ella subjetas que se rebelaron. Enla qual ciudad ⁊ di
chas p₂ouincias el dicho capitan y españoles consiguieron grandes y se
ñaladas victo₂ias dignas de perpetua memo₂ia. Assi mesmo baze rela
cion como bá descubierto el mar del Sur: ⁊ otras muchas ⁊ grãdes p₂o
uincias muy ricas de minas de o₂o: y perlas: y pied₂as p₂eciosas: ⁊ avn
tienen noticia que ay especeria.

the Bible in the several ancient tongues in which it was preserved. The Old Testament of this six-volume Bible is in four ancient languages, the New Testament in Latin and Greek. The Greek type of the New Testament, based on ancient forms, is considered to be the purest ever cut. As court printer to Charles V, Brocar printed many fine books.

The leading general printers of the time were the Crombergers, father and son, Germans working in Seville. Jakob Cromberger had taken over the press of Ungut and Polonus in 1904. The Crombergers printed a great many romances with woodcut illustrations and blackground arabesque initials. They also printed a large number of theological works.

Cortés,
Carta tercera
page 208
Tristan
page 211

When Archbishop Zumárraga of Mexico wanted a catechism in Spanish and Nahuatl to aid in the conversion of Mexican Indians, the Crombergers were asked to print it. The difficulties of producing this work in Spain decided Juan Cromberger to send a printer and a press to Mexico. An Italian, Giovanni Paoli (Juan Pablos in Spanish) was sent out in 1539 under a ten-year contract, and in that same year he completed the catechism in Mexico—one hundred years before the first book was printed in North America. The catechism, a twelve-leaved quarto, has been described in a book of 1877, but it no longer exists. Other books of Pablos' are known by mention but not by examples. From 1544, however, we have four sizable books, all of them of religious nature. The earliest of them is thought to be Zumárraga's *Doctrina Cristiana*, dated 1543 on its title page and decorated with an ecclesiastical symbol and an assortment of border pieces put together in a somewhat improvised way.

Zumárraga,
Doctrina Cristiana
page 210

Pablos completed his contract, whose terms seem incredibly harsh, and stayed on to print thirty-seven known books before his death. Most, but not all of them, were religious books; some were scientific books made for the newly founded University of Mexico. A good number of them were the first of their kind in the New World.

Around 1530 Spanish books began to decline in quality. The number of presses and the output of books had increased considerably, and neither trained artisans nor sufficient paper of good quality existed to meet this increase. The greater number of types and ornaments in a printer's supply were put together with less discrimination. Furthermore, Spain was financially drained by the wars of expanding empire. The styles of other countries, especially Italy and the Netherlands, began to filter into Spanish books. From the forties on, an increasing number of books were printed in roman type, sometimes accompanied by italics. Foreign influence became decisive when in Madrid, seat of the newly founded court, presses were set up and equipped with roman types. The taste of the court quickly dominated all others, and smaller books set in roman type became common, decorated with lighter capitals and ornaments, and boasting Renaissance borders. Woodcut illustrations were used less, and around 1580 copperplate engravings were introduced. But the changeover had not come at a propitious moment; Spanish printed books were not remarkable until the last quarter of the eighteenth century. They never again had the strong national flavor of the Spanish Gothic book.

Dotrina breue muy p̃ = uechofa delas cofas q̃ p̃ene = cen alafe catholica y a n̄ra cri ftiandad en eftilollano p̃a co = mũ íntelígẽcia. Cõpuefta por el Reuerẽdiff.mo. S. dõ fray Juã çumarraga primer obpo õ Merico. õelcõfeío õ fu ma geftad. In p̃ffa ẽla mifma ciu = dad õ Merico por fu mãda.ᵒ y a fu cofta. Años M̃. ơrlii.

de l co llegta
des fran.ᶜᵒ deçala ya

ZUMÁRRAGA, *Doctrina Cristiana*. Mexico, Juan Pablos, dated 1543. John Carter Brown Library, Brown University
Tristan. Seville, Juan Cromberger, 1528. Pierpont Morgan Library

ribera dla mar:y la reyna no fazia sino llo
rar por el prometimiēto del rey su señor/y
dezia. Ay el mi caro amigo tristan dōde so
ys vos:agora os topasse yo por este cami
no:por tal q̃ me tirassedes deste mal caua
llero. Ay agora fuesse yo muerta. E quan
do palomades saco la reyna dela corte tri
stan no era ende/que era ydo a caça por la
mañana. En aq̃l tiēpo era venido enla cor
te vn cauallo el qual era ferido de vna lā
çada/y venia ala reyna que lo guaresciese
τ aquel cauallero auia nōbre sagramor/y
demādo que por q̃l razō erā todos tristes
y ellos le cōtarō como ſPalomades lleua
ua la reyna:τ luego dixo a su escudero. yo
al palacio y ved si ay algū cauallo que to
me armas pa yr en pos de palomades. E
el escudero paro miētes por todas partes:
τ no vio q̃ niguno tomasse armas:saluo q̃
todos llorauā τ fazian grā duelo. Luego
sagramor dixo.dad me el mi escudo τ la lā
ça:que no descaualgare d mi cauallo: avn
que muriesse hasta que halle el cauallero q̃
lleua la Reyna/que assi como assi muerto
so τ si a dios pluguiere ella me sanara/y se
re preciado τ amado entre los caualleros/
que por la mi fe el no la lleuara sin batalla
el escudero dixo a su señor. Como tan abo
rrido soys que vos quereys matar/y me
ter en peligro de muerte que avn non soys
sano:por mi fe dixo sagramor. Mas quie
ro morir a manos de buen cauallero/que
no beuir entre los couardes caualleros de

cornualla:que nō osan defender a su seño
ra de vn solo cauallero:y el cauallero salio
dela corte:τ anduuo tāto fasta que alcāço
al cauallo que lleuaua la reyna:τ llamo lo
τ dixole.Esperad cauallero q̃ cōbatir vos
cōuiene:o dexareys la reyna q̃ lleuays fal
samente.E palomades se torno/τ desmin
tiole:τ dixole. Por cierto la reyna vos no
la podeys leuar sin batalla:τ boluiose el v
no cōtra el otro τ dierō se tan grandes gol
pes q̃ la reyna pēsaua q̃ eran muertos/se
gū la grā cayda que dierō:τ al caer que ca
yo sagramor rebētō le la llaga que traya/
τ corria le mucha sangre. Mas tanto era
el de buen cauallero:que lo no sintio antes
se leuanto en pie con gran essuerço τ pusie
ron mano alas espadas τ dieron se gran
des golpes que fuego salia delas espadas
muy alto.E palomades pensaua q̃ era tri
stan por los grādes golpes q̃ le daua Sa
gramor:τ mientra ellos se cōbatian.la rey
na se metio por la floresta:τ fuesse lo mas a
priessa que ella pudo a vn charco de agua
por se afogar antes que la lleuasse paloma
des porque era grā enemigo d tristan que
bien sabia ella que no era dō tristan aquel
cauallero que enlas armas y enel cauallo
lo conoscio:τ quādo ella se yua al charco/
encontro con vn ciudadano q̃ yua a caça/
τ luego conocio q̃ era la reyna:τcorrio cō
tra ella/τ dixole. Señora por dios no os
ahogueys enesse mal lugar/que es de vos
o como soys aqui venida.y ella le conto to
da la razō punto por punto :q̃ no le mintio
nada. E dixo como se q̃ria ahogar en aq̃l
charco/antes q̃ ninguno la ouiesse saluo el
rey su señor.E el cibdadano dixo.plazeme
que os he fallado:q̃ yo vos lleuare aq̃ cer
ca a vna mi torre q̃ ninguno no vos aura si
no el rey:y sereys biē seruida d todo mi po
der.porq̃ os ruego señora q̃ no me digays
de no/τ la Reyna fue alegre:τ dixo que le
plazia de se yr conel : el cibdadano la lleuo
delāte si:y anduuierō hasta q̃ llegaron ala
torre: y alli descaualgaron y metiose den
tro dela torre/τ fue bien seruida de gran

ENGLAND

English printing made no great strides in the sixteenth century; on the contrary, tightening legislative restrictions all but throttled its vitality. In the first thirty years of the century Wynken de Worde and Richard Pynson dominated the scene, producing between them about two-thirds of the books printed in England. They worked commonly in black letter, though in 1518 Pynson printed the first English book in roman type, imported from Paris. Wynken de Worde followed shortly afterward, and even obtained an italic font from Antwerp.

Pynson's production was largely centered on legal books, but he printed a few illustrated books which, if not particularly original, were well produced. His 1509 edition of the *Ship of Fools* had excellent copies of the Basel woodcuts. But his best work was to be found in the handful of liturgical books he printed—an Horae and three Missals. The *Missale ad usum Sarum* of *Missal* 1520, a large folio beautifully printed in red and black on vellum, is set in textura with square *page 213* black-ground initials. The music in it is printed in square black notes on red staff lines, and a large heraldic cut of French character with red and black type set into it is used twice.

About this time Oxford University and Cambridge had presses briefly, both operated by Germans, for a period of about two years each. But they were far slower than the European universities to establish permanent presses of their own. It was not until late in the century, in 1585, that the Oxford University Press opened on a firm basis, never to shut down again.

The series of restrictive legislations bearing on printing that began at the end of the first quarter of the century had two targets: the preponderance of foreign printers working in England, and the printing of heretical works. The opening gun against foreign printers was the prohibition of foreign-born apprentices. As for heretical printing, the changing opinions of the heads of state made all polemical printing dangerous. Henry VIII broke with the Catholic Church and declared himself head of the Church of England in 1534. His policies toward the printing of the Bible in English serve to illustrate the extent of his about-faces: In 1536 he sent William Tyndale to the stake for his translation of the New Testament, printed on the Continent. Two and a half years later he commissioned Richard Grafton to print the complete English Bible.

Missale ad usum Sarum. London, Richard Pynson, 1520. Pierpont Morgan Library. 15 x 9¼ in.

Mnes gentes plaudite
manib⁹ iubilate deo in
voce exultationis. Pſal
m⁹. Subiecit populos no
bis: et gentes ſub pedibus
noſtris. Oratio.

Eus virtutũ cuius eſt totũ quod
eſt optimũ.inſere pectozibus no
ſtris amoʒẽ tui nois.τ pʒeſta in nobis re
ligionis augmẽtum: vt q̄ ſunt bona nu
trias.ac piefatis ſtudio: que ſunt nutrita
cuſtodias.Per. C Ad romanos.   vi.

Ratres. Humanũ dico: ppter in
firmitatem carnis veſtre. Sicut
cĩ exhibuiſtis mẽbʒa veſtra ſeruire im
mundicie. τ iniquitati ad iniquitatẽ.ita
nũc exhibete mẽbʒa veſtra ſeruire iuſti
cie in ſctificationẽ. Cũ enim ſerui eſſetis
peccati:liberi fuiſtis iuſtitie. Quez ergo
fructũ habuiſtis tũc in illis.in q̄bus nũc
erubeſcitis? Naʒ finis illoʒum moʒs eſt.
Nũc vero liberati a pctõ:ſerui autē facti
deo. Habetis fructũ veſtrũ in ſanctifica
tionẽ:finẽ vero vitã eternã. Stipendia
enim peccati:moʒs. Gratia aũt dei:vita
eterna. In rp̄o ieſu:dño noſtro.Gʒ. Te
nite filii audite me timoʒem dñi docebo vos.v̄.
Accedite ad eũ et illuminamini et facies veſtre
non cõfundentur. Alla. v̄. Te decet hymnus
deus in ſyon:et tibi reddetur votum in hieruſa
lem. C Secundũ Marcum.   viii.

N illo tpe. Cuz turba multa eſſet
cũ ieſu.nec haberent q̄d manduca
rẽt.cõuocatis diſcipulis ait illis. Miſere
oʒ ſup turbã:quia ecce iã triduo ſuſtinẽt
me:nec habẽt q̄d mãducẽt.Et ſi dimiſe
ro eos ieiunos in domũ ſuã: deficient in
via. Quidã enim ex eis de lõge venerũt
Et reſpõderũt ei diſcipl’ ſui.Unde iſtos
poterit q̄s hic ſaturare panibus in ſolitu
dine? Et interrogauit eos. Quot panes
habetis? Qui dixerũt. Septem. Et pʒe
cepit turbe: diſcumbere ſuper terram.
Et accipiẽs ſeptẽ panes.gratias agens.
fregit.et dabat diſcipulis ſuis: vt appo
nerent. Et appoſuerunt turbe. Et habe
bant piſciculos paucos.et ipſos benedi
xit.et iuſſit apponi. Et manducauerunt
et ſaturati ſunt. Et ſuſtulerunt quod ſu
perauerat de fragmentis:ſeptẽ ſpoʒtas.

Erant autem qui manducauerunt.qua
ſi quatuoʒ milia:et dimiſit eos. Offeri.
Sicut in olocauſtum arietum et tauroʒũ et ſ
cut in milibus agnoʒum pinguiuz ſic fiat
ficium noſtroʒum in conſpectu tuo hodie: ι
placeat tibi:quia non eſt confuſio confidẽti
in te domine.   Secretā
Ropiciare dñe ſupplicationibus
noſtris:et has oblationes populi
tui benignus aſſume. et vt nullius ſit ir
ritũ votũ.nullius vacua poſtulatio p̄ſta
q̄s:vt q̄d fideliter petimus.efficaciter cõ
ſequamur.Per do. Cõto. I nclina aurem
tuam accelera vt eruas nos.   Poſtcõo.
Epleti dñe munerib⁹ tuis.tribue
q̄s vt eoʒũ mundemur effectu. et
muniamur auxilio. Per dñm noſtrum
C Feria quarta. Ad romanos.   viii.
Ratres. Nihil nũc dãnationis eſt
his.qui ſunt in rp̄o ieſu:q̄ nõ ſcdʒ
carnẽ ambulant. Lex enim ſp̄ũs vite in
rp̄o ieſu:liberauit me a lege pcti et moʒ
tis. Naʒ q̄d impoſſibile erat legi:in quo
infirmabatur per carnẽ. deus filiũ ſuuʒ
mittens in ſimilitudinez carnis peccati.
Et de peccato dãnauit peccatum in car
ne:vt iuſtificatio legis impleretur in no
bis. qui nõ ſcdm carnẽ ambulamus:ſed
ſcdm ſpiritũ. Qui eĩ ſcdm carnez ſunt:
que carnis ſunt ſapiũt. Qui vero ſcdm
ſpiritũ ſunt:que ſunt ſp̄ũs ſentiunt. Nã
pʒudẽtia carnis moʒs eſt.Pʒudẽtia autẽ
ſpiritus:vita et pax. In chʒiſto ieſu:dño
noſtro. C Secundum Matheum.   xii.
N illo tpe. Abiit ieſus ſabbato per
ſata:diſcipuli aũt eius eſurientes
ceperũt euellere ſpicas τ mãducare.Pha
riſei autẽ videtes:dixerunt ei. Ecce diſci
puli tui faciunt:q̄d nõ licet eis facere ſab
batis.At ille dixit eis. Non legiſtis quid
fecerit dauid q̄n eſuriit et q̄ cũ illo erant?
Quõ itrauit in domũ dei. et panes ppo
ſitiõis comedit quos nõ licebat ei edere:
neq̄ his q̄ cũ eo erant.niſi ſolis ſacerdoti
bus? Aut nõ legiſtis in lege: q̄a ſabbatis
ſacerdotes in tẽplo ſabbatũ violant:et ſi
ne crimine ſunt? Dico autẽ vobis: qʒ tẽ
plo maioʒ eſt hic. Si autẽ ſciretis q̄d eſt
miam volo τ nõ ſacriticiũ:nũq̄ cõdẽnaſ
ſetis innocẽtes. C Dñica. viii. Officium

Henry had issued a list of banned books in 1529; by 1538 he established a censorship. Two decades later Catholic Queen Mary instituted a powerful means of control of the press by granting a charter in 1557 to the printer-publishers' organization, the Stationers' Company, to regulate all printing. Protestant Elizabeth, Queen two years later, extended the control: all books had to be licensed, and those already printed could be abolished. The granting of monopoly privileges for certain classes of books put a final straitjacket on printing. But despite the risks, controversial books continued to appear in England bearing foreign imprints —either printed in some London cellar or actually smuggled in from outside the country.

The large number of English books produced abroad continued to bring the influence of foreign typography to England. By the second half of the century John Day, the leading printer, was producing roman and italic books that used every stylistic mannerism of Basel, Paris, and Lyons. Day cut some of his own roman and italic types, which were not far inferior to the best the Continent could offer.

The Cosmographicall Glass by William Cuningham, printed in 1559, is Day's most distinguished book. His own italic type appears in it, with historiated initials and some of the best woodcuts of the century. His *Aelfredi regis res gestae* (1574) is another fine typographical specimen, set in Day's roman.

*Foxe,
Book of Martyrs
page 215*

Foxe's *Book of Martyrs,* an illustrated folio which Day printed in 1563, is not particularly handsome, but it was one of the most widely read books in England. The book's body type is a small, even black letter; roman and italic types, capitals and lower case letters are used with it in many sizes for various purposes, along with a variety of initials. The richly shaded illustrations, which jut awkwardly into the margins, depict the martyrdoms in grisly detail, and must have contributed much to the popularity of the book. Despite the lack of taste of the ensemble, Day's merit is shown in an introductory italic page with an enormous initial bearing a portrait of Queen Elizabeth.

In 1545, at a place and time little famed for book illustration, a significant event took place: the first really successful book illustrated with copperplate engravings was produced. Thomas Geminus, a Flemish surgeon, at the command of Henry VIII issued a pirated edition of Vesalius' great *Anatomy*, with a finely engraved title page and illustrations copied after the original woodcuts. The enthusiastic reception it met did much to help launch the era of the engraved book.

English printing, like printing elsewhere, had fallen into different and more commercial hands towards the end of the century. Scholarly books were mostly imported from the Continent. It was as a cheap little popular edition that Shakespeare's first printed work appeared—*Venus and Adonis*—a crudely printed quarto in roman type.

JOHN FOXE, *Book of Martyrs (Acts and Monuments).* London, John Day, 1563. Pierpont Morgan Library. 12¼ x 8 in.

TO THE QVENES MOSTE EXCEL-

Lent Maiestie Quene Elizabeth, by the grace of God Quene of England, Fraunce &
Ireland, defendour of the faith, and supreme gouernour of the saide Realme of Englande and Irelande, next
vnder the Lorde, as well in causes ecclesiasticall, as also to the temporall state appertaining, her humble
subiect IOHN FOX hartely wisheth and desireth with increase of Gods holy spirite and grace,
long to florishe and reigne in perfect health, and much honour, through the mercie and
fauour of Christ Iesus, our Lorde and æternall Sauiour, to the come
fort of his churche, and glorie of his
holy name.

ELISABETHA

Onstantine the greate
and mightie Emperour, the
sonne of Helene an Englyshe
woman of this youre Realme
and countrie (moste Christian
and renowmed Princesse
Queene Elizabeth) after he
had pacified and established
the churche of Christ, being
long before vnder persecution, frō the tyme ofour sauia
our Christ almost 400 yeres:
and comming in his progresse
at length to a citie called Cæ-
saria, (where Eusebius wry-
ter of the Ecclesiasticall story
was then placed Byshop) required of the sayde Eusebius
vpon his owne free motion, to
demaund and aske of him what so euer he thought expediēt or necessary for the state
and commoditie of his Churche, promising to graunt vnto him the same, whatsoeuer
he should aske. whiche Eusebius, if he had thē required what terrene benefite soeuer
he would, either of possessions to be geuen, or of impositiōs to be released, or any other
lyke &c. he had no doubt obtained his request of that so lyberall, and so noble harted
Emperour. But the good and godly Byshop, more nedy then gredy, more spiritually
geuen, then worldly minded, who had learned rather to take a litle, thē to aske much,
setting all other respectes aside, made this petition, onely to obtaine at his maiesties
hande, vnder his seale and letters autentique, free leaue and license through al the mo-
narchie of Rome, going to all Cōsulles, Procōsulles, Tribunes and other officers in all
cities and countries, to searche out the names, sufferinges and actes, of all such as suffered in al that time of persecution before, for the testimonie and faith of Christ Iesus.
The nomber of all whiche holy and blessed Martyrs, vpon the sayd licence being sear-
ched out, amounted to the accompt, for euery daye in the Calendary to be ascribed (as
Hierome wryting to Chromatius and Heliodorus doth wytnesse) fiftie thousande
Martyrs, sauing only the first daye of Ianuary excepted. For that day beyng assigned
to the chousing of their Consules, was therfore festiually solennized throughout all
the Romaine Empire.

In whiche Historie (moste excellent and noble Queene) twoo thynges put me in
a variable doubt, whether of these two rather to cōmend and extolle: the good Emperour, or the godly Byshoppe: the one for his Princely proferre, the other for his godly

B.j. and sincere

LES
OEVVRES
DE PIERRE
DE RONSARD
GENTILHOMME
VANDOSMOIS PRIN-
CE DES POETES
FRANÇOIS,

Reueues et augmentees

A PARIS,
Chez NICOLAS BVON
au mont S. Hilaire à
l'enseigne S. Claude.

L. Gaultier sculp.

Auec priuilege du Roy.
M. DC. IX.

THE
SEVENTEENTH
CENTURY

The book in the seventeenth century was in the process of transition from the sober and rather ponderous style spread by the Plantin press to the light and elegant one of the pre-Revolutionary French court. With few exceptions, standards of printing had been worsening since the latter part of the sixteenth century. In the Netherlands, where this was not true, the tradition of the hereditary scholarly printing-house still held, but elsewhere printers were often merely jobbers working for a publisher. The very institutions that had fostered printing in its early days—both Church and State—now feared and restricted it. The few printers licensed, under close control, had a virtual monopoly, and their work suffered from lack of competition. Types were still based on the French types of the sixteenth century, but they were poorly cut and unevenly set, and the cheap paper they were printed on made them even rougher. The fine sense for the relation of sizes of display and body types, of type ornaments and margins, had disappeared along with the men of culture who had been printers. The attention of the seventeenth-century printer or publisher was elsewhere; when he wanted a book to have more distinction than usual, he covered its insufficiencies with an engraved title page.

The taste of the first twenty years of the century was essentially that set by Plantin in the previous century. The Antwerp house of Plantin, under the son-in-law Moretus, continued to turn out well-printed volumes, often provided with title pages designed by Rubens. Their usual form was that of an arch against which classical and allegorical figures leaned, or from which they arose as sculptural elements. Despite Rubens' splendid sense of weighty form, these title pages now seem overblown. The figures of flesh appear sculptured and the sculptural figures fleshlike—a concept perhaps appealing to the Baroque taste, which wished to break down the barriers between reality and art, and between the arts themselves. The books of the Plantin Press were popular all over Europe, and Netherlands engravers and printers were imported into France and England in the first quarter of the century.

The Netherlands, actively engaged in trade, showed a continued interest in the printing of atlases and books of travel. A great new printing house was founded in Amsterdam at the beginning of the century by William Janzoon Blau, who had studied with the Danish astronomer Tycho Brahe. The well-run presses, named after the nine Muses, turned out maps and atlases that were world-famous, as well as enormous numbers of scientific and general books. Throughout the century the house of Elzevir was printing its rather compressed pocket editions of classic and contemporary literature that were popular from England to Italy. Their chief claim to handsomeness lay in the types of Van Dyck in which they were printed.

Both the Netherlands and England were well provided with a bourgeois reading public, and for that reason had a relatively good general production of books. In France and Italy the story was different. The general run of books was poor, but special editions commissioned by princely patrons were magnificent. Especially the commemorative books celebrating royal weddings, births, funerals, or victories reflected the pomp and extravagance of an era of enormous staged festivities, with parades, regattas, dramatic presentations, and fireworks. Frequently the commemorative volumes were merely albums of engravings and not properly books at all.

Buonanni,
Ricreatione dell'Occhio
e della Mente
page 219

The engraved title pages that universally formed the most important element of all books that sought to rise above the commonplace were indeed remarkable. They gave free reign to the extravagant fantasy of the Baroque era. The classic arch of the early part of the century became more and more laden with free-standing figures and architectural divisions; some soared into giddy triumphal arches with many tiers of figures. Perhaps out of this architectural compartmentalization grew the idea of the simply compartmented title page, made up of a series of boxes containing the title and symbols, scenes, portraits, or figures.

As the century progressed, bolder and freer compositions were brought forth. Sometimes the architectural element was reduced to a volute-framed central panel in which the title was engraved, surrounded by appropriate figures: animals in an Aesop edition, skeletons in a medical treatise. Allegorical and classical figures continued to play an important part in title page decoration. They often abandoned their architectural framework later in the century and floated or lolled, holding a banner with the engraved title suspended between them. The devices by which a surface was provided for the title were varied and ingenious. The stomach of a spread-eagled grotesque beast might serve, or a pelt stretched between the beaks of two birds, a sail supported between oars, a drapery held by putti. (In all cases the artist went to extreme lengths to show how the text-bearing material was secured, whether with nails, cords, or whatever.) Some later title pages were simply engraved scenes with figures, their titles engraved in a bare spot in the composition.

It seems strange that the brilliant literary productions of the period—the works of Shakespeare, Milton, Corneille, Racine, Molière, La Fontaine, Cervantes—were seldom printed in a worthy manner. It was not until the eighteenth century that novels and plays received the full attention of printers and public. The most carefully produced books of the seventeenth century, in the aristocratic countries, were books of horsemanship, military science, of travel and exploration,

FILIPPO BUONANNI, *Ricreatione dell'Occhio e della Mente*. Rome, 1681. Yale University Library
I numi a diporto su l'Adriatico. Venice, 1688. Engravings by Alessandro della Via. New York Public Library
Foldout 27¼ x 19½ in.→

PARTE QVARTA

Si esprimono i Gusci de' Testacei,
nella Parte seconda descritti.

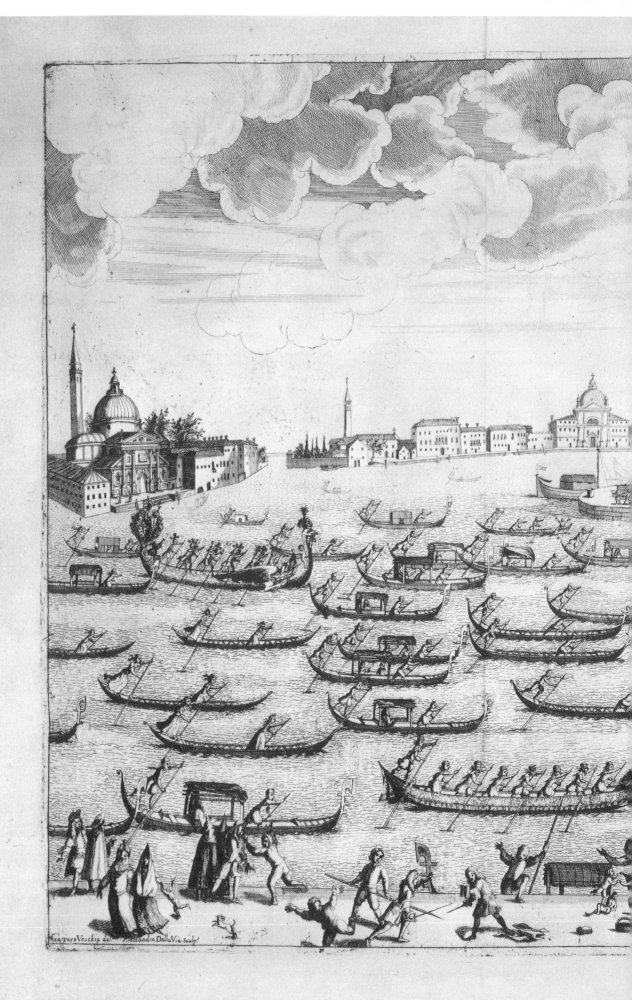

Gasparo Vecchia del. Alessandro Dalla Via sculp.

of the arts and sciences. Emblem books and handsome religious service books continued to be printed. At the other end of the scale, very cheap and ephemeral printing was greatly increased; pamphlets and, for the first time, newspapers were widely circulated.

Ronsard, Oeuvres page 216
In the first quarter of the century the French book was dominated by foreign craftsmen and foreign style. Thomas de Leu and Leonard Gaultier, of Flanders and Germany, decorated most of the books printed in France with engraved title borders in the severely architectural style of Plantin. Crispin de Passe of Utrecht was for some years the leading illustrator of fashionable novels. He also made the illustrations for Pluvinel's *Maneige Royal* (1623), a manual of horsemanship with Louis XIII as royal pupil.

About 1630 a fresh breeze seemed to be blowing. The technique of etching, which permitted a quicker, freer line, was coming into favor. Jacques Callot, a Frenchman who had worked in Italy, brought back with him a dashing, sketchy style, the very antithesis of the Netherlands manner. He brought out many albums of prints which ranged from *commedia dell'arte* figures to scenes of public squares, carnivals, battles, court festivities — vast in perspective yet peopled with telling little individual figures. Among the books he illustrated were two delicately fresh *Lux claustri page 223* emblem books, the *Lux claustri* (1646) and the *Vie de la Mère de Dieu* (1626). Their small vignettes fit neatly into the type page in a way not usual until the next century. In Callot's hands, the soberest book décor of the time becomes gayly vivid. The traditional arched title page has light figures perched on it restlessly, as if for the moment only. The frontispiece portrait has eyes which speak from beyond the exuberant Baroque frame. Callot influenced a succession of illustrators in France and abroad.

The court of the Roi Soleil, Louis XIV, who reigned from 1643 until 1715, dominated the *Courses de testes et de Bague page 219* taste of the period. The *Courses de testes et de Bague* is one of the large commemorative books printed for Louis, in 1670. It contains the plan and costumes of a festivity designed to show the infant Dauphin the military powers of his father through the magnificence of a public *fête*. The caparisoned horses and riders are shown and described in detail, and a double-spread view of the field of action shows all the participants and guests. The title page has a large bust of Louis against the courtyard of Versailles.

An event of major importance to French printing occurred when Cardinal Richelieu opened a printing office in 1640 in the Louvre itself, the *Imprimerie Royale*. Its intent and effect were to set standards of excellence in typography, engraving, and paper. The painter Poussin was commissioned to design the frontispiece engraving for the works of Virgil — a task which he carried out in a rather vacuous classical style. The *Imprimerie* set about also to acquire punches and matrices of fine types. Jean Jannon's *charactères de l'Université* (close enough to Garamond's types to have been erroneously attributed to him) were used at first. In 1692 Louis XIV

PRINCIPIIS OBSTA.

Resiste au mal à son commencement.

Dirige dum teneris curuescit frondibus arbor.
Paruula quod patitur, nescit adulta pati.

❧❧❧

LE prudent Iardinier en émondant son ENTE,
Ses debiles rameaux, dresse d'vn ART secret;
Du ieune inferieur retien l'humeur ardente,
De peur qu'il ne s'eschappe, & te porte au regret.

G ij

VIDI VICI

Courses
de Testes et de Bague
Faittes
Par Le Roy,
et par
Les Princes et Seigneurs
de sa Cour,
En l'Année 1662.

Ægid. Rousselet sculp.

A Paris,
De l'Imprimerie Royale 1670.

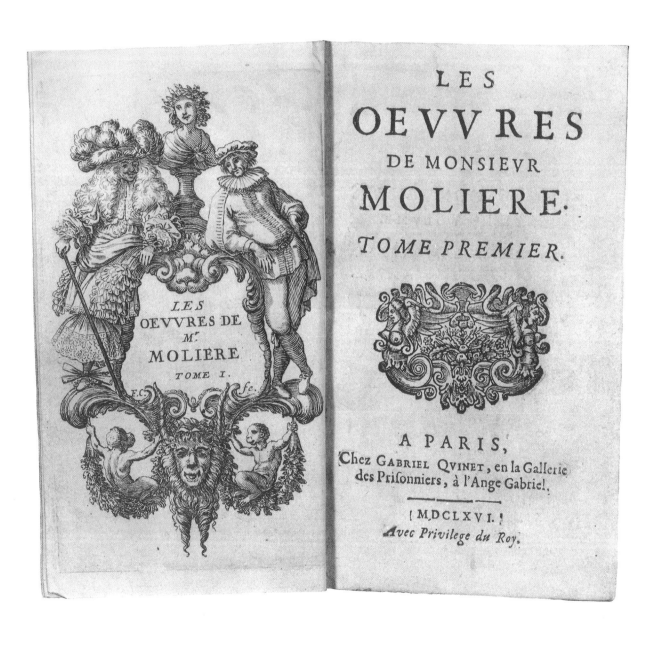

MOLIÈRE, *Oeuvres*. Paris, 1666. Engravings by François Chauveau. Pierpont Morgan Library

← *Courses de testes et de Bague*. Paris, Imprimerie Royale, 1670. New York Public Library. 16 x 11 in.

Panáq; cum prensam sibi jam Syringa putaret
Corpore pro Nymphæ calamum tenuiße. ——

Syrinx

Ouid. I. Metam.

commissioned the design of a new typeface for the exclusive use of the royal printing house. Philippe Grandjean after much scientific experiment developed the *romain du roi,* a precisely cut type with thin, straight serifs—the first real step towards the "modern" type face.

The result of all this activity was an improvement in the printing of books from midcentury on. Under the auspices of the *Imprimerie* some superb book decorators came to the fore, among them Claude Mellan, Abraham Bosse, and François Chauveau. Chauveau made the tasteful elaborations in the *Délices de l'esprit* of Jean Desmarets (1658)—interlaced scrolls used on the title page and above and below his engraved illustrations. He also made the two sprightly frontispiece engravings for a two-volume *Oeuvres de Molière* printed in 1666, which give a gay distinction to an edition not otherwise remarkable. For Michel de Marolles translation of Virgil, printed in 1649, Chauveau made large richly toned engravings of a romanticized classicism.

Oeuvres de Molière page 225

Another of De Marolles books, the *Tableaux du Temple des Muses,* printed in 1655, contains some of the most beautiful illustrations of the century, which bring a heavy, sleepy sensuousness to the figures of classic legend. They were engraved by Cornelis Bloëmaert after an existing collection of paintings.

De Marolles, Tableaux du Temple des Muses page 226

In the last quarter of the century Sébastien Leclerc illustrated books with a lighter touch learned from Callot. He provided Benserade's *Métamorphoses d'Ovide en rondeaux* (1676) with small vignettes that lead directly into the Rococo book. Chauveau collaborated with Leclerc on this book. Leclerc's *Pratique de la Géométrie* is illustrated with tiny landscapes. In Perrault's *Labyrinte de Versailles* (1677) he uses larger plates but preserves a light quality in his etchings of the fantastic Versailles fountains planned to represent fables from Aesop.

In Italy as in France, books for the general reader were poor, special productions for the nobility superb. The commemorative books made for the display of princely pomp reached particularly exuberant heights of Baroque excess. One such book printed in 1688, *I numi a diporto su l'Adriatico,* describes a Venetian regatta staged for his serene highness Ferdinand III, prince of Tuscany, on his visit during Carnival. Its fourteen large plates engraved by Alessandro della Via depict the various floats. They are all complex and symbolic; in one, Venus in triumph, nude on her shell with two amorini, is supported by a lion (Venice) and by figures pouring water from vases (the rivers Arno, Tiber, and Po). A fold-out plate shows the regatta in progress. The type that accompanies the illustrations is uneven and sometimes coarse. Italian typography fared no better than that of other countries, though some of the italic types had a lively quality.

I numi a diporto su l'Adriatico pages 220 and 221

In most Italian books the title pages bore the same heavy burden they did elsewhere; they often constituted the sole artistic interest of the book. The rolling vitality they had by midcentury is

DE MAROLLES, *Tableaux du Temple des Muses.* Paris, 1655. Engravings by Cornelis Bloëmaert. New York Public Library. 17 x 11 in.

easy to imagine. Italian title pages were typically composed of weighty figures in violent motion, those aloft bearing a banner with the title engraved on it, while other figures postured or reclined below.

Germany, devastated and impoverished by the Thirty Years War, somehow managed to print a rather sizable number of books. Frankfurt was an important typefounding center, supplying many types to the Netherlands. From that city the De Brys, father and sons, issued their remarkable series of travel books, the *Grands Voyages* and *Petits Voyages*, beginning in 1590. The long series ranged through the north and south continents of the New World, Africa, India, China, and the Polar North. The typography of the large, well-printed volumes is in the best sixteenth-century French manner. The De Brys illustrated them after the drawings of travellers with half-page engravings showing the costumes, habitat, and unusual customs of far-flung peoples. The pages suffer only from the inherent difficulties of engraved illustrations; they are sometimes out of position, and they lack continuity with the type page. Not all German books fared so well; many were not only badly printed but tastelessly elaborate.

De Bry,
Petits Voyages
page 229

Every country suffered restrictions of the press. France instituted a royal censorship in 1624, and sent hundreds of persons to the Bastille for having printed or sold books judged to be "against the honor of God, the service of the King and the peace of the State." Large numbers of the books in circulation came from clandestine presses or were smuggled across borders. Louis XIV, while encouraging printing on the one hand, on the other hand limited the number of licensed printers in Paris to thirty-six.

English printing suffered under the heaviest restrictions. All privilege and control remained centered in the tight little group known as the Stationers' Company, which had the right to raid any other printing office. By the Star Chamber Decree of 1637 the number of licensed printers was limited to twenty. The number of printers increased somewhat during the rule of Cromwell. Charles II, on assuming power, ordered that they be reduced once more to twenty "by death or otherwise."

Despite these unpropitious circumstances, books were turned out in England in good number. The title pages that adorned them were less sophisticated than those of the Continent, but they had a peculiarly British forthrightness. The archway prevalent in the early part of the century might be surmounted by an allegorical female figure with spurting breasts, but she had a no-nonsense look about her. The river gods at the base of the title page for a book on coastal piloting were as doughty a set of gentlemen as the knee-breeched English explorers above them. There were many designers of engraved title pages. Some of the best, such as Wenzel Hollar,

DE BRY, *Petits Voyages*. Frankfurt, late XVI - early XVII centuries. Engravings by the De Bry brothers. Pierpont Morgan Library. 12 x 7½ in.

S Amogithios hos offendimus in Continente quadam, VVaygat dicta. Externa specie quidem feri, sed illicò tamen ad colloquium nostrum humani, & bene morati inuenti sunt. Staturæ sunt breuis, vultus lati & depressi, oculorum paruorum. Genua ipsis extrorsum prominent. Crines alunt promissos, quos intortos ab occipite religant. Vestitum gerunt ex pellibus hispidis sartum, quo à vertice ad pedes vsque conteguntur. Hi trahis necessaria conuehunt : quarum singulis duas damas præfigentes cursum tam concitatum agunt, vt celeritatem eam nec expeditus equus æquare queat.

m

Wither,
Juvenilia
page 231

were foreigners. Among the designers who showed both fantasy and skill in the early years of the century were Renold Elstrack and William Hole, both of whom favored architectural constructions in their title pages. William Faithorne, later in the century, preferred the scenic title page.

Francis Barlow, a painter of animals, made some distinguished illustrations for an edition of Aesop's *Fables* printed in 1665. His title page for it was an oval with engraved script surrounded by birds and beasts of a shaggy realism. Wenzel Hollar, who often engraved Barlow's designs, made his own illustrations to the *Aesopics* of 1668. Later in the century Medina made a dramatic set of designs for engravings in Milton's *Paradise Lost*.

Oxford and Cambridge maintained their right to operate presses against the attacks of the Stationers' Company and made important contributions to scholarly printing in England. The Dutch types procured in the latter half of the century by Dr. Fell, Bishop of Oxford and patron of the press, are still cast and used today.

A landmark in the history of printing was the exportation by the Rev. Jose Glover sailing aboard the *John* in 1638, bound for the Massachusetts Bay Colony, of a complete outfit for printing. The Rev. Dr. Glover died in passage, but the locksmith he had indentured to operate the press landed with it in good order.

The Massachusetts Bay Colony had been settled by uncommon men, among whom were a number of clerics, mostly graduates of Cambridge. Although the colony had been in existence a scant twenty years, Harvard University had already been founded, and the press was a planned adjunct to it. The locksmith, Stephen Day, and his son Matthew, installed the press at Cambridge, the seat of the new university, and operated it for ten years. The earliest extant

The Whole Book
of Psalmes
page 233

piece of printing from it is *The Whole Book of Psalmes*, often referred to as the *Bay Psalm Book*, a quarto of 294 pages set in the usual mixture of English types, and ambitious enough to have a border of scrolled ornaments around its title page.

The press at Cambridge retained a unique position among the subsequent early presses of the Colonies, which were more utilitarian in their function. Among its notable books was a primer of Indian language prepared by John Eliot and printed around 1654. This book was a prelude to a far more visionary project of Eliot's, the printing of the whole Bible in the language of the Natick Indians. The problems were enormous. Not only did the language have to be transcribed into sounds represented by the English alphabet, but concepts meaningful to the Indians had to be substituted for certain European Christian ones. The word "virgin" posed such a problem: the idea of a chaste female being without meaning to the Indian mind, "virgin" had to be transcribed as "a chaste young man." Indian words had to be invented even for the

IVVENILIA.

A
Collection
of those
POEMES
which were
heretofore imprin-
ted, and written by
George wither.

LONDON
printed for John
Budge in pauls Church
yard at ẙ signe of the
green dragon.
1622

RE
scul

title of the book. The New Testament was completed in 1661, and the entire *Up-Biblum God* in 1663. It was printed by the Days' successor, Samuel Green, with the assistance of an imported assistant and an Indian boy later christened James Printer.

Marmaduke Johnson, the Englishman who came to the New World to assist Samuel Green in the printing of the Indian Bible, returned to England but came back to the colony in 1665 with a press of his own. In that same year a court order had been issued to the effect that "there shall be no printing press allowed in any town within this jurisdiction but Cambridge." Johnson printed in Cambridge as he was forced to, but he made repeated efforts to have the law repealed. Nine years later he was able to move his press to Boston, where in 1674 he set up the first privately owned press in America.

Boston saw a succession of printers within the next decades. By 1690 the first newspaper in the New World was printed there by Boston's fifth printer, Richard Pierce, for the publisher Benjamin Harris. *Publick Occurrences both forreign and domestick* was a three-page publication about 6″ x 10″, neatly set in two columns and bearing heading and initials in large, bold type. The issue of September 25, 1690, was the only one produced, however. The provincial council, apparently not pleased with its contents, banned the publication. Not until 1704 was a newspaper, the Boston *News-Letter*, firmly established.

At the colony of Jamestown in Virginia a press was set up in 1682 by William Nuthead, but it was silenced by the authorities before it produced a single completed piece of printing. The Press Restriction Acts operative in England were not generally applied to the colonies, but colonial printers were subject to the approval of the governor and his council. It was not until 1730 that a press was permitted in Williamsburg, the capital of Virginia.

The enterprising young William Bradford, who had first come to the New World as a boy of nineteen in the company of William Penn, set up a press in or near Philadelphia in 1685. Five years later he built, with two partners, a paper mill near Germantown. But Bradford too ran afoul of the authorities and was arrested for printing matter not to their liking. Governor Fletcher of New York obtained the release of the printer and his press, and installed Bradford as Royal Printer of New York—an office he served for the next fifty years.

The early books printed in America looked like what they were: English books printed under frontier circumstances. The types used were imported from England, and they were set, as much as conditions permitted, in the English manner. The fact that many of the early publications were governmental documents and that many of the printers themselves were in the service of the colonial governments gave a certain dignity to their official work and set standards for the more commonplace products: the business forms, the legal papers, and that central item of the colonial press, the weekly newspaper.

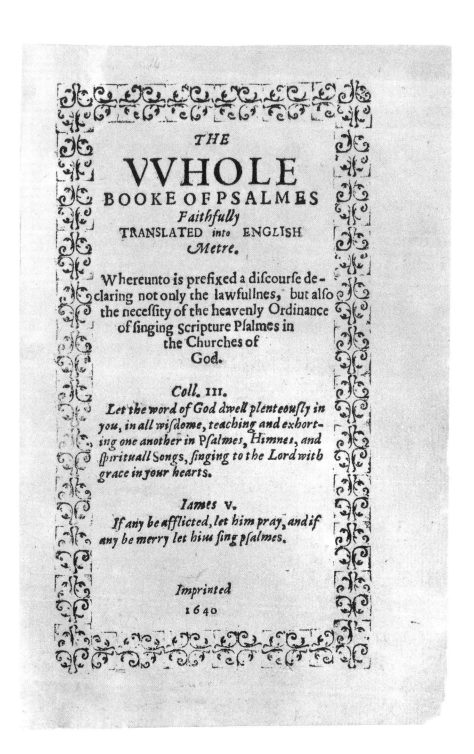

THE
VVHOLE
BOOKE OF PSALMES
Faithfully
TRANSLATED *into* ENGLISH
Metre.

Whereunto is prefixed a difcourfe de-
claring not only the lawfullnes, but alfo
the neceffity of the heavenly Ordinance
of finging Scripture Pfalmes in
the Churches of
God.

Coll. III.
*Let the word of God dwell plenteoufly in
you, in all wifdome, teaching and exhort-
ing one another in Pfalmes, Himnes, and
fpirituall Songs, finging to the Lord with
grace in your hearts.*

Iames v.
*If any be afflicted, let him pray, and if
any be merry let him fing pfalmes.*

Imprinted
1640

Colonial books were often ornamented with borders of type flowers on their title pages, but illustrations were rare. The first of any sort was a woodcut map of New England in Hubbard's *Narrative of the Indian Wars*, printed in Boston in 1677. The printer, John Foster, the second in Boston, made the cut himself. A copperplate-engraved portrait of Increase Mather was used as a frontispiece to two of Mather's works in 1701 and 1702, but it was another fifteen years before engraved illustrations were established in the New World. Not until after 1800 did illustration of any sort really come of age.

THE EIGHTEENTH CENTURY

The eighteenth century, in the realm of books, was above all the time when novels and plays came into their own. Throughout the seventeenth century religious books still outnumbered all others. The balance shifted in the eighteenth century; the habit of reading and collecting books became widespread among the leisure class, and with it grew an enthusiasm for beautifully illustrated copies of old and new literary classcs.

In all things, French taste dominated the century. The French court, enamored of the arts, conceived a particular passion for the illustrating and even the printing of their own editions on little private presses. Louis XV, while still Dauphin, was one such enthusiast; he, his brother the Duke of Burgundy, and his mother all had private presses at which they delighted to work. Madame de Pompadour, Louis's mistress, engraved illustrations to Corneille's *Rodogune* after drawings made by Boucher and had twenty copies of the book printed from silver type at Versailles.

The transition from rich Baroque style to the lighter, gayer Rococo had been well prepared by the end of the preceding century. Grandjean's *romain du roi*, Leclerc's vignettes, the growing taste for the novel, all led toward the smaller, more delicate book which could conveniently be held in the hand. As early as 1719 De la Motte's *Fables nouvelles* were printed in a transitional type, with much space between the lines, and illustrated with dainty half-page etchings by Watteau's teacher, Claude Gillot. Some few folios were still printed at midcentury. The splendid edition of La Fontaine's *Fables* with full-page engravings after pen-and-wash drawings by Oudry is in four large folios; but large books were exceptional. "No period," says Hind, "has shown a greater genius for refinement in the little things of art, and no country has produced artists whose graceful talent was more fitted to miniature creations than France." Grandjean's *romain du roi* appeared in print in 1702 in the *Médailles sur les événements du regne du Louis-le-Grand*, prepared with utmost care and skill by the *Imprimerie Royale*. The monopoly held by the Crown for the use of this cooler, lighter type did not prevent its being copied as closely as possible by many admirers. The new trend in typography was given a decisive impetus by the typefounding house of Fournier. Pierre Simon Fournier cut a fine transitional type in a number of weights and condensations and, to go with it, invented an assort-

V. ARTICLE.

NOTES
De Musique & de Plein - chant.

PETITE MUSIQUE.

Lorsque sur ta musette Tu

chante ton ardeur, Une langueur

secrette s'empare de mon cœur.

Ah! sur un ton si tendre, Pour-

quoi te faire entendre? pourquoi

Colin m'allarmer chaque jour?

Ne peut-on pas vivre heureux

sans amour?

ment of light ornamental capitals based on engravers' lettering. His delicate typeflowers launched a new style: They were made up into gentle borders to frame title pages and arranged to form a variety of head- and tail-pieces. Fournier's own *Manuel typographique*, printed in 1764, the first historical and technical manual of the art of printing, is a masterpiece of this style. The pages, with countless specimens of domestic and exotic types as well as Fournier's own excellent music types, are framed in his borders and sprinkled with his typeflowers. Barbou, one of the leading printers of the time, published Fournier's work and made wide use of his types and ornaments.

Fournier, Manuel typographique page 236

Fournier's types were a perfect accompaniment for the illustrations enjoyed by the French aristocracy—illustrations in a combination of etching and engraving technique, by turns mannered, voluptuous, boisterous and naughty, but always delicate in execution. The best talents in France turned their hands to book illustration. Boucher's warm sensuality and Fragonard's lively depictions of the manners of the time found their way into book engravings. Yet some of the most successful books of the eighteenth century were the work of artists like Charles Eisen and Moreau le jeune who were primarily book illustrators. Less successful were the books illustrated by too many artists in collaboration.

The *Contes et nouvelles en vers* of La Fontaine, published by Barbou in 1762 for a subscription group known as the *fermiers généraux*, is a superb example of Eisen's talent and of eighteenth-century French books. The two volumes each open with an engraved portrait facing a title page made up of Fournier's light types and a small symbolic vignette—a typical arrangement of the time. The preface is in a small italic. The neat body type has Fournier's open capitals and little heading bars for gentle ornament. At the end of each of the *contes* are tail-pieces, sometimes called *culs-de-lampe*, executed by the engraver Choffard, who was the master of this highly specialized art. Composed of elements symbolic of each story, the *culs-de-lampe* are minutely delicate concoctions of rose garlands, floating clouds, nets, and a whole host of eighteenth-century paraphernalia. They provide a setting for Eisen's illustrations, which run the gamut of Rococo grace, sly amorousness, and deliberate licentiousness. Some of the illustrations were made in two versions, "uncovered" and "covered" (as in "fig leaf").

La Fontaine, Contes et nouvelles pages 238 and 239

One of Eisen's loveliest books is Montesquieu's *Le temple de Gnide* (1772), a prose poem in which both the text and the radiant illustrations are engraved. There was evident concern, in the latter part of the eighteenth century, with breaking down the disunity between type printed by one system and illustration printed separately by another. A text engraved throughout was one solution. Another was the use of an engraving plate so large that the marks of its impression were all but lost at the edges of the page. This effect was aided by the excellent laid paper used at the time, with ridges made by the parallel wires on which it drained.

Montesquieu, Le temple de Gnide pages 240 and 241

Mais il fçut la dorer ; & pour me fatisfaire,
D'un bon contrat de quatre mille écus,
Qu'autrefois pour femblable affaire,
Il avoit eu de fon beau-pere,
Il augmenta la dot : je ne m'en plaignis plus.
Ce contrat doit paffer de famille en famille :
Je le gardois exprès ; ayez-en même foin :
Vous pourrez en avoir befoin,
Si vous mariez votre fille.
A ce difcours le gendre moins fâché
Prend le contrat, & fait la révérence.
Dieu préferve de mal ceux qu'en telle occurrence
On confole à meilleur marché.

S ij

LA FONTAINE, *Contes et nouvelles en vers*. Amsterdam (Paris), Barbou, 1762. Illustrations by Charles Eisen, *culs-de-lampe* by Choffard. Yale Beinecke Rare Book Library

LE FAISEUR D'OREILLES,

ET

LE RACCOMMODEUR

DE MOULES.

*Conte tiré des cent Nouvelles nouvelles, & d'un
conte de Bocace.*

Sire Guillaume allant en marchandise,
Laissa sa femme enceinte de six mois,
Simple, jeunette, & d'assez bonne guise,
Nommée Alix, du pays Champenois.
Compere André l'alloit voir quelquefois :
A quel dessein ? besoin n'est de le dire,
Et dieu le sçait : c'étoit un maître Sire ;
Il ne tendoit guère en vain ses filets ;
Ce n'étoit pas autrement sa coutume :
Sage eût été l'oiseau qui de ses rets
Se fût sauvé, sans laisser quelque plume.
Alix étoit fort neuve sur ce point.
Le trop d'esprit ne l'incommodoit point ;
De ce défaut on n'accusoit la Belle.
Elle ignoroit les malices d'Amour :
La pauvre Dame alloit tout devant elle,

MONTESQUIEU, *Le temple de Gnide*. Paris, 1772. Illustrations by Charles Eisen. Pierpont Morgan Library

QUATRIÈME CHANT

PENDANT que Thémire étoit occupée avec ses Compagnes au culte de la Déesse, j'entrai dans un bois solitaire; j'y trouvai le tendre Aristée: nous nous vîmes le jour que nous allâmes consulter l'Oracle, c'en fut assez pour nous engager à nous entretenir; car Vénus met dans le cœur, en la présence d'un habitant de Gnide, le charme secret que trouvent deux amis, lorsqu'après une longue absence ils sentent dans leurs bras le doux objet de leurs inquiétudes.

60   LES BAISERS.

Ainsi s'exhale une étincelle.
Oui, plus que Tantale agité,
Je vois, comme une onde infidelle,
Fuir le bien qui m'est présenté.
Ton baiser m'échappe, cruelle!
Le désir seul m'en est resté.

III. BAISER.

L'ABEILLE
JUSTIFIÉE.

Dans la chaleur d'un jour d'Été,
Non loin d'un ruisseau qui murmure,
A l'abri d'un bois écarté,
Thaïs dormoit sur la verdure.
La voûte épaisse des rameaux
Brisant les traits de la lumière,

Les Baisers, a dainty book in whose illustration Eisen participated, has a typeset text illustrated only with vignette head-pieces and *culs-de-lampe.* The plates of these small engravings were made large enough to extend to the outermost edges of the margin, allowing a perfect marriage of type and illustration. The more essential charms of the book are those of zestful liveliness and sensuality reduced to a pretty and orderly microcosm. The physical attributes of *Les Baisers* far outdistanced the merit of Dorat's poetic text—a fact which caused the witty Abbé Galiani to remark, "Ce poet-là se sauva du naufrage de planche en planche."

Dorat,
Les Baisers
page 242

One of the most delightful eighteenth-century illustrators was J. M. Moreau, known as "le jeune." His full-page illustrations accompany the first volume of a song book dedicated in 1773 to the Dauphine, the *Choix de chansons* by M. de la Borde. The songs themselves are engraved within simple black borders. Each is preceded by a full-page illustration in a similar border, facing a plain bordered page with the song title. Both songs and illustrations are printed in a strikingly black ink on excellent paper. Moreau le jeune's illustrations are full of movement, grace, *éclat,* and endowed with a witty observation of the small details of life. His effects of light and shade, or of illumination at night, are startlingly effective.

De la Borde,
Choix de chansons
page 244

French illustrative technique was almost uniformly that of etching, touched up with the engraver's tool—a process which gave warmth and variety of tone and also the crisp precision that seems to be a French characteristic. The technical work was generally carried out by engravers, the artist supplying only the design, though some few did their own engraving.

England, unlike other European countries, remained independent of France. In competition rather than sympathy with France, England pursued her own soberer ideals. The England of expanding Empire, of rising trade and tradesmen, was not likely to find much in common with the finesse and frivolity of the French aristocracy. English books were for a broader, commoner group of readers with a more puritanical cast of mind. The excellence of eighteenth-century English printing lay in a strong, clarified typography. English illustrations, through Hogarthian satire or Blakean mysticism, showed a deeply moral feeling or else reflected the English love of countryside.

In the early part of the century, which was otherwise dominated by foreign artists, Hogarth emerged as the great illustrator. Hogarth's central works, however, were the series of prints such as *The Rake's Progress* which spoke for themselves without text. The books that he illustrated, among them Butler's *Hudibras* of 1726, show a Hogarth who has not yet attained his mature style.

William Caslon cut important new fonts of type in 1722 which remained throughout most of the century the popular type in England and the American colonies. Caslon's letters were based on the Dutch types used at the beginning of the century, refined in form and cut for

M. DE LA BORDE, *Choix de Chansons.* Paris, 1773. Illustrations by Moreau le jeune in the first of four volumes. Pierpont Morgan Library →

HORACE, *Oeuvres.* London, John Pine, 1733 and 1737 (vols. 1 and 2). Illustrations and text engraved by John Pine. Yale Beinecke Rare Book Library →

78.

Fuyés cher Cidamant
Dit-elle en soupirant.

J.M. Moreau le Jeune. Inv. 1773.

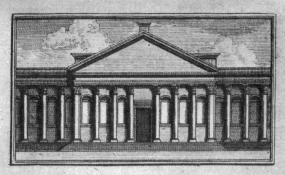

QVINTI
HORATII FLACCI
EPISTOLARVM
LIBER I.

EPISTOLA I.
AD MAECENATEM.

RIMA dicte mihi, summa dicende
 Camena,
  Spectatum satis, et donatum jam rude,
   quaeris,
Maecenas, iterum antiquo me includere ludo.
Non eadem est aetas, non mens. Veianius, armis
Herculis ad postem fixis, latet abditus agro,   5
Ne populum extrema toties exoret arena.
Est mihi purgatam crebro qui personet aurem;
Solve senescentem mature sanus equum, ne

fluent combination. But a new trend had been surging up since the introduction of Grandjean's *romain du roi* in France—a trend toward the more geometrically cut modern letter.

Horace,
Oeuvres
page 245

Something of a forecast of the new typography is to be found in the Horace whose text and decorations were engraved by John Pine. In the two octavo volumes published in 1733 and 1737 Pine used condensed roman letter-forms for his text and for his striking capitals which had strong contrasts of thick and thin. He showed great inventiveness in composing the facing pages of his book, which were full of classical decorations in headpieces, intials, and *culs-de lampe*. They have nothing of French liveliness, however; even the fauns are rather wooden, and the female figures tend to look like men with breasts. Even so, in its rigid way it is a fine classical book, far ahead of its time and an influence on the future.

The heavy use of capitalization began to give way around midcentury, changing considerably the look of the type-page. John Baskerville, a wealthy Birmingham manufacturer with typographic ambitions, made another step in the development of a new typography. Baskerville recut Caslon's letter in a somewhat wider, rounder, and lighter form. The type itself was not remarkably different, but the way of setting it was. Baskerville used very open spacing between the lines and extremely wide margins. The type was printed with unusual care on a smooth "wove" paper developed by Baskerville, using fine wire gauze instead of parallel wires to drain the pulp. (Later, not content with the smoothness of his paper, Baskerville had it hot-pressed.) Type ornaments and rules, popular with other printers of the time, were abandoned; Baskerville wanted only the harmony of type, paper, and printing to constitute the beauty of his pages.

Juvenal and
Persius Flaccus,
Satyrae
page 247

The first product of Baskerville's efforts, a Virgil printed in 1757, went far toward achieving his ideals. The *Satyrae* of Juvenal and Persius Flaccus which he printed in 1761 was even finer. Its simple title page is set in spaced-out capitals. The beauty of its text pages derives from the handsome size and spacing of the body type and the contrasting weight of the titles and initials. Baskerville made a few essays into illustrated books. He produced a charming little Aesop, with all its illustrations grouped in tiny compartments on one page. His *Orlando Furioso*, illustrated by Moreau le jeune, Eisen, Cochin, and other notable French artists, could have ranked as an excellent example of French bookmaking. But Baskerville's real contribution was his approach to typography.

The response to Baskerville's books was stronger and more immediate on the continent than in England. In France the Didots, a learned family of publishers, printers and typefounders, cut a type which increased the contrasts of thick and thin and reduced the serifs to hairlines. In Italy, Giambattista Bodoni had been printing charming books in the characters and style of Fournier for many years at the court of Parma. He had brought the world to the door of his out-of-the-way aristocratic press. He was patronized by such foreign celebrities as Napo-

JUVENAL AND PERSIUS FLACCUS, *Satyrae*. Birmingham, Baskerville, 1761. Yale University Library. 11½ x 8½ in.

SATYRA II.

In eos qui severioris vitae studio foedum animum obte-
gentes, aliorum vitiis iniquiores sunt.

ULTRA Sauromatas fugere hinc libet et glacialem
Oceanum, quoties aliquid de moribus audent
Qui Curios simulant, et Bacchanalia vivunt.
Indocti primum: quamquam plena omnia gypso
Chrysippi invenias: nam perfectissimus horum est,
Si quis Aristotelem similem, vel Pittacon emit,
Et jubet archetypos pluteum servare Cleanthis.
Fronti nulla fides: quis enim non vicus abundat
Tristibus obscœnis? castigas turpia, cum sis
Inter Socraticos notissima fossa cinædos.
Hispida membra quidem, et duræ per brachia setæ
Promittunt atrocem animum: sed podice lævi
Cæduntur tumidæ, medico ridente, mariscæ.
Rarus sermo illis, et magna libido tacendi,
Atque supercilio brevior coma: verius ergo,
Et magis ingenue Peribonius: hunc ego fatis
Imputo, qui vultu morbum, incessuque fatetur.

Horum

leon and the King of Spain. Joaquín Ibarra, the Spanish court printer, produced handsome books which reflected Bodoni's influence. Even Benjamin Franklin wrote a letter praising his work, which was happily translated and circulated under the misconception that it was from the President of the United States.

Perhaps it was the edition of Baskerville's *Orlando Furioso* printed in Italian which caught Bodoni's attention, perhaps a book of Didot's. In 1791 he began printing in an entirely different style, with types based on Didot's and Baskerville's, but far stronger in their effect of vertical shading. He also emphasized the open spacing, the wide margins, the play of richly black ink against white paper. To enhance the effect he often used a large folio format against which his splendidly contrasting types could resound fully, in an effect which has been described as "sumptuous austerity."

Bodoni, Manuale tipografico page 249

The modern letter reached its fullest expression in the books which Bodoni printed at the turn of the century and for some years after. Copied, recopied, and distorted, it dominated the books of the nineteenth century.

In England Caslon's types had prevailed; now, toward the end of the century, publishers wanted types in the lighter modern style. Baskerville's types had dispersed after his death in 1775. New fonts were cut along similar lines by William Martin for the printer William Bulmer. Bulmer was one of a number of English printers consciously dedicated to ideals of fine typography. His best work is exemplified by the folio edition of the *Poems by Goldsmith and Parnell*, printed in 1795. In it Martin's types, simply set and finely printed, are combined with small vignettes by Thomas and John Bewick. These vignettes are wood engravings—a technique which the Bewicks perfected. Thomas Bewick's finely textured illustrations in this book, in Gay's *Fables* and particularly in the *History of Quadrupeds* and *British Birds* set off a wave of wood engraving at home and abroad.

Poems by Goldsmith and Parnell page 251

Outside of all trends and traditions are the books which William Blake produced, mingling in unorthodox patterns his strangely powerful illustrations and the poetic texts which are often a part of his plates. Blake conceived of many of his books as illuminated books for which his plates formed only the basis; later he and his wife painted over and added to the imprint. The *Songs of Innocence*, issued in 1789, and the *Songs of Experience*, in 1794, were illuminated in this way; even the tiny lettering is covered with paint strokes. These early books show a gentle and compassionate side of Blake's nature. Full of delicacy, shy grace, and soft color, they are so miniature and inward that they seem hardly intended for the outward eye. Through their awkward and inept quality Blake's feeling somehow emerges.

Blake, Songs of Innocence and of Experience page 250

At the same period Blake wrote and illustrated his socially and morally critical books, *America, a Prophecy; Europe, a Prophecy* and the *Visions of the Daughters of Albion*. He printed

GIAMBATTISTA BODONI, *Manuale tipografico*. Parma, printed by his widow five years after his death, 1818. Yale Beinecke Rare Book Library. 12 x 8 in.

numero di piccioli diversi segni, che
vanno aggiunti e sopra, e sotto, e in
mezzo alle lettere, quando appor si
vogliono tutte le note destinate a to-
gliere ogni dubbietà di lettura non
che nella pronunzia di ciascuna voce, nella total modulazione de' pe-
riodi, e in ogni ancorchè minimo ri-
poso, che debba aver luogo più dopo
questa che dopo quella parola con-
forme al senso; con tutto ciò lo stesso Abramo figlio di Chajìm, ch'eb-
be parte alle prime stampe Ebree,
quando nel 1476 furono colle pure
lettere impressi in Mantova il primo, e in Ferrara il secondo de' Quat-
tro Ordini della rabbinica giurispru-
denza di Giacobbe figlio di Ascèr, lo
stesso recolla a compimento, impri-

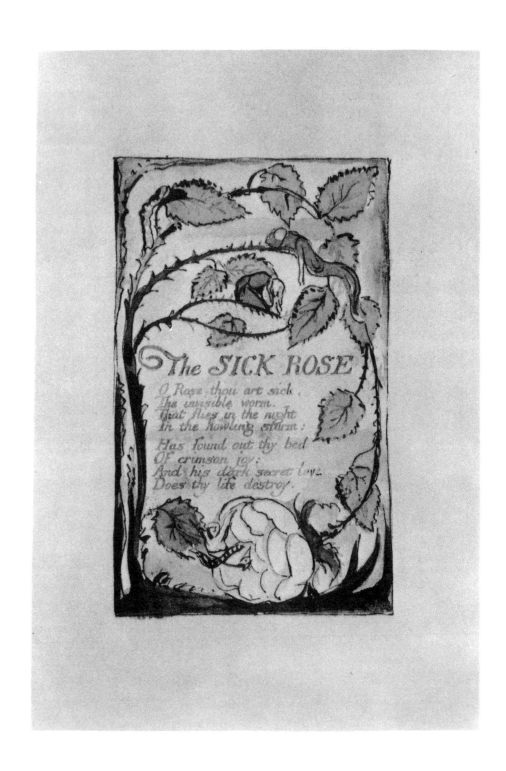

The SICK ROSE

O Rose thou art sick.
The invisible worm.
That flies in the night
In the howling storm:

Has found out thy bed
Of crimson joy:
And his dark secret love.
Does thy life destroy.

WILLIAM BLAKE, *Songs of Innocence and Experience*. London, 1789 and 1794. Pierpont Morgan Library

Poems by Goldsmith and Parnell. London, William Bulmer, 1795. Wood engravings by Thomas and John Bewick.

Yale Beinecke Rare Book Library. 11½ x 9 in.

THE TRAVELLER.

Remote, unfriended, melancholy, slow,

Or by the lazy Scheld, or wandering Po;

Or onward, where the rude Carinthian boor

Against the houseless stranger shuts the door;

Or where Campania's plain forsaken lies,

A weary waste, expanding to the skies;

Where-e'er I roam, whatever realms to see,

My heart, untravell'd, fondly turns to thee:

Still to my Brother turns, with ceaseless pain,

And drags at each remove a lengthening chain.

their combined texts and illustrations in different techniques—relief etching with watercolor tints, woodcut with pen and wash. Evidently, these books were not issued in large editions. Blake was best known to the public of his own time by works published through normal channels: his illustrations to Young's *Night Thoughts* and Blair's *Grave*. In *Night Thoughts*, a large folio issued in 1797, Young's poetic text is typeset, and Blake's large, dreamlike figures move freely in the space around them, buoyant, weightless, surreal. The engravings are executed in open line, palely tinted. Blake's poetic imagination makes itself felt here. It found its most powerful expression after the turn of the century in his masterpiece, *Illustrations of the Book of Job*.

In America printing spread gradually through the colonies, which in the course of the century became the United States. Boston kept her lead in printing until the middle of the century, when Philadelphia rose into prominence. An important press was founded at Williamsburg, Virginia, where William Parks began printing in 1730. Parks achieved a distinguished typography with simple means, working first in the Dutch types used in England and later in William Caslon's letters, available around 1734 and popular in the New World throughout the century. James Franklin, Benjamin's elder brother, established a lively press in Boston in 1717, at which the boy Benjamin served his early apprenticeship. Benjamin Franklin was, of course, the most prominent printer of the century in the New World. With eleven years of printing experience behind him (two of them spent in England) he set up his own shop in Philadelphia with a partner in 1728, at which time he was twenty-three years old. He shortly began to publish the *Pennsylvania Gazette*, which became the leading colonial newspaper.

Almanacs had been a staple item of publication since the inception of printing in America. Franklin introduced *Poor Richard's Almanack* in 1733 and both edited and printed it every year thereafter until 1757. It was full of his wise saws, which became household phrases throughout the colonies, and, later, in Europe as well.

The first magazines to appear in America were produced competitively and almost simultaneously by Franklin and a rival printer, the son of William Bradford. (Bradford's first issue beat Franklin's by several days.) Both publications had the same general intent: to provide a digest or review of the news, and both survived but a few issues.

Benjamin Franklin's career as a printer was as full of "firsts" as his career as an inventor. He published the first novel in the New World, Samuel Richardson's *Pamela*, in 1744. His classical editions were among the first printed in America: the translation of Cato's *Moral Distichs* in 1735, and of Cicero's *Cato major* in 1744. The *Cato major*, with its handsome title page in black and red, was considered by Franklin to be his finest piece of printing.

Cicero, Cato major page 253

M. T. CICERO's
CATO MAJOR,
OR HIS
DISCOURSE
OF
OLD-AGE:

With Explanatory NOTES.

PHILADELPHIA:
Printed and Sold by B. FRANKLIN,
MDCCXLIV.

Germany was not notable for her books during the eighteenth century. German typography became less excessive, and toward the end of the century even tried to assume a French lightness, but the effect was more one of feebleness than of delicacy.

Some of the best illustrated German books were architectural ones. Among illustrated novels, those of Chodowiecki stood out. His work was best in tiny formats—little 32mo editions, or the pocket almanacs popular at the time, in which much of the new literature appeared.

A considerable influence on German book decoration was exerted by the illustrated books of Venice. Venice was in an artistic heyday, and her exuberance springs at the reader from the pages of Venetian Rococo books. Scenes from life on the canals give a special cachet to some of these books; so do the symbols of carnival: the mask and the fan. A zest for Rococo detail—for the ornamented frames, the amorini and garlands, the vignettes composed of graceful groups of objects or of figures—animates the pages. These pages are often overdone, but it is difficult to resist the charm of their very vitality.

Tasso,
Gerusalemme liberata
page 255

The large folio edition of Tasso's poem *Gerusalemme liberata* published by Albrizzi in 1745 is illustrated with Piazzetta's full-page plates, framed with Rococo borders, at the beginning of each canto. The cantos themselves are preceded by an "argument," set apart from the balance of the page by typically Venetian vignette frames, formed very freely of figures and architectural motifs. A pictorial initial introduces the body of the text in a somewhat heavy type. At the end of each canto is a sizable tailpiece in the form of figures supported on an architectural scroll. What a difference between these figures and their French counterparts! Where the French figure, clad and unclad, is self-conscious and lightly self-contained, the Italian Rococo body is heavy, fluent, indolent, and totally unself-conscious.

The French Revolution broke in 1789 and even in Italy resulted in a change of style. Goldoni's comedies had been published in 1761 with spirited illustrations very French in appearance. Between 1788 and 1795 one of Venice's best publishers, Zatta, undertook to produce the plays in forty-four 16mo volumes, with illustrations in a dainty classical style. The change was great from the elaborate Rococo settings and gestures of the edition of a few decades earlier, but the new classicism was still light and charming.

In France a wave of sober classicism followed the Revolution. Rococo was rejected as a style of the overthrown regime. With the coming of Napoleon the "Romanization" of French style was seriously pursued. The ideal in painting was David. Moreau le jeune, particularly gifted for the fripperies of Rococo, abandoned his natural bent to follow the new severer goals. The Didots reigned as typographers and publishers in the neoclassic style. They published many 32mos, very appropriate and neat with their small, light type and little engravings, but they moved also into the production of folios such as the coldly splendid Virgil of 1798, intended to rival Bodoni's.

TORQUATO TASSO, *Gerusalemme liberata*. Venice, Albrizzi, 1745. Illustrations and decorations by Piazzetta. Yale Beinecke Rare Book Library. 17¼ x 11 in.

Entrano i duo guerrier nell'ampio tetto,
Ove in dolce prigion Rinaldo stassi:
E fan sì, ch'ei, pien d'ira e di dispetto,
Move al partir di là con loro i passi.
Per ritenere il cavalier diletto,
Prega e piange la Maga; egli al fin vassi.
Essa per vendicare il suo gran duolo,
Strugge il palagio, e va per l'aria a volo.

CANTO DECIMOSESTO.

I.

TONDO è il ricco edifizio, e nel più chiuso
Grembo di lui, ch'è quasi centro al giro,
Un giardin v'ha, ch'adorno è sovra l'uso
Di quanti più famosi unqua fioriro.
D'intorno inosservabile e confuso
Ordin di loggie i Demon fabbri ordiro:
E tra le obblique vie di quel fallace
Ravvolgimento impenetrabil giace.

As a lovely anachronism, the *Contes et nouvelles* of La Fontaine with sixteen engravings after Fragonard appeared in an incomplete Didot edition in 1795. Fragonard had begun these illustrations almost twenty years earlier, and they had all the grace and dash of the high period of Rococo. But Fragonard as an illustrator was out of phase; his designs for a number of books— *Orlando Furioso*, La Fontaine's *Fables, Don Quixote*—never appeared in published form.

Technical innovations cropped up throughout the course of the century. One stimulant was the persistent desire to reproduce paintings by graphic means. In 1729 in France one such group of reproductions known as the *Cabinet Crozat* was made, using the engraved plate combined with wood blocks printed in tone.

Attempts to render the soft effect of crayon or pastel resulted in the invention of the "crayon method" and stipple engraving, in both of which the engraved line was broken into a number of dots. The resulting plates were sometimes printed in color, producing a clean, fresh effect. Towards the end of the century, aquatint was much used in England for its softened ground, capable of rendering the effect of water color. It was a perfect medium for illustrating the albums of scenic views popular at the time.

Early in the century a German named Le Blon, working in England under subsidy, applied Newton's theory of the three primary colors to printing. In 1723 he produced a book, *Coloritto*, explaining his process and using, if to poor effect, what were actually the first three-color process plates. Le Blon's invention was not perfected until 1892, after printing methods had been completely revolutionized.

THE
NINETEENTH
CENTURY

The revolutions and counter-revolutions in style that characterize the nineteenth-century book reflect a civilization in the throes of far-reaching inner changes. The old social orders were being overtaken by a rising bourgeoisie and working class. At the same time the craft methods of production were being rapidly replaced by mass-production machinery. Very early the books begin to have a familiar look; we recognize them as belonging to our world.

Bodoni's formally perfect books set the style for the first twenty years of the century. His title pages eliminated every excess element; the types were carefully chosen and placed to balance, and to give the proper importance to each word. His folios and his 16mo editions both had generous proportions of white margin to offset their brilliant black type areas.

In France the Didots printed similar books in their even more mechanically precise types. They ornamented them with strict engraved classical headpieces and with engraved illustrations after the dramatically classic school of David. Bodoni had said proudly, "I want only the magnificent, and I do not work for common readers." The Didots were broader in their scope. Their folio editions such as the three-volume *Oeuvres* of Racine printed by Pierre Didot the elder in 1801 and his folio Aesop of 1802 were flawless in typography and craftsmanship. They also produced fine 16mo editions after the tradition of Bodoni. At the same time they produced many inexpensive books by the new process of stereotyping, making plates of the type from which they could print much larger editions. *Racine, Oeuvres pages 258 and 259*

The illustrations of the Didot Racine were engraved after designs by a number of artists working in the manner of David. They are precisely engraved and sternly classic; gone are both the frivolous gaiety and the warmer technique of the recent past. Like the Didot type, the illustrations are sharp in contrast of dark and light. The engravings in the Aesop have a lighter touch, perhaps because of their subject matter. They are contained in headpieces which make brilliant use of classic architectural perspectives.

Curiously enough, the painter David himself foresaw the end of the classical rage, at a moment when he, classicism—and Napoleon—were at their height. In 1808 he predicted, "Within ten years the study of the antique will have become neglected...all these gods and heroes will be replaced by knights and troubadours." David was only a little premature in his forecast. The

A.L. GIRODET *INV.*   ORESTE.   MATHIEU *SCULP*.

ET QUI SAIT CE QU'UN JOUR CE FILS PEUT ENTREPRENDRE? TEL QU'ON A VU SON PERE EMBRASER NOS VAISSEAUX,
PEUT-ÊTRE DANS NOS PORTS NOUS LE VERRONS DESCENDRE, ET, LA FLAMME A LA MAIN, LES SUIVRE SUR LES EAUX.

ANDROMAQUE.   ACTE I.er   SCENE II.me

ANDROMAQUE,

TRAGÉDIE.

....

ACTE PREMIER.

———

SCENE I.

ORESTE, PYLADE.

ORESTE.

Oui, puisque je retrouve un ami si fidele,
Ma fortune va prendre une face nouvelle;
Et déja son courroux semble s'être adouci
Depuis qu'elle a pris soin de nous rejoindre ici.
Qui l'eût dit, qu'un rivage à mes vœux si funeste
Présenteroit d'abord Pylade aux yeux d'Oreste;
Qu'après plus de six mois que je t'avois perdu
À la cour de Pyrrhus tu me serois rendu?

PYLADE.

J'en rends graces au ciel, qui m'arrêtant sans cesse
Sembloit m'avoir fermé le chemin de la Grece,

romantic revolution did not hit full force for another twenty years.

The romantic spirit appeared in books with an appropriate suddenness and force when Delacroix made illustrations to Goethe's *Faust* in 1828. These illustrations were large full-page lithographs made without any concern for their typographic setting. They sought, however, to interpret the very essence of the text. The new technique of lithography, which permitted the artist to draw directly on the reproductive surface, had been used in a few other books in France. Delacroix took full advantage of its richness and flexibility to make a set of illustrations full of verve, excitement, and color. Nothing could have been farther from the classic style, and nothing could have toppled it more completely.

Beginning in 1832, Célestin Nanteuil made his richly medieval etchings for the works of Victor Hugo. Especially dramatic are the frontispieces for *Marie Tudor* and *Lucrèce Borgia*, with an intense scene from the play in a central panel surrounded by a border full of figures and ornament. The title lettering is formless and "handmade," etched as a part of the border; letter forms shared in the freeing of fantasy. Tony Johannot, among others, illustrated Hugo's *Notre Dame de Paris* in 1836 with darkly romantic steel engravings. Steel, newly adopted for engraving, had an advantage over copperplate in that it permitted finer lines and held up for more impressions.

In 1835 LeSage's picaresque novel *Gil Blas* was printed with spirited illustrations—scenes of adventure and highway robbery—some of which were full-page, but many in the form of vignettes. They were used as headpieces and tailpieces, and—for the first time—inserted in the midst of running text. These illustrations by Jean Gigoux were wood engravings, a medium made popular by Thomas Bewick in England. A pupil of Bewick's, brought to France by the Didots, taught the technique to a generation of Frenchmen. For a quarter of a century wood engraving became the most popular of the several media used concurrently in France.

Gil Blas introduced another English feature, the thin double-line border around the type-page. The small, condensed modern type is further embellished with a great many large, decorative initials of a definitely nineteenth-century fantasy.

Saint-Pierre,
La Chaumière indienne
page 261

The edition of Saint-Pierre's *Paul et Virginie* published in 1838 by Curmer, along with *La Chaumière indienne*, is richly interlarded with wood engravings. Some of them are in the form of vignettes; others make a kind of fanciful historiated initial in which the shape of the letter emerges from some aspect of the small illustration. The book has been called over-decorated, but it is an undeniably handsome example of the romantic book.

Around 1840 a new trend appeared, diametrically opposed to the romantic. A satirical and highly contemporary vein of literature and illustration began to be explored. Daumier led the way with *Les cent et un Robert-Macaire*, printed in 1839-40, in which a slight and sardonic text was accompanied by his bitter caricatures in lithograph. *Les Français peints par*

J. H. BERNARDIN DE SAINT-PIERRE, *Paul et Virginie*, with *La Chaumière indienne*. Paris, Curmer, 1838. Wood engravings by Tony Johannot and others. Yale Beinecke Rare Book Library

Il y a environ trente ans qu'il
se forma à Londres une compagnie de savants anglais, qui
entreprit d'aller chercher,
dans diverses parties du mon-
de, des lumières sur toutes les sciences, afin d'é-
clairer les hommes et de les rendre plus heureux.
Elle était défrayée par une compagnie de sous-

41

eux-mêmes, another book of caricatures with wood engravings by Daumier and others, printed in 1840, started a wave of caricature books.

Delord,
Un autre monde
page 263

A strangely fascinating satiric talent was revealed by Grandville, who made surreal woodcut illustrations for a book by Delord called *Un autre monde*, printed in 1844. This world of "transformations, visions, incarnations, ascensions, locomotions…metamorphoses…apotheoses and some other things" was clearly a source for some of Tenniel's illustrations for *Alice's Adventures in Wonderland*. Grandville had a particular flair for animals as well as for the dreamlike. He showed this to advantage in illustrations for La Fontaine's *Fables*, published in 1839, and in the satire on human behavior entitled *Scènes de la vie privée et publique des animaux*.

The Didots' modern types, condensed for economy, prevailed all this while and in fact became a deeply rooted French style which persists till this day. But a Lyons printer, Perrin, perhaps under the influence of a similar move in England, in 1846 revived the old style types. He had the Garamond type recut in a more mathematically exact version, and called it "Augustaux." Other printers took it up, and under the misapplied name of "Elzévir" it formed a second style of French typography. Antique (sans-serif) and Egyptian (square serif) types were now in existence, but they were used mostly in posters; they appeared in books, if at all, on title pages, which were often conglomerate atrocities of fat, thin, expanded, contracted, script, and fantastic types.

The Second Empire, after the turn of mid-century, was dominated by the stream of books illustrated by Gustave Doré, "the last of the Romantics." Doré's gift and curse was his great facility. He seemed unable to stop the outpourings of his imagination, and the pages of the books he illustrated were overrun. His ability to portray a world of demonic fantasy or of dramatic grotesquerie was the basis of his fame, but he had other less obvious talents. The

Balzac,
Contes drôlatiques
page 264

Contes drôlatiques of Balzac, published in 1855, though one of the earliest, is one of his best books. Among its overabundant illustrations are many tiny vignettes tucked everywhere into the type-page, which portray with incredible life and movement such scenes as a rabble storming a castle or a cortège at full gallop, draperies fluttering. Sometimes there is a Callot-like piquancy to his lighter figures, just as some of his darker fantasies remind one of details from Bosch. Doré was able to achieve an astonishing fluency of line in his wood engravings, which often have the quality of having been sketched with a hasty brush. The great depth of color—the sudden light areas within brooding blacks—give his work much of its dramatic vitality. Doré's later illustrations, such as those for *Don Quixote*, are more labored and lack the spontaneity of his early work.

One does not readily associate the names of Doré and Manet, but in 1869 an ambitious book, *Sonnets et eaux-fortes*, was published by Lemerre with etchings by the two artists among a

TAXILE DELORD, *Un autre monde*. Paris, H. Fournier, 1844. Illustrations by Grandville. Yale Beinecke Rare Book Library

Hahblle, portant ses regards vers une fenêtre de l'atelier
qui donnait sur la campagne, aperçut deux paysagistes qui,
pleins d'ardeur et exposés aux rayons d'un soleil non moins
ardent, s'évertuaient à peindre une vaste étude de bouleaux.

Il apprit avec admiration qu'un de ces consciencieux
artistes, s'étant imposé la tâche de reproduire un palmier
dans ses moindres détails, avait vu trois fois fleurir et
défleurir son modèle avant que cette œuvre de patience
fût parachevée.

à elle, de braves capitaines, archers et seigneurs, curieux de la
servir en tout poinct. Elle n'avoyt qu'ung mot à souffler, à ceste
fin d'occire ceulx qui faisoyent les faschez. Une desconficture

d'hommes ne luy coustoyt qu'ung gentil soubrire; et, souventes
fois, ung sire de Baudricourt, capitaine du Roy de France, luy
demandoyt s'il y avoyt, ce iour-là, quelqu'un à tuer pour elle, par
manière de raillerie à l'encontre des abbez. Sauf les potentats du
hault clergié, avecques lesquels madame Impéria accommodoyt
finement ses ires, elle menoyt tout à la baguette, en vertu de son
cacquet et de ses fassons d'amour, dont les plus vertueux et in-
sensibles estoyent enlassez comme dans de la glue. Aussy vivoyt-
elle chérie et respectée autant que les vrayes dames et princesses,
et l'appeloyt-on Madame. A quoy le bon empereur Sigismond res-
pondoyt à une vraye et preude femme qui se plaignoyt de ce : —
Que, elles, bonnes dames, conservoyent les costumes saiges de
la saincte vertu, et madame Impéria les tant doulx erremens de
la déesse Vénus. Paroles chrestiennes dont se chocquèrent les
dames, bien à tort.

Une desconficture d'hommes ne luy coustoyt qu'ung gentil soubrire.

number of others. Manet illustrated the poem *Fleur exotique* with an etching of a Spanish girl in a dark rectangle. The text is set in a somewhat florid old style italic with arabesque head- and tail-piece. These facing pages remain in the format of preceding generations, but Manet illustrated two books a few years later that led toward a different style. In 1874 he made etchings for Charles Cros' poem *Le Fleuve*, which follows the course of a river from its source to the sea. At first the etchings are barely wider than the poetic text they are set into, but for the scene of the river in the city the etching plate becomes much wider and its lines seem to break out of the rectangular boundaries. On the following page Manet has used two etching plates, one above the text and a smaller one below, so that they effectively surround it.

Manet made woodcuts for the slim leaflet containing Mallarmé's *L'après-midi d'un faune* two years later. The one illustrated text page contains a few lines of airily set poetic text and, above it, a sketchy woodcut of nymphs bathing. The woodcut's lines breathe outward into the margins and form a perfect unity with the text. Manet's illustrations for *Le Fleuve* and *L'après-midi d'un faune* lead forward to a new kind of book format in which the illustration permeates the page and weaves with the type into a lightly textured unity.

Cros, Le Fleuve page 267

At the same period, in 1875, Manet illustrated quite another type of book. For Mallarmé's translation of Poe's *Raven* he made free full-page lithographs, completely separate from the printed text but deeply interpretive of its mood. Manet's *Raven*, along with Delacroix's *Faust* of 1828, were the forerunners of the *livres de peintre* which were the most important French contribution to publishing in the twentieth century.

England, with France, led the world in book production in the nineteenth century. England was already on familiar terms with the industrial revolution at the beginning of the century and was receptive to new methods of production. The finest English printer of the time, William Bulmer, was experimenting in 1800 with the iron Stanhope press which could print a large enough sheet to almost double production. Thomas Bensley, another of England's best printers, encouraged the invention of the cylindrical press which was the basis of the revolution in printing. By 1814 the *London Times* was being secretly printed on two steam-powered cylindrical presses. Steam presses were, however, not much used for book printing until the late forties and early fifties. A papermaking machine which Didot began to develop in France before the turn of the century was perfected in England and from 1812 was operating commercially. By 1853 wood pulp was being processed to make an inferior but apparently boundless supply of paper which rapidly supplanted rag paper.

English typography continued in the tradition set at the end of the eighteenth century. Types were modern, but less extremely so than on the continent. The neat classical formats persisted. A liberal use of rules remained a characteristic British feature.

Job printing, hitherto in the same style as book printing, in industrial England was beginning to develop characteristics of its own. For bold display, Robert Thorne cut a modern type broadened out to merit the name "fat face." It was copied on the Continent by everyone from Bodoni to the *Imprimerie Royale*. Two similar inventions came from England around 1815: the Egyptian letter and the sans-serif, both intended for display.

Bulmer and Bensley were the leading printers of the early years, though the typographic purity of their books gave way somewhat to commercialism. The Chiswick Press was also printing fine books when in 1824 the young Charles Whittingham became a partner. In a few years he took it over entirely and made it the greatest press of the Victorian era.

Whittingham produced his best books in cooperation with the publisher William Pickering. Pickering was a man of extraordinary taste, who had been a publisher and antiquarian book-seller since 1820. He had begun by publishing a series of books in extremely small type which he called the "Diamond Classics." At that time books were either sold in loose sheets, to be privately bound in leather or half-leather, or else in paper-covered boards intended as a temporary cover. Around 1822 Pickering had the idea of covering his Diamond Classics with cloth and pasting a paper label on their spine. The title pages of these books were also revolutionary; they avoided the endlessly long titles common at the time. Only the few essential words were set in carefully spaced capitals the size of the text.

The Vision and the Creed of Piers Plowman page 268

Pickering and Whittingham first got together in 1830 to publish a series of books called the "Aldine Edition of the British Poets." These books were in a more legible type but the same simple style; their only decoration was Aldus' mark on the title page, and an oval frontispiece portrait. Pickering and Whittingham went on to print poetic editions with woodcut title borders and other ornaments copied freely after books of earlier times. They also printed many handsome editions of prayer books in antique styles, some of them set in black-letter type and printed in black and red on handmade papers. Their masterpiece in this line was *Queen Elizabeth's Prayerbook*, printed in 1869, with over a hundred vigorous woodcuts by Mary Byfield, who made many of their ornaments.

Pickering's familiarity with old books and admiration for their styles led him to revive Caslon's type, which he used on several title pages in the forties. In 1844 he set two books fully in Caslon. One of them was *Lady Willoughby's Diary*, the other, George Herbert's *Temple*. Both were produced in the style of eighteenth-century books. From the time of their publication a revival of old style types spread in England, France, and America.

English illustrated books were still largely concerned with landscape, which they depicted in a manner at once realistically detailed and highly romantic. Many of the early topographical books were in aquatint, which was often hand colored. Landscapes by Turner, Gainsborough and Constable appeared in these books. In the thirties Turner made a number of small vignette

CHARLES CROS, *Le Fleuve*. Paris, 1874. Etchings by Manet. Harvard College Library

Qu'on se lise entre soi ce chant tranquille et fier,
dans les moments de fièvre et dans les jours d'épreuve;
qu'on endorme son cœur aux murmures du Fleuve.

Va, chanson! Mais que nul antiquaire pervers
n'ose jamais changer rien à tes deux cents vers!

The vision and the creed of
Piers Ploughman
newly imprinted

London William Pickering
M dccc xxxxij

The Vision and the Creed of Piers Plowman. London, Pickering, Chiswick Press, 1842. Library of Philip Sperling,
New York

illustrations for books of poems by Byron, Scott, Milton, and other poets less known to our day. Turner achieved an extraordinary atmospheric quality in these small steel-engraved scenes by using the delicate gray tones that the medium permitted for distant mountains, clouds, or skies with pale rays of light.

Rogers, Italy page 270

William Blake pursued his inner voices in the early decades of the century, expressing them in his illuminated books in symbols not readily understood by the public. In 1821 he participated in the illustration of Thornton's Virgil, a book intended for school use; he made small wood engravings for it, full of a moody, pastoral mystery. In 1825 he completed his masterpiece, the series of engraved plates illustrating the *Book of Job*—a powerful vision in which the words and illustrations work together as voices succeeding and sustaining one another. Blake was in the midst of making engraved illustrations for Dante's *Inferno* when he died in 1827.

Lithography became a popular medium for botanical and bird studies in the twenties and thirties, as well as for topographical books. A new viewpoint was added when the railroad came on the scene, and books with titles such as *London-Birmingham Railway* appeared (1839), with views from a railway journey in hand-colored lithography. The railway provided a new market as well as a new subject for books; the first railway bookstall was opened in 1848, and the Railway Library was begun in 1849, a cheap series in printed paper covers that numbered thirteen hundred titles in half a century.

The English had a natural bent for caricature and satire, as Hogarth had shown in the eighteenth century. Early in the nineteenth century Rowlandson made his lively, rollicking commentaries on British character and behavior in such books as *The Tour of Dr. Syntax in Search of the Picturesque*, published in 1812. Illustrated magazines such as *Punch* and *The Illustrated London News* appeared in numbers in the decade between 1832 and 1842. From the ranks of the magazine artists came Dickens' illustrators—George Cruikshank with his sinisterly realistic etchings for *Oliver Twist*, and "Phiz," who made the more ordinary illustrations for *Pickwick Papers*, *David Copperfield*, and a great many other Dickens novels.

Books for children were developing rapidly in England. In 1840, under the name of Felix Summerly, Henry Cole began the Home Treasury series of children's books "to cultivate the Affections, Fancy, Imagination and Taste of Children." The early books in this series had frontispieces printed in lithography at the Chiswick Press and colored by hand. Later the Chiswick Press introduced color wood engravings in the series; but color-printed children's books were not really established until the Toy Books of the sixties.

Children's books of the past had been made primarily for moral or other instruction. Now books of adventure and pure fun began to appear. Edward Lear's first *Book of Nonsense* came out in 1846 with his humorous black-and-white drawings and verses. A whole series of Lear nonsense books followed. Carroll's *Alice's Adventures in Wonderland* was published in 1865

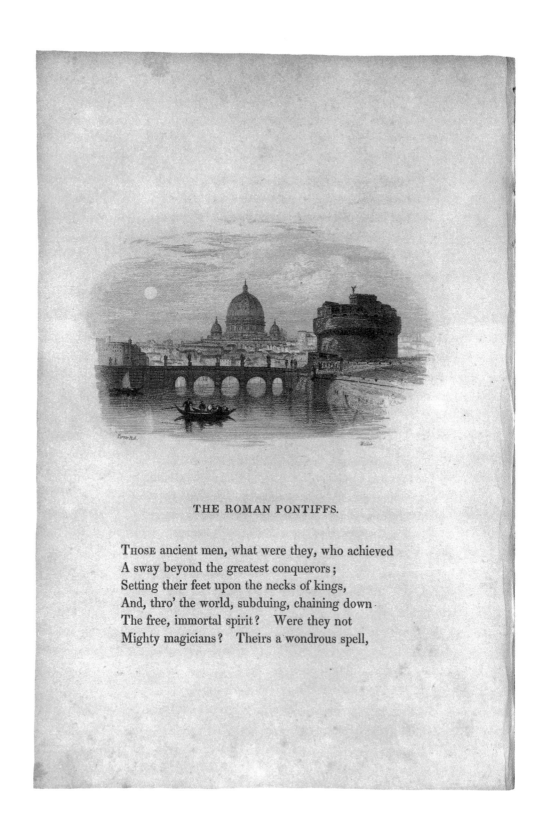

THE ROMAN PONTIFFS.

THOSE ancient men, what were they, who achieved
A sway beyond the greatest conquerors;
Setting their feet upon the necks of kings,
And, thro' the world, subduing, chaining down
The free, immortal spirit? Were they not
Mighty magicians? Theirs a wondrous spell,

and *Through the Looking-Glass* in 1871 with wood engravings by the magazine illustrator Tenniel.

Color printing in books for adults was the innovation of the forties. Chromolithography, color printed from a series of lithographic plates, was most often used, but it was sometimes supplemented with color wood blocks. Art books with reproductions of paintings were popular, as well as those of a less sober nature, such as *Pearls of the East*, an album with two-color plates of voluptuous ladies of the harem as drawn by Fanny and Louisa Corbaux. The strong antiquarian interest of the middle years brought books with color plates of the art and architecture of the past. Henry Shaw's fine books of this sort were mostly produced by Pickering and the Chiswick Press, in sumptuous format with fine typography and printing. They were usually hand colored, but some, such as his *Encyclopedia of Ornament* of 1836, had several plates printed in color wood engraving.

The antiquarian taste of the times led to "illuminated" gift books, with a text often—but not always—taken from the Bible. Owen Jones and Noel Humphreys were masterly designers of these, freely adapting the decorative styles and motifs of manuscripts to make rich, imaginative books printed in chromolithography.

In the fifties a monumental curiosity was produced by chromolithography: Digby Wyatt's great two-volume folio, too cumbersome to handle, of *The Industrial Arts of the Nineteenth Century*. It contained 160 plates of choice objects from the Great Exhibition, printed in gold and colors, using from seven to fourteen impressions per plate.

Color wood engraving began to gain popularity in the late fifties at the hands of Edmund Evans, the leading wood engraver of his time. Evans began his career by printing in that process the bright cover designs for cheap yellow-paper-covered editions known as "yellowbacks." In 1856 he printed *Sabbath Bells*, his first book with full-color wood engravings of the soft, delicate drawings of Birket Foster. It was followed by a number of books with Foster's illustrations, including *The Poems of Oliver Goldsmith*, whose scenes were achieved with nine or ten printings, and *Common Wayside Flowers*, with free, naturalistic flowers beside a simple text. Evans began to print the Toy Books published by Routledge and Warne in the sixties. These were at first bright, simple books by anonymous artists. Walter Crane was the first name attached to the Toy Book illustrations. Crane was much impressed by Japanese wood-block prints, and he used large areas of flat color in his *Sing a Song of Sixpence Toybook* of 1866, and others. He designed his books throughout, with an attention to the harmony of facing pages that he also learned from the Japanese. Later his work grew rich and dense under pre-Raphaelite influence.

Common Wayside Flowers page 272

Edmund Evans launched the careers of two other children's book illustrators, Randolph Caldecott and Kate Greenaway, both of whom became known for their delicately colored

WOOD ANEMONÉ.

Some Grecian poet,
    Where it grew
Lay dreaming, while
    The sweet South blew
Its white-streak'd petals
    To and fro ;
And through his eyes,
    Half shut, he saw
A God-like shape,
    Form'd of the wind,
And thus a name
    Did for it find :
For seeing all
    Its bells in motion,
He thought this young god
    Of the ocean
Had left fair Thetis'
    Pearly side,
Upon its drooping
    Bells to ride ;
And ever since
    That dreamy hour,
It has been call'd
    The Wind-flower.

wood-engraved illustrations that harked back to an idealized past. Like Crane, Kate Greenaway designed her books throughout and, further, often wrote their verses. Her gentle, quaint depictions of childhood were apparently irresistible to Victorian parents.

In 1851 Langton had found a way to photograph on wood, so that the wood-engravers had an accurate copy to cut. In 1850 in France, Gillot had used zinc plates as a substitute for lithographic stone, and mounted them on wood blocks so that they could be printed with the type. Gillot's son combined these two advances in 1872 and produced the photoengraved line-cut. Shortly afterward, around 1880, the half-tone cut was produced in France, England, and America at roughly the same time.

The mechanical line-cut did not print so well as wood-engraving, but it offered certain possibilities to illustrators which they needed time to become aware of. Aubrey Beardsley was one of the first to do so. He quickly abandoned the techniques suitable for wood engraving and developed a system of small dotted patterns and other patterns that gave areas of textured tone. He used these with particular skill to suggest fabrics. Beardsley belonged to the group of aesthetes centered about Oscar Wilde. His illustrations for Wilde's *Salome*, printed in 1894, show a Japanese influence mixed with Beardsley's unique patterns. They so successfully express depravity and wild tragedy that Wilde said, "They are cruel and evil and so like dear Aubrey who has a face like a silver hatchet with grass-green hair."

Beardsley illustrated Pope's *Rape of the Lock* in 1896 and his own romance, *Under the Hill*, in 1903. His drawings became more complexly patterned and took on some of the mannerisms of the eighteenth century. They have an inescapably dated look, for all their skill.

Beardsley and his Art Nouveau group were one reaction to industrialized England; another was the pre-Raphaelite brotherhood. A group of young artists pledged themselves to fight the poor standards and bad taste of the era by reviving what they considered to be the artistic ideals of the Middle Ages. Their movement included both the fine arts and the useful arts; they felt that the useful should also be beautiful. Their aim was to supplant the tawdry products of the machine with products of fine craftsmanship. William Morris was the prime mover of the pre-Raphaelite Arts and Crafts movement. Aided by the artists Burne-Jones and Rossetti, he designed and produced textiles, stained glass, carpets and furniture in factories run according to pre-Raphaelite social and aesthetic philosophy.

Interest in a typographic revival had been shown by Herbert Horne and Selwyn Image in their publication, the *Hobby Horse*, as early as 1886. A lecture given by the printer Emery Walker before the Arts and Crafts Exhibition Society excited Morris's interest. In order to apply his ideals to the printed book, Morris founded the Kelmscott Press in 1891. Morris owned and admired many fifteenth-century printed books, and he wanted to achieve the spirit and quality of these books in the products of his press. He designed types after the early

Common Wayside Flowers. London, Edmund Evans for Routledge, Warne and Routledge, 1860. Color wood engravings by Birket Foster. From Ruari McLean, *Victorian Book Design*

273

German round gothics, and after Jensen's roman. With them he used woodcut illustrations, and woodcut borders and initials which he designed. Morris was particularly concerned that his books be conceived as a total unity. He used handmade papers, specially prepared inks, and a hand press for printing.

Morris,
The Story of
the Glittering Plain
page 277
The Water of
the Wondrous Isles
page 276

The Story of the Glittering Plain, written by Morris, was the first Kelmscott book, printed in 1891. A new edition of 1894 was more elaborate than the first, with Morris's woodcut borders surrounding dense illustrations by Walter Crane. To the modern eye the less heavily decorated books are preferable, such as *The Water of the Wondrous Isles* (1897), another of Morris's own texts. Fifty-three books in all came from the Kelmscott Press. The last and most ambitious was the folio *Works of Chaucer*, set in two columns of the large gothic type and heavily embellished with Morris's black-ground vine-leaf borders and with woodcut illustrations by Burne-Jones.

For all his love of the fifteenth century, Morris did not achieve its qualities in his books. He worked with a too lavish hand and lost the most essential quality of the earlier era, that of simplicity. Morris's books remain thoroughly Victorian, closer to some of Beardsley's pages than to those of a more innocent age. Nevertheless, their effect on the printers of his time was immense. Morris led the way back to a unified typography in place of a needless assortment of types. He reinstated the book with illustrations by one artist, related to the overall design. He established, in short, the ideal of the book as a unified work of art.

Morris's books crystallized a desire for better design and printing that had been growing in England, the Continent, and America. In England a number of private presses were formed, dedicated to fine printing and a revival of fifteenth-century styles. The Ashendene and the Eragny Press were founded in 1894, the Vale Press in 1896. In 1900 Emery Walker, who had been Morris's advisor, established the Doves Press with Cobden-Sanderson. Charles Ricketts at the Vale Press and Lucien Pissarro at the Eragny Press both produced woodcut-illustrated books that were close in spirit to Morris's. The Ashendene and the Doves Press directed their ideals to pure typography. They sought the simplest and most orderly pages, decorated only with calligraphic initials.

The private presses cut their own types based on types of the past. Jensen's roman was the basis of the Vale and Doves types. The Ashendene Press used Caslon and the type of Dr. Fell revived by the Oxford Press. In 1902 they cut a semi-roman based on the type used in the first Italian printed books. Ashendene books came closest to the actual appearance of incunabula, with their heavy types, often printed on vellum, surrounded by wide margins of handmade paper and completed with rubrics in red, blue and gold.

For a while the strong, black effect of well-inked, closely spaced type and heavy woodcut borders was pursued in England, Germany, and America. Germany was especially influenced

OSCAR WILDE, *Salome*. London and Boston, 1894. Illustrations by Aubrey Beardsley. Yale Beinecke Rare Book Library

WILLIAM MORRIS, *The Water of the Wondrous Isles*. Hammersmith, Kelmscott Press, 1897. Yale Beinecke Rare Book Library. 11¼ x 8 in. →

WILLIAM MORRIS, *The Story of the Glittering Plain*. Hammersmith, Kelmscott Press, 1894. Yale Beinecke Rare Book Library. 11¼ x 8¼ in. →

SALOME
A TRAGEDY IN ONE
ACT : TRANSLATED
FROM THE FRENCH
OF OSCAR WILDE :
PICTURED BY
AUBREY BEARDSLEY

LONDON : ELKIN MATHEWS
& JOHN LANE
BOSTON : COPELAND & DAY
1894

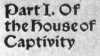

not be seen, or kind and had no will to scare the simple maiden; or else maybe there were none such in those days. Anyhow, nought evil came to her out of Evilshaw.

Chapter VI. Herein is told of Birdalone's raiment ✿ ✿

LANK and long is Birdalone the sweet, with legs that come forth bare & browned from under her scant grey coat and scantier smock beneath, which was all her raiment save when the time was bitter, and then, forsooth, it was a cloak of goat-skin that eked her attire: for the dame heeded little the clothing of her; nor did Birdalone give so much heed thereto that she cared to risk the anger of her mistress by asking her for aught.

BUT on a day of this same spring, when the witch-wife was of sweeter temper than her wont was, and the day was very warm and kindly, though it was but one of the last of February days, Birda-lone, blushing and shame-faced, craved timidly some more womanly attire. But the dame turned gruffly on her and said: Tush, child! what needeth it? here be no men to behold thee. I shall see to it, that when due time comes thou shalt be whitened & sleeked to the very utmost. But look thou! thou art a handy wench; take the deer-skin that hangs up yonder and make thee brogues for thy feet, if so thou wilt.

EVEN so did Birdalone, and shaped the skin to her feet; but as she was sewing them a fancy came into her head; for she had just come across some threads of silk of divers colours; so she took them and her shoon & her needle up into the wood, & there sat down happily under a great spreading oak which much she haunted, and fell to broidering the kindly deer-skin. And she got to be long about it, & came back to it the next day and the next, and many days, whenso her servitude would suffer it, and yet the shoon were scarce done.

SO on a morning the dame looked on her feet as she moved about the cham-ber, and cried out at her: What! art thou barefoot as an hen yet? Hast thou spoilt the good deer-skin and art yet but shoe-less? ❧ Nay, our lady, said Birdalone, but the shoon are not altogether done ❧ Show them to me, said the dame.

BIRDALONE WENT to her little coffer to fetch them, & brought

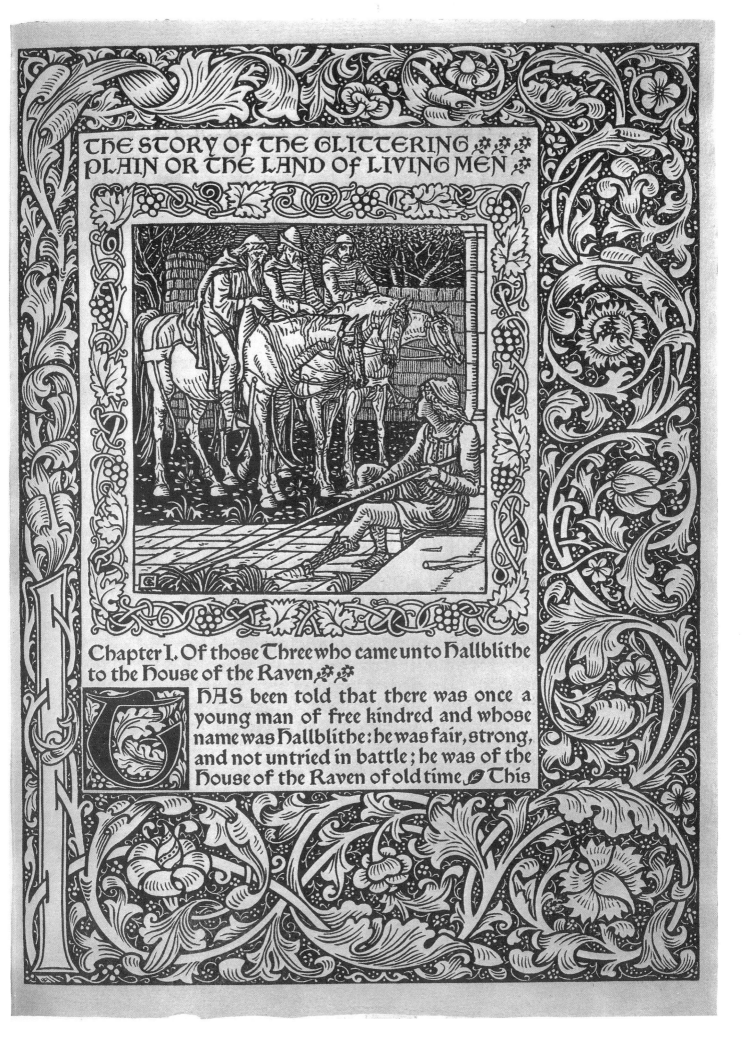

THE STORY OF THE GLITTERING ❦ ❦ PLAIN OR THE LAND OF LIVING MEN

Chapter I. Of those Three who came unto Hallblithe to the House of the Raven ❦❦

IT HAS been told that there was once a young man of free kindred and whose name was Hallblithe: he was fair, strong, and not untried in battle; he was of the House of the Raven of old time. This

by Morris's books. German printing between 1550 and 1580 had been particularly cheap and tasteless. A "secession" movement against the state of all the arts was under way, and its journal, *Pan*, reproduced some of Morris's pages. Their effect was immediate and far more general than in England. Commercial presses such as the Insel-Verlag, and the German type foundries participated in the revival along with the private presses. Pure typography became a consuming interest. There was also great interest in calligraphy, which began to lead to new type designs.

Certain nineteenth-century German children's books have a special interest. Just before mid-century Dr. Hoffman wrote and illustrated *Struwelpeter*. Its horrifying and delightful pictures were reproduced by chromolithography and did much to popularize that medium for children's books. Most German children's books were sentimental, but in the '70's Wilhelm Busch, a magazine illustrator, began his comical adventures of *Max und Moritz, Die Fromme Helene*, and other characters. His lively woodcut illustrations arranged in series on the page, each accompanied by a short line of verse, led a step closer to the modern comic strip.

America was still dependent on England's leadership in the early part of the nineteenth century. Two Scotsmen, Binny and Ronaldson, established the first substantial type foundry in Philadelphia and brought out a specimen book that was probably the first in America. They cut a good transitional type, Oxford (revived at the end of the century), and modernized American printing by eliminating the long S. An English printer, John Wilson, brought the sound typography of the period of Bulmer and Bensley to American books. Later, when Pickering and the Chiswick Press revived old style types in England, Caslon types were again imported to America. American book design remained simple and rather uniform until after the Civil War. The modern type face dominated, wood engraving was most often used for illustrations, and the general style of books was classic, changing to romantic, as overseas.

Early in the century Alexander Anderson popularized wood engraving with his copies of Bewick's illustrations for an American edition of the *General History of Quadrupeds* (1804). Anderson's illustrations were the first in America with any sophistication or real competence. The American Tract Society issued from the twenties on its long series of religious booklets neatly adorned with wood engravings. The reading public was broadening rapidly, and publishers realized that illustrations extended the appeal of their books. The many history books and biographies of historical figures that reflected a period of patriotic self-consciousness were often illustrated with wood engravings.

In the 1830's and '40's "gift books" and annuals became popular. These were anthologies of literature gotten up with a presentation plate, a decorative title page, and a number of engraved plates. For this purpose, metal engraving was considered more elegant than wood.

By far the most ambitious book produced in the first half of the century was Harper's Illuminated Bible, printed in 1846, a folio decorated with 1600 meticulous wood engravings. The large illustrations, after copies of Italian paintings, were surrounded by a nineteenth-century version of Italian Renaissance borders. Decorative initials and small engravings were dispersed so that every opening page was embellished. The book was an immense financial success for its publishers, Harper Brothers.

The development of American books was greatly influenced by the fact that magazines and newspapers were, as they still are, the most important branches of publishing there. *The Illustrated London News* had been widely read in America; in 1855 Frank Leslie left its staff and crossed the seas to found *Frank Leslie's Illustrated Newspaper*. Leslie used wood engravings to illustrate the news and also as a muckraking device to mobilize public opinion against social abuses. *Harper's Weekly* was founded, and a series of other magazines followed. They became part of every literate household.

A large group of illustrators was kept employed by the magazines. The taste for profuse illustration carried over into books, and all sorts of editions were plentifully illustrated, many of them in the style of Cruikshank. Felix Darley was known for his wood engravings and etchings in Washington Irving's books around 1850, which owed something to both Cruikshank and Doré. Harry Fenn gained attention with his realistic wood engravings for Whittier's poem *Snow-bound* in 1868. Fenn produced two volumes of illustrated travels called *Picturesque America* and followed them with *Picturesque Europe* and *Picturesque Palestine*. The popularity of views was reflected in *Harper's Weekly*, which published country scenes and contrasted them with the squalor of the crowding cities. Winslow Homer drew scenes from the Civil War, sitting in Harper's home office.

The end of the Civil War brought the industrialized segment of America clearly into the ascendancy. America had ceased to be a receiver nation and was making contributions which influenced European publishing, especially in the way of technical inventions. The German-American Othmar Mergenthaler in 1886 invented the Linotype machine which, operated by a keyboard, set and cast a line of type at a time and returned the matrices to their places. The following year another American, Tolbert Lanston, invented the Monotype machine which cast individual letters. American inventors contributed heavily to the bookbinding processes which were racing to keep up with the greatly increased production of the perfected cylindrical presses.

By the eighties, when the half-tone plate became practical for reproducing illustration, *Harper's Magazine* was a pioneer in its use. As if to compete with it, wood engraving undertook to imitate the effect of any other medium. Color half-tones were possible by 1892. The fine lines of reproductive wood engraving and the fine dots of the half-tone plate called for clay coated and polished papers.

American illustrators, without the weight of tradition to inhibit them, took to the new photo-mechanical effects more quickly than their European counterparts. There was a mania for tonal effects, resisted only by the illustrator Howard Pyle in the eighties. Pyle kept strictly to woodcut technique in his illustrations for *The Merry Adventures of Robin Hood* (1883) and *The Wonder Clock* (1888), but even he eventually succumbed to the effect of paintings reproduced by half-tone.

The leading printer from midcentury on was Theodore Low DeVinne, who during his long productive years worked to maintain standards in the face of increasing mechanization. DeVinne was not a great stylist, but he kept a much-needed soundness in his publications.

In 1884 the Grolier Club was founded for the "promotion of the arts pertaining to the production of books." Other bibliophiles' societies followed.

Consciousness of style sprang up in America under the influence of William Morris, whose books and whose ideals attracted a new type of personality to book design and printing. Will Bradley was one of Morris's admirers who emulated his rich borders and initials. Bradley founded the Wayside Press in 1895. As art director of the *Century Magazine* and editor of *The Chapbook* published by the American Type Founders, he also adapted Morris's style for commercial printing.

Daniel Berkeley Updike founded the Merrymount Press in 1893 as a commercial enterprise under scholarly direction. The early products of this press were also in the Morris manner. The publishing industry as a whole was little affected by the revival, however. The idea of well-made trade books did not really take hold in America until after World War I.

In France, toward the end of the century, well-designed and printed books were rare. Concern over the deterioration of the quality of books showed itself in several ways. A number of bibliophiles' societies was formed from 1873 on; these societies produced their own limited editions which, though conservative in taste, were devoted to fine printing. The publisher Edouard Pelletan reiterated Morris's tenets to the French press between 1896 and 1912, with considerable effect. A Society of Printers and Engravers was organized in 1889 to stimulate the interest of the best artists in book illustration and to improve standards. One of the aims of this group was to avoid the photographic reality of current illustration, which ignored the overall appearance of the book. The painter Maurice Denis called for "the decoration of a book, without servitude to the text, but with an embroidery of arabesques on the pages, an accompaniment of expressive lines." Independently, the French illustrators were arriving at opinions remarkably close to those of William Morris.

Denis himself made unusual illustrations for André Gide's *Le voyage d'Urien*, published in a refreshing square format in 1893. The title page was still in a poor mixture of types, but the text pages were simple and good. Denis's simplified, crayony lithographs, fitted into the text in a variety of ways, were printed against different tinted backgrounds which were sometimes cut away to expose the creamy page color.

Forain made an etched frontispiece for Huysmans' *Marthe* in 1879, and illustrations for his *Croquis parisiens* in 1886. The latter book was in a new elongated format and had green-printed headings. Redon and Renoir made frontispieces for volumes of poems in the eighties and nineties. Toulouse-Lautrec, whose lithographed posters were causing a stir, made his first book illustrations in 1893: eleven of the twenty-two lithographs in Montorgueil's *Le Café-concert*, an album. The next year he illustrated a large square folio devoted to the singer Yvette Guilbert. The type in this folio was set in very widely spaced lines and printed in green. The lithographs of the singer, in the same soft green, flow easily into the text and sometimes under it.

The publisher Floury engaged Lautrec in 1898 to illustrate Clemenceau's *Au pied du Sinaï* with lithographs that once again tapped his intimate knowledge of the theatrical world. The next year Floury had him illustrate Jules Renard's *Histoires naturelles*. The typography of the resulting folio is very attractive; even the title page is in well-related types. The album is in unbound folded sheets, with a section title on each first fold in large capital-and-lowercase type, accompanied by Lautrec's lithographs. Lautrec's drawings display his brilliant understanding of the natural stance and movements of animals.

French publishers, in short, were beginning to employ the talents of the avant-garde painters. The sheer style of these artists was refreshingly new, but their use of the page was even newer, and broke all the boundaries of the past. Pierre Bonnard's first illustrated book was a poorly produced little edition of Peter Nansen's *Marie*, published in 1898. The tactile pleasure of his lithographs was all but obliterated by the cramped format and the hard black reproduction by photogravure. Two years later Ambroise Vollard published Verlaine's *Parallèlement* with Bonnard's lithographs and gave the folio every luxury of realization. The poetic text was set in a beautiful Garamond italic with ample space around it. Bonnard's delicately sensuous drawings of forbidden loves among rumpled bourgeois trappings are as light and fresh as if they had been drawn in soft red crayon on the cream-colored handmade paper. Nothing could be more contemporary than this book made in 1900.

*Verlaine,
Parallèlement
pages 282 and 283*

VERLAINE, *Parallèlement*. Paris, Ambroise Vollard, 1900. Yale University Library, Graphic Arts Collection. 11½ x 9¼ in. →

A LA PRINCESSE ROUKINE.

Capellos de Angelos.
(Friandise espagnole.)

C'est une laide de Boucher
Sans poudre dans sa chevelure,
Follement blonde & d'une allure
Vénuste à tous nous débaucher.

Mais je la crois mienne entre tous,
Cette crinière tant baisée,
Cette cascatelle embrasée
Qui m'allume par tous les bouts.

23

The Prologue of the Wisdom of Jesus the son of Sirach
by the Translator [Grandson of the original Author].

WHEREAS many and great things have been
delivered unto us by the law & the prophets,
and by the others that have followed in their
steps, for the which things Israel ought to be commended
for learning and wisdom; and since not only the readers must needs become skilful themselves, but also they
that love learning must be able to profit them which are
without, both by speaking & writing; my grandfather
Jesus, having much given himself to the reading of the
law, and the prophets, and the other books of our fathers, and having gotten therein good judgement, was
drawn on also himself to write something pertaining to
instruction and wisdom; to the intent that those which
are desirous to learn, and are addicted to these things,
might make progress much more by living according to
the law. Wherefore let me intreat you to read it with
favour and attention, and to pardon us, if in any parts
of what we have laboured to interpret, we may seem to
fail in some of the phrases. For the same things uttered
in Hebrew, & translated into another tongue, have not
the same force in them: and not only these things, but
the law itself, and the prophecies, and the rest of the
books, have no small difference, when they are spoken
in their original language. For having come into Egypt
in the eight & thirtieth year of Euergetes the king, and

5

THE
TWENTIETH
CENTURY

The strongest new influences on the design of books in the early part of the twentieth century were the English private presses and the painter-illustrators. The revolution in painting which began in the late nineteenth century changed the illustration and layout of books. At the same time, the revival of fifteenth-century styles and standards begun by Morris animated the English private presses and, through them, fine printing in Germany and America.

The work of the English private presses was slow to have an effect on commercial printing in England. In Germany, on the other hand, it evoked a response in both commercial and private presses. Morris's heavy ornament and the sinuous line of Art Nouveau appeared in German books through the early years of the century. The pure typography of the Doves and Ashendene books was also taken up, and the Englishmen who had designed them were brought over to design German books. The Insel-Verlag began to print a series of German classics in 1905 designed by Emery Walker of the Doves Press. Their title pages were by England's leading calligrapher, Edward Johnston, and the English designer Eric Gill.

Ecclesiasticus
page 284

The Bremer Press, a private press founded at Munich in 1911, produced books in a strong, simple typography. Like its British counterparts, the press had special types cut and relied on calligraphic details for decoration.

The Cranach Press founded at Weimar in 1913 by the Graf von Kessler, printed fine books which drew on the talents of both England and France. Kessler commissioned the French sculptor Maillol to illustrate Virgil's *Eclogues* with woodcuts which Maillol began in 1912. The war delayed production of the book, but it was brought out in 1925-26. The types in which the book was set were designed by Johnston and Edward Prince, the initials by Eric Gill. Maillol, in the true Morris spirit, made the paper on which the book was printed.

In 1929 the press printed a handsome edition of Shakespeare's *Hamlet* in types designed by Johnston after those of Fust and Schoeffer, set in a block and bordered by commentary in the way common in the fifteenth century. Edward Gordon Craig, the English illustrator, made the woodcut illustrations.

The German type foundries participated strongly in the revival of interest in fine book production. They cut new types and set up their own small presses to produce exemplary books.

Calligraphy, made popular by English example, became once again the basis of type design, as it had been in the early years of printing. E.R. Weiss designed some of the most important new types, beginning with a Fraktur cut by Bauer in 1913. He also designed entire books, some in a rather light fifteenth-century style, others dense and black, with close-packed gothic types. Rudolph Koch made important contributions to the new German books in the twenties and thirties. He favored a heavy Germanic typography, and used his own heavy woodcut initials and illustrations with it.

Das Evangelium des Markus page 287

In their own characteristic ways many German illustrators worked in the archaic woodcut style that continues to be one of Germany's most successful contributions. Fritz Kredel, Richard Seewald, Willi Hawerth, and the sculptor Ernst Barlach are among them. At the same time artists such as George Grosz were making light pen-and-ink sketches for books. The Austrian expressionist painter Kokoschka had an important influence on German illustrated books, beginning with the children's book *Die träumenden Knaben* that he wrote and illustrated in Vienna in 1908, a startling mixture of Art Nouveau and folk art. From 1917 on Kokoschka made lithographs for a number of German books.

In America the English revival was the central influence for the first quarter century and more. The men who designed books were for the most part also typographers. Frederick Goudy, who, inspired by Morris, founded the Village Press in Chicago in 1903, designed over a hundred typefaces, often producing a new one especially for a book he was designing. Bruce Rogers, in charge of limited editions and general typography at the Riverside Press in Boston in the early part of his career, and later advisor to the presses of Cambridge, Oxford, and Harvard, designed the Montaigne and Centaur types, based on Jensen's roman. Both Rogers and Daniel Updike at his Merrymount Press worked in an allusive style, using types and ornaments to suggest the era or content of the books they designed. Updike, at first under the spell of Morris's heavy books, gradually turned to the restrained taste of the English eighteenth century. Rogers ranged freely and tastefully among all periods, choosing and adapting what he

De Guérin, The Centaur page 289

liked for a given work. He was able to produce first-rate fifteenth-century Italian pages, complete with woodcuts; frivolous eighteenth-century French ones with feminine borders; or dignified British pages reminiscent of Bulmer and Bensley. When the Oxford Press undertook to print a splendid Bible in 1935, Rogers was chosen to design it in his Centaur type. Calm, dignified, monumental, the Oxford Lectern Bible is considered Rogers' greatest work.

While the best designers and publishers in England, America, and Germany were preoccupied with typography and the overall quality of the book, France concentrated on illustration. The illustrated book had a particularly high status in France; it was considered a worthy vehicle

Das Evangelium des Markus. Offenbach-am-Main, 1923. Typography and design by Rudolf Koch. From Schauer, *Deutsche Buchkunst 1890 bis 1960.* 11¼ x 7½ in.

die ganze Welt gewönne und nähme an seiner Seele Schaden? Oder was kann der Mensch geben, damit er seine Seele löse? Wer sich aber mein und meiner Worte schämet unter diesem ehebrecherischen und sündigen Geschlecht, des wird sich auch des Menschen Sohn schämen, wenn er kommen wird in der Herrlichkeit seines Vaters mit den heiligen Engeln.

DAS IX. KAPITEL:

Und er sprach zu ihnen: Wahrlich, ich sage euch: Es stehen etliche hie, die werden den Tod nicht schmecken, bis daß sie sehen das Reich Gottes mit Kraft kommen. ¶ Und nach sechs Tagen nahm Jesus zu sich Petrus, Jakobus und Johannes, und führte sie auf einen hohen Berg besonders allein und verklärte sich vor ihnen. Und seine Kleider wurden helle und sehr weiß wie der Schnee, daß sie kein Färber auf Er-

for the finest artists. There was a public willing to pay high prices for the *livre de luxe* illustrated with direct prints by an esteemed artist. Ambroise Vollard, the art dealer who spent his accumulated fortune producing fine illustrated books, slowly led their taste to the appreciation of his extraordinary editions, illustrated by such painters as Bonnard, Derain, Chagall, Dégas, Dufy, Rouault, and Picasso. Vollard was a perfectionist; he spared nothing in the full realization of the artist's intentions. In his determination to be the greatest publisher of illustrated books the world had ever known, he exacted the most scrupulous care in the typography and production of his books and was loath to consider them complete or perfect enough for publication. As a result, a great many of his *livres de peintre* were in an unfinished state at his death in 1939. Some have been published since under other auspices.

Vollard's first great publications—Verlaine's *Parallèlement* and the *Daphnis et Chloé* of Longus, both illustrated by Bonnard—remain unsurpassable, but it required some time for even the cultivated taste of the bibliophiles to catch up with them. The edition of 250 copies of the *Daphnis et Chloé* was not bought up for twenty years. Nevertheless, Vollard continued to commission and prepare books illustrated by avant-garde painters with an art dealer's instinct for what must come to be recognized as great.

Some of Vollard's most magnificent books were those illustrated by Rouault, whose early training in stained-glass techniques is strongly reflected in his powerful prints. Rouault worked on the illustrations for *Les réincarnations du Père Ubu* for fifteen years before the volume came out in 1933, photographing his original gouache sketches on the printing plates and then enriching them with drypoint, aquatint, and etching. His own text accompanied the intense color etchings for *Le Cirque de l'étoile filante*, peopled with clowns and acrobats. Rouault's broad manner of working called for a large page; his books for Vollard were monumental. The last one, the *Miserere*, which was to have had a text by Suarès, was finally brought out as a volume of prints accompanied by captions. The artistic magnitude of the prints is almost matched by the size of the gigantic volume.

In 1931 Vollard commissioned Picasso to illustrate Balzac's tragicomedy *Le chef d'oeuvre inconnu*, in which a painter seeks for years to create the ideal expression of female beauty and ends up with an inscrutable abstraction. Picasso combined cubist woodcuts with romantic-classic linear etchings without the slightest incongruity. But abstract art, for some reason, never became an important direction in book illustration. Picasso himself favored a classic, romantic, or expressionistic approach. The illustrations commissioned by Vollard for the *Histoire naturelle* of Buffon (which Picasso did not finish until after the publisher's death) are in a rough expressionistic technique that achieves the essence of animality.

Gogol's *Les Ames mortes* and La Fontaine's *Fables* with Chagall's mysterious Hebraic illustrations were a part of the treasure-store of books begun by Vollard but not published during

MAURICE DE GUÉRIN, *The Centaur*. Montague, Mass., Montague Press, 1915. Typography and design by Bruce Rogers. Yale Beinecke Rare Book Library. 12 x 8 in.

❡ THE CENTAUR. WRITTEN BY MAURICE DE GUÉRIN AND NOW TRANSLATED FROM THE FRENCH BY GEORGE B. IVES.

I Was born in a cavern of these mountains. Like the river in yonder valley, whose first drops flow from some cliff that weeps in a deep grotto, the first moments of my life sped amidst the shadows of a secluded re‑ treat, nor vexed its silence. As our mothers draw near their term, they retire to the cav‑ erns, and in the innermost recesses of the wildest of them all, where the darkness is most dense, they bring forth, uncomplaining, offspring as silent as themselves. Their strength‑giving milk enables us to endure with‑ out weakness or dubious struggles the first difficulties of life; yet we leave our caverns later than you your cradles. The reason is that there is a tradition amongst us that the early days of life must be secluded and guarded, as days engrossed by the gods.

❡ My growth ran almost its entire course in the darkness where I was born. The innermost depths of my home were so far within the bowels of the mountain, that I should not have known in which direction the opening lay, had it not been that the winds at times blew in and caused a sudden coolness and confusion. Some‑ times, too, my mother returned, bringing with her the perfume of the valleys, or dripping wet from the streams to which she resorted. Now, these her home‑comings, although they told me naught of the valleys or the streams, yet, being attended by emanations there‑ from, disturbed my thoughts, and I wandered about, all agitated, amidst my darkness. 'What,' I would say to myself, 'are these places to which my mother goes and what power reigns there which sum‑ mons her so frequently? To what influences is one there exposed,

fut bien aise de la voir, et l'ayant baisée, la
remit chantant toujours dans son sein.

Une autre fois ils entendirent du bois prochain un ramier, au roucoulement duquel
Chloé ayant pris plaisir, demanda à Daphnis
que c'étoit qu'il disoit, et Daphnis lui
fit le conte qu'on en fait communément.
« Ma mie, dit-il, au temps passé y avoit
« une fille belle et jolie, en fleur d'âge

50

LONGUS, *Daphnis et Chloé*. Paris, Les Frères Gonin, 1937. Woodcuts by Maillol. Museum of Modern Art, New York

his lifetime. The etchings for Hesiod's *Theogony* begun by Braque for Vollard were not published until 1955. Intransigent, demanding to a fault, Vollard established a standard for *éditions de luxe* that came close to his desires.

At the beginning of the century the *Imprimerie Nationale* began to print many of the fine books of private and commercial publishers. Vollard's *Parallèlement* was set in the beautiful Garamond italics of the *Imprimerie* and was to have borne its imprint, but the nature of the erotic text caused the reconsideration and withdrawal of the official imprint. The *Imprimerie* has continued to produce some of France's finest books. In 1951 it printed Goethe's *Promethée* in the translation of André Gide, set in the old *romain du roi* of 1700 and illustrated with the unmistakably twentieth-century color lithographs of Henry Moore.

Vollard had a rival in excellence in the firm of Albert Skira of Lausanne, which produced *livres de peintre* in the best French tradition. Skira commissioned Picasso's first important book, the *Métamorphoses* of Ovid, published in 1931. Picasso made fluent line etchings for this edition, chaste in its typography and serenely classic in effect. Léon Pichon, a leading French publisher, printed the book for the Swiss firm.

In 1932 Skira published the *Poésies* of Mallarmé, set in Garamond italics and decorated with Matisse's engravings, which fill out the pages with their linear volumes. Matisse was an artist who took the illustrated book as seriously as the framed print or painting and gave much thought to the problems of balancing areas of type and of illustration. In one instance, the *Pasiphaë* of Montherlant, he set himself the task of balancing the type pages against totally black linoleum prints, incised with thin white line. *Mallarmé, Poésies pages 292 and 293*

Three of the classical works which Maillol illustrated with woodcuts were published by the Gonin brothers of Paris and Lausanne: *L'Art d'aimer* of Ovid in 1935; two years later, Longus' *Daphnis et Chloé*; and in 1950, Virgil's *Géorgiques*. The *Daphnis et Chloé*, unlike most *livres de luxe*, was in a relatively small format. Maillol cut the blocks in a pure, classic line, less consciously archaic than the cutting of the *Eclogues* printed by the Cranach Press. The woodcuts and type blend with a lucid harmony seldom seen outside the fifteenth century. *Longus, Daphnis et Chloé page 290*

Some of the French books we have considered were consciously new in their approach; others harked back to the past. Not a few books seem to go in both directions at once. The strong, primitive woodcuts made by Dérain for Guillaume Apollinaire's *L'Enchanteur pourrissant* in 1909 and by Raoul Dufy for his *Le Bestiaire* in 1911 have a blackness and a crude vigor reminiscent of some of the earliest German printed books. They are matched very knowingly with rather black and none-too-even types. Both Dérain and Dufy showed later that they were masters of a fine linear technique at the opposite pole. Dufy, in Montfort's *La belle Enfant* (1930), surrounds the type-page with sophisticated etchings in the lightest line. His watercolors for Dorgelès *Vacances forcées*, printed in 1956, have been reproduced *Apollinaire, Le Bestiaire page 295*

MALLARMÉ, *Poésies*. Lausanne, Albert Skira, 1932. Etchings by Matisse. Museum of Modern Art, New York. 13 x 9¾ in. →

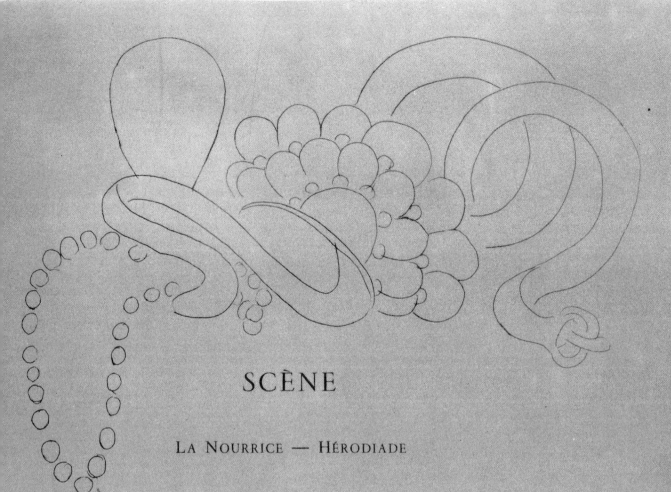

SCÈNE

LA NOURRICE — HÉRODIADE

N.

Tu vis! ou vois-je ici l'ombre d'une princesse?
A mes lèvres tes doigts & leurs bagues & cesse
De marcher dans un âge ignoré..

H.

Reculez.
Le blond torrent de mes cheveux immaculés
Quand il baigne mon corps solitaire le glace

by wood engravings that preserve almost incredibly the effect of transparent washes dashed across the page.

Dufy and Derain both belonged around 1910 to the group of painters led by Matisse who called themselves "Fauves"—Wild Beasts. They were much influenced by African sculpture and sought a forceful expression of their own. The Cubists and the Fauves in France were contemporary with the Futurists in Italy. The Futurists had organized themselves under the poet Marinetti, who proved to be a master of the manifesto. His first, issued in 1909, constituted a frontal attack on bourgeois culture. The Futurists scorned intellect and logic as part of the despised past; they exalted movement and speed as belonging to the world of the future. They expressed these attitudes in their publications by a conscious violation of all the accepted laws of typography. Types of all kinds and sizes were used together; they proceeded (within the limits of communicating at all) in any direction but the expected ones. Marinetti went even further: he invented *Tipografia in libertà* and *Parole in libertà*, which "freed" words and letters from logical use in sentences and used them as independent expressive elements.

Marinetti,
Les mots en liberté
futuristes
page 296

In a manifesto of 1911 the Futurists declared, "The language of the old art is dead. Traditions are dead. We have a new and exciting idiom, a set of personal symbols compounded of anything and everything. We will express the dynamic energy of modern life....We will jerk your sensibilities into the most acute responses." The movement that issued this clarion call soon died out, but its spirit seems to be essentially the one that continues to animate the art of our time.

The Dadaist movement that originated in Zurich in 1916 used the same shock tactics as Futurism, but toward a different end. Where Futurism wanted to overthrow the traditional order for a world dominated by the machine, Dada was a protest against the world of machines and the folly of war. Dadaist typography was just as assiduous as the Futurists' in its flouting of conventions. When the first book of Tristan Tzara, the literary leader of Dada, was published in 1916—*La première aventure céleste de Mr Antipyrine*—it was set as a sort of blank verse with no capital letters or punctuation and illustrated with nonobjective woodcuts by the painter Marcel Janco.

An unpunctuated lowercase text was new to books. Nonobjective illustrations had already appeared in Germany in 1913 in a book of poems, *Klänge*, written and illustrated by the Russian painter Kandinsky. The artistic revolt had not been confined to Western Europe. In Russia it led to various forms of nonfigurative art. Kandinsky's early abstractions were relatively lyric; the severe abstract art of the Russian Constructivists also came to Germany with the Russian Exhibition in Berlin in 1922. The Constructivist El Lissitsky had a strong influence on the recently formed Bauhaus.

GUILLAUME APOLLONAIRE, *Le Bestiaire*. Paris, 1911. Woodcuts by Dufy. Yale University Library, Graphic Arts Collection. 14 x 10¼ in.

LA CARPE.

Dans vos viviers, dans vos étangs,
Carpes, que vous vivez longtemps !
Est-ce que la mort vous oublie,
Poissons de la mélancolie.

853 305
128 155
1 165 156
1 022 173
468 466
308 780
186 265
-59 066
565 898
147 887
1 007 661
1 881 484
184 620
180 188
650 995
84 995

FRANCE

VIVE LA FRAANCE

MORT AUX BOCHES

LÉGER LOURD

Mon Amiiiii

vitesssssss sxxxxx xssssssss

BEL + LE

virer virer vir
vir
spirales 5 spirales
spirale pneumatique de volant
coup
vir
8
629 =

MaAA
AAapetite

VICTOIRE

ta-tatata tatata ta
tap tap tap
ta ta ta ta ta ta

fooooooooooc

GUERRE

V forrrrrrrrrrr
traac craac craa
craac craa
croc
TOUMB TOUM

496 578
1 688 415
4 031 054
673 053
1 543 437
280 514
198 034
981 995
2 679 823
1 463 513
758 733
1 341 933

PRUSSIENS

Verbalisation
dynamique
de
la route

mocastrinar fralingaren donl
donl donl × × + × vronkap
vronkap × × × × × angolò
angoll angolà angolin vronkap
+ diraor diranku falasò fala-
sòhh falasò picpic viaAAAR
viamelokranu bimbim
nu ranu = = = = + =
rarumà viar viar viar

The Bauhaus was created in 1919 when the Weimar Arts and Crafts School and the Academy of Art were merged under the direction of Walter Gropius in recognition of the unity of all design. The school was from the first a clearinghouse for all the "isms," from which it distilled its own synthesis. The Bauhaus tenet of the indivisibility of the arts can be traced back to the English Arts and Crafts movement. From Futurism came an acceptance of the machine as basic to modern production. Dadaist and Futurist destruction of accepted modes played a part, countered by the functional Constructivist approach. The Dutch movement known as De Stijl, whose aim was to change life through art and architecture, was an important influence in the first years of the school. When the Hungarian designer Moholy-Nagy was appointed to the Bauhaus in 1922, Russian Constructivism definitely took the upper hand.

The basic idea which the Bauhaus applied to all design was: "Form follows function." In typography the prototypes were the poster and the publicity announcement. Moholy-Nagy stated in the first book which he designed for the Bauhaus, "The new typography must impart information clearly and in the most forcible form." Order, simplification and clarity were the typographic ideals. In practical terms, sans-serif and square serif types were favored, arranged asymmetrically on the page. The types ran not only horizontally but also at right angles and sometimes diagonally. In 1925 capital letters were dropped.

Lissitsky and Arp,
Die Kunstismen
page 298

The decorative elements of Bauhaus typography were simple geometric forms—squares, circles, triangles—basic signs such as arrows, enlarged letters or numerals, and primary colors. A particular Bauhaus characteristic was the use of heavy black bars for interest or emphasis. White space was also consciously manipulated for these purposes. The poster prototype suggested photography as a natural counterpart of the new typography, and Bauhaus books began to incorporate the experimental photographs made at the school into their designs.

The new typography spread throughout the Germanic cultures of Europe—those of Switzerland, Austria, the Netherlands and Scandinavia—and into Italy, disseminated partly through the writings of Jan Tschichold. England and America received it later, around the time of the second World War. Advertising design was the most affected by it; in publishing, technical books took on the organization and the typography of the new style.

In Germany, both the fifteenth-century influence and the new typography flourish side by side. The designer and typographer Hermann Zapf, who has worked for the leading type-founders and publishers, is fundamentally oriented in the early style. Besides calligraphic types like Palatino, he has designed the sans-serif Optima with something of calligraphic sensitivity. In his books Zapf shows an extraordinary sense for the balancing of type and space. He often uses a calligraphic letter, a handwritten word, or a chaste ornament (perhaps blind-embossed) to set off his otherwise perfectly simple, harmonious title pages.

Zapf,
Typographische
Variationen
page 299

MARINETTI, *Les mots en liberté futuristes*. Milan, 1919. Typography and design by Marinetti. Harvard Houghton Library. Foldout page 10¼ x 9¼ in.

EL LISSITSKY AND HANS ARP, *Die Kunstismen*. Erlenbach-Zurich, 1925. Typography and design by El Lissitsky. Yale University School of Fine Arts →

HERMANN ZAPF, *Typographische Variationen*. Frankfurt am Main, 1963. Yale University Library, Graphic Arts Collection. 12 x 8¼ in. →

Die Gegenwart ist die Zeit der Analysen, das Resultat aller Systeme, die jemals entstanden sind. Zu unserer Demarkationsgrenze haben die Jahrhunderte die Zeichen gebracht, in ihnen werden wir Unvollkommenheiten erkennen, die zur Getrenntheit und Gegensätzlichkeit führten. Vielleicht werden wir davon nur das Gegensätzliche nehmen, um das System der Einheit aufzubauen. MALEWITSCH.

Le temps actuel est l'époque des analyses, le résultat de tous les systèmes qui aient jamais été établis. Ce sont des siècles qui ont apporté les signes de notre ligne de démarcation, nous y reconnaîtrons les imperfections qui menaient à la division et à la contradiction. Peut-être que nous n'en prendrons que les propos contradictoires pour construire notre système de l'unité. MALEWITSCH.

The actual time is the epoca of analyses, the result of all systems that ever were established. Centuries brought the signs to our line of demarcation, in them we shall recognise the imperfections that led to division and contradiction. Perhaps we hereof only shall take the contradictory to construct the system of unity. MALEWITSCH.

KUBISMUS

Das, was den Kubismus von der älteren Malerei unterscheidet, ist dieses: er ist nicht eine Kunst der Nachahmung, sondern eine Konzeption, welche strebt sich zur Schöpfung herauszuheben. APOLLINAIRE.

Statt der impressionistischen Raumillusion, die sich auf Luftperspektive und Farbennaturalismus gründet, gibt der Kubismus die schlichten, abstrahierten Formen in klaren Wesens- und Maßverhältnissen zueinander. ALLARD.

FUTURISMUS

Die Futuristen haben die Ruhe und Statik demoliert und das Bewegte, Dynamische gezeigt. Sie haben die neue Raumauffassung durch die Gegenüberstellung des Inneren und Äußeren dokumentiert.
Die Geste ist für uns nicht mehr ein festgehaltener Augenblick der universalen Bewegtheit: sie ist entschieden die dynamische Sensation selbst und als solche verewigt. BOCCIONI.

EXPRESSIONISMUS

Aus Kubismus und Futurismus wurde der falsche Hase, das metaphysische deutsche Beefsteak, der Expressionismus gehackt.

CUBISME

Ce qui distingue le cubisme de la peinture précédente c'est qu'il n'est pas un art de l'imitation, mais une conception qui tend a s'élever en création. APOLLINAIRE.

Au lieu de l'illusion impressioniste de l'espace basée sur la perspective de l'air et le naturalisme des couleurs, le cubisme donne les formes simples et abstraites en leurs relations précises de caractère et de mesures. ALLARD.

FUTURISME

Les futuristes ont démoli la quiétude et la statique et démontré le mouvement, la dynamique. Ils ont documenté la nouvelle conception de l'espace par la confrontation de l'intérieur et de l'extérieur.
Le geste pour nous ne sera plus un moment fixé du dynamisme universel: il sera décidément la sensation dynamique éternisée comme telle. BOCCIONI.

EXPRESSIONISME

C'est du cubisme et du futurisme que fût fabriqué le hachis, le mystique beefsteak allemand: l'expressionisme.

CUBISM

What distinguishes cubism from precedent painture is this: not to be an art of imitation but a conception that tends to rise itself as creation. APOLLINAIRE.

Instead of the impressionist illusion of space based on the perspective of air and the naturalism of colour, cubism offers the simpel and abstracted forms in their precise relations of character and measure. ALLARD.

FUTURISM

Futurists have abolished quietness and statism and have demonstrated movement, dynamism. They have documentated the new conception of space by confrontation of interior and exterior.

For us gesture will not any more be a fixed moment of universal dynamism: it will decidedly be the dynamic sensation eternalised as such. BOCCIONI.

EXPRESSIONISM

From cubism and futurism has been chopped the minced meat, the mystic german beefsteak: expressionism.

Typographische Variationen

Ein Buch über Ausdruck und Form der Buchstaben

78 Buchtitel und Textseiten als

in den verschiedensten Anwendungen klassischer und

Gestaltungsmöglichkeiten der

neuzeitlicher Drucktypen. Mit Einleitungen von

Typographie und Buchgraphik

G. K. Schauer, Paul Standard und Charles Peignot

entworfen von Hermann Zapf

Gotthard de Beauclair, since 1951 director of the Trajanus-Presse at the Stempel Typefoundry, like Zapf, Georg Trump, and other leading German book designers, is also a typographer. At the Trajanus-Presse he produces small editions of finely printed books which are rather light and open in effect.

Saint-Soline, Antigone, oder Roman auf Kreta page 301

The tradition of the dark woodcut combined knowingly with close-set type—an effect which has its origins in incunabula—is continued today by illustrators such as Werner Klemke, Eugen Sporer, Otto Rohse, and Gerhard Marcks. In Switzerland Imre Reiner has evolved a highly personal modern style in both his lettering and his wood-engraved illustrations.

In England, the private presses had begun to wane after about 1925. Only one, the Golden Cockerel Press, continued to produce fine books, many of which were the work of Eric Gill in his roles of typographer, designer, and illustrator. They owe much to their superb paper and presswork. Gill had a sleek and decorative medieval approach to design. His woodcuts are often contained in short side borders or worked into the beginnings of sections, as in *The Canterbury Tales* of 1931. In *The Four Gospels*, printed the same year, he made beginning words the decorative element, twining the woodcut letters with human forms in a way that was new but strongly reminiscent of manuscript illumination. There is a great unity to these pages, set in Gill's own Cockerel type.

The Nonesuch Press, founded in 1923 by Francis Meynell, has filled some of the functions of the private press under commercial auspices. Its aim has been to produce books with "significance of subject, beauty of format, and moderation of price." The typesetting, printing, and binding of these books was mostly done by machine, but they were produced with great care, and their design and illustration has been of high quality. A wide variety of media and styles have been used in their illustration, from Stephen Gooden's line engravings of seventeenth-century inspiration to the stencil-colored illustrations of poster artist McKnight Kauffer. Nonesuch books did something the private presses had not done: they put fine books within the scope of the general public.

British illustration of this century is not in a class with the best French work, but some of it, such as the satirical drawings of Edward Bawden, is very much suited to books. British style is at its best in the work of Rex Whistler, who, before his death in World War II, worked in an imaginative revival of Baroque style, using many architectural details.

The so-called "paperback revolution" of our time originated in 1932 with Albatross Books, a series of contemporary English books printed in Hamburg, Paris, and Milan in inexpensive but pleasant format. The idea was not precisely new. Paper-covered sixpenny reprints were common in Victorian England. The little booklets of sacred plays and romances sold in the streets of late fifteenth- and sixteenth-century Florence were in a real sense paperbacks, pictorial cover and all.

CLAIRE SAINT-SOLINE, *Antigone, oder Roman auf Kreta*. Frankfurt, 1958. Woodcuts by Otto Rohse. From Schauer, *Deutsche Buchkunst 1890 bis 1960*

Claire Sainte-Soline

Antigone *oder Roman auf Kreta*

Büchergilde Gutenberg, Frankfurt

When Penguin Books started in England in 1935 they filled a need for inexpensive, handy editions generated by the economic depression and soon intensified by the war. The Penguin series, which has expanded to include many fields in publishing, has consciously tried for good typography and even good illustration within the limits of its methods of production. In 1947 Jan Tschichold set up standards of typography and layout which are flexibly applied to all the books. Penguin has put it with typical British conciseness: "What is cheap need not be nasty." The innumerable paperback series that have sprung up on both sides of the Atlantic have not always borne this out.

In America after World War I the general run of books began to improve. Certain of the large presses such as William E. Rudge of Mount Vernon, N. Y., and the Lakeside Press in Chicago became concerned with the design and production of good books. William E. Rudge employed designers of the caliber of Bruce Rogers and Frederic Warde; the Lakeside Press was guided by the sound standards of William Kittredge.

A number of smaller printers were from the start dedicated to fine book production. Among them were the Grabhorn brothers in San Francisco, and Elmer Adler's Pynson Printers and Joseph Blumenthal's Spiral Press in New York. The Spiral Press, which began work in 1926, continues to turn out both good, conservative commercial work and fine limited editions such

Ecclesiastes,
pages 304 and 305

as the *Ecclesiastes* published in 1965, with Ben Shahn's illustrations and letters, and Blumenthal's own Emerson type.

In 1929 the Limited Editions Club, founded by George Macy, began to publish books of more than ordinary interest for its fifteen hundred subscribers at the rate of one a month. They were designed by the leading typographers and artists of both continents and produced in a manner which if not *de luxe* was the next thing to it. A peculiarly democratic feature was that the book titles were selected by the readers by ballot.

The Limited Editions Club acquainted Americans with the work of outstanding European designers and printers. Among them was Giovanni Mardersteig whose Officina Bodoni at Verona has the official right to use Bodoni's matrices; with the Bodoni types and others he prints fine editions in a pure and controlled typography. Jan van Krimpen of the long-established Enschedé Press in Haarlem designed one of the Limited Editions books in his handsome Romanée type. French and Russian illustrators, Czech typographers, Swedish printers, all contributed to the series which ran for thirty years.

Other limited edition series and illustrated edition series turned out books which made a conscious effort to please. From soberer motives, more akin to those of the early scholar-printers, the university presses also became important contributors of well-designed books. The books of the Yale Press, in particular, continue to be remarkable, many of them in the clean, sensitive typography of Alvin Eisenman. Museum publications are another source of well-designed books. Peter Oldenburg and Joseph Blumenthal maintain a conservative good taste in their work for New York museums, and Carl Zahn has done some imaginative publications for the Boston Museum of Fine Arts.

Individual book designers, working for a publisher or free lance, have done much to further the quality of American books. W. A. Dwiggins, besides designing such important book types as Electra and Caledonia, early set a style for Knopf books that made them unmistakable. Knopf has continued to maintain high standards with such designers as George Salter and Warren Chappell. Marshall Lee has designed books which are often unusually sensitive for a number of publishers.

Illustration is of relatively small importance in contemporary American publishing, except in books for children. Some painters have illustrated and designed children's books that are fresh and inventive: Leo Lionni's *Little Blue and Little Yellow* (1950) and *Inch by Inch* (1960) are good examples of the American juvenile version of the *livre de peintre*. Joseph Low has made amusing illustrations that fit well with type. Alexander Calder's continuous-line illustrations of some years back for Aesop's *Fables* (probably not intended for children), and Thurber's drawings for *Fables for Our Time* and many other books (surely not intended for children) are in their own way unsurpassable.

Among the private presses that have cropped up here and there is the Gehenna Press, founded in 1942 by the artist Leonard Baskin to print books with his own wood engravings and linoleum cuts or those of other artists. Baskin has a personal touch even in his typography. The Uruguayan artist Antonio Frasconi also likes to design and print his own books, such as *Birds from my Homeland* (1958), though he works sometimes for commercial publishers.

This necessarily incomplete listing of persons, presses, and publishers at least indicates from what sources the ideas, the skills, and the standards come for the best books in our time. The American Institute of Graphic Arts, an organization of all those connected with book publishing, has since 1923 held an annual exhibition of the "Fifty Books of the Year," meant to act as a yardstick and stimulus. These exhibitions have been taken up by a number of European countries.

The homogenizing forces of our time have broken many barriers of national style, and sometimes it is difficult to tell at a glance the origin of a book. But local differences in production or taste still exist, and where they are manifest they bring the pleasure of variety. Czechoslovak books, for example, often have a unique peasant quality in their decorations and a corresponding strength in their typography. British books, at their best, have a typically British sound and forthright quality, which may stem largely from their use of well-cut, snug-

דברי קהלת בן־דוד מלך
בירושלם : הבל הבלים
אמר קהלת הבל הבלים

Ben Shahn

ECCLESIASTES
OR, THE PREACHER

IN THE KING JAMES TRANSLATION OF THE BIBLE

WITH DRAWINGS BY BEN SHAHN, ENGRAVED
IN WOOD BY STEFAN MARTIN

CALLIGRAPHY BY DAVID SOSHENSKY

PRINTED AND PUBLISHED AT THE SPIRAL PRESS
NEW YORK 1965

setting monotype faces. French books, even when they are not illustrated by great painters and printed by hand, have a characteristic sensitivity; there is often a soft charm even to a cheap little French edition. A good German book has its characteristic typography and a sense of the press that reminds one that Germany was, after all, the place where printing originated. American books all too often bespeak technical facility and mass production, along with the attempt to look like "a lot for the money." We are the country in which the Linotype machine took over fastest, and now the photo typesetter is seeking to replace it. Offset lithography is practiced in American book publishing far more than in any other country.

For the lover of fine books, nothing can replace the bite of type or plate into good paper, the play of well-cut, well-set text against illustration or decoration of deep artistic value. But an inexpensive edition can carry its own aesthetic validity through imaginative or appropriate design. These are not matters of concern only for aesthetes; if, in an era of uncertain values, we want to keep alive respect for ideas and knowledge, it is important to give books a form that encourages respect. The style and production of books, for all the centuries they have been made, still have much to offer the designer and publisher in challenge, the reader in pleasure.

BIBLIOGRAPHY

BAKER, C. H. COLLINS. *Catalogue of William Blake's Drawings and Paintings in the Huntington Library*. San Marino, Calif., 2nd. ed. 1957

BECHTEL, EDWIN DE T. *Jacques Callot*. New York: G. Braziller, 1955

BELLONI, DR. CARLO. "Italian Pioneers of Graphic Design," *New Graphic Design*, No. 3, Oct. 1959

BINYON, LAWRENCE. *The Drawings and Engravings of William Blake. London:* The Studio, 1922

BLAND, DAVID. *A History of Book Illustration*. Cleveland and New York: The World Publishing Co., 1958

BREWER, FRANCES J. (ED.). *Book Illustration*. Papers presented at the Third Rare Book Conference of the American Library Association in 1962. Berlin: Gebr. Mann Verlag, 1963

BRONSON, BERTRAND H. *Printing as an Index of Taste in Eighteenth-Century England*. New York: The New York Public Library, 1963

BUHLER, CURT F. *The Fifteenth-Century Book*. Philadelphia: The University of Pennsylvania Press, 1960

BURKHARDT, JACOB. *The Civilization of the Renaissance*. Oxford and London: Phaidon Press. New York: Oxford University Press, 1945

ČERNÝ, JAROSLAV. *Paper and Books in Ancient Egypt*. London: H. K. Lewis and Co. Ltd. for the University College, London, 1947

COUDERC, CAMILLE. *Les enlumières des manuscrits du moyen âge de la Bibliothèque nationale*. Paris: Editions de la Gazette des beaux-arts, 1927

DIRINGER, DAVID. *The Hand-Produced Book*. London: Hutchinson's Scientific and Technical Publications, 1953

——*The Illuminated Book, its History and Production*. London: Faber and Faber, 1958

ETTENBERG, EUGENE M. *Type for Books and Advertising*. New York: D. Van Nostrand Co., Inc., 1947

GUPPY, HENRY. "Human Records: A Survey of their History from the Beginning." Bulletin of the John Rylands Library, Vol. 27, pp. 182-222. Manchester, 1942-43

HAEBLER, KONRAD. *The Early Printers of Spain and Portugal*. London: Printed for the Bibliographical Society, 1897.

HERBERT, J. A. *Illuminated Manuscripts*. London: Methuen and Co., 1911

HIND, ARTHUR M. *A History of Engraving and Etching*. Boston: Houghton Mifflin and Co., 1923

——*An Introduction to a History of Woodcut*. Boston: Houghton Mifflin and Co., 1935

HOFER, PHILIP. *The Artist and the Book: 1860-1960*. Boston Museum of Fine Arts, 1961

——*Baroque Book Illustration*. Boston: Harvard University Press, 1951

HOLMES, CHARLES (ED.). *The Art of the Book*. London, Paris, New York: "The Studio" Ltd., 1914

IVINS, WILLIAM M., JR. *Artistic Aspects of Fifteenth-Century Printing*. Papers of the Bibliographical Society of America. Chicago: The University of Chicago Press, 1932

——*The Malermi Bible and the Spencer Collection*. Bulletin of the New York Public Library, Vol. 33, No. 11. New York, Nov. 1929

JOHNSON, ALFRED F. *A Catalogue of Engraved and Etched English Title-pages*. London: Oxford University Press for the Bibliographical Society, 1934

——*A Catalogue of Italian Engraved Title-pages in the Sixteenth Century*. London: Oxford University Press for the Bibliographical Society, 1936

——*The First Century of Printing at Basle*. London: Ernest Benn Ltd., 1926

——*French Sixteenth Century Printing*. London: Ernest Benn Ltd., 1928

——*The Italian Sixteenth Century*. London: Ernest Benn Ltd., 1926

KENYON, FREDRIC G. *Books and Readers in Ancient Greece and Rome*. Oxford: Clarendon Press, 1932

LANCKOROŃSKA, MARIA AND OEHLER, RICHARD. *Die Buchillustration des XVIII. Jahrhunderts in Deutschland, Oesterreich und der Schweiz*. Hamburg: Maximilian-Gesellschaft, 1932

LANCKOROŃSKA, MARIA. *Die Venezianische Buchgraphik des XVIII. Jahrhunderts*. Hamburg: Maximilian-Gesellschaft, 1950

LEHMANN-HAUPT, HELLMUT. *The Book in America*. New York: R. R. Bowker, 1939

LEJARD, ANDRE (ED.). *The Art of the French Book*. Paris: Les Editions du Chêne, 1947

LOHSE, RICHARD P. "The Influence of Modern Art on Contemporary Graphic Design," *New Graphic Design*, No. 1, Sept., 1958

MACROBERT, T. M. *Printed Books, a short introduction to fine typography*. London: Victoria and Albert Museum, 1957

MADAN, FALCONER. *Books in Manuscript*. London: K. Paul, Trench, Trübner and Co., Ltd., 1893

MCLEAN, RUARI. *Victorian Book Design*. London, Faber and Faber Ltd., 1963

MCMURTRIE, DOUGLAS C. *The Book—The Story of Printing and Bookbinding.* New York: Oxford University Press, 1937

Modern German Book Design. Offenbach am Main, Klingspor-Museum, 1959

MOREY, C. R. Introduction to *Illuminated Manuscripts,* Catalog of an exhibition at the Pierpont Morgan Library, New York, 1933-34

——Introduction to *The Greek Tradition,* Catalog of an exhibition of the Baltimore Museum of Art and the Walters Art Gallery, 1939

MORISON, STANLEY. *A Brief Survey of Printing History and Practice.* London: 1923

——*Four Centuries of Fine Printing.* London: Ernest Benn Ltd., 1914

——*German Incunabula in The British Museum.* London: 1928

——AND DAY, KENNETH. *The Typographic Book, 1450-1935.* Chicago: The University of Chicago Press and London: Ernest Benn Ltd., 1963

MUSPER, H. TH. *Die Urausgaben der holländischen Apokalypse und Biblia pauperum.* Munich: Prestel-Verlag, 1961

NEUMANN, ECKHARD. "Typography, Graphic Design and Advertising at the Bauhaus." *New Graphic Design,* No. 17, 18, Feb. 1965

OSWALD, JOHN CLYDE. *Printing in the Americas.* New York: Gregg Pub. Co., 1937

POLLARD, ALFRED W. *Early Illustrated Books.* London: K. Paul, Trench, Trübner and Co., 1893

——*Facsimiles from Early Printed Books in the British Museum.* London: 1897

——*Fine Books.* London: Methuen and Co., Ltd., 1912

——*Old Picture-books.* London: Methuen and Co., 1902

——*The Pierpont Morgan Library Catalog of Manuscripts and Early Printed Books.* London: The Chiswick Press, 1907

Printing and the Mind of Man. Catalogue of the exhibitions at the British Museum and at Earls Court. London: F. W. Bridges and Sons Ltd. and the Association of British Manufacturers of Printers' Machinery (Proprietary) Ltd., 1963

Publications of the A.I.G.A.

Quarto-millenary—The first 250 publications and the first 25 years of the Limited Editions Club. New York: The Limited Editions Club, 1959

RANSOM, WILL. *Private Presses and their Books.* New York: R. R. Bowker and Co., 1929

SABBE, MAURITS. *Plantin, the Moretus, and their Work.* Brussels: Musée Plantin-Moretus, 1926

SANDER, MAX. *Le livre a figures italien depuis 1467 jusqu'à 1530.* New York: G. E. Steckert Co., 1941

SCHAUER, GEORG KURT. *Deutsche Buchkunst 1890 bis 1960.* Hamburg: Maximilian-Gesellschaft, 1963

SCHMUTZLER, ROBERT. *Art Nouveau.* New York: Abrams, 1962

SKIRA, ALBERT. *Anthologie du Livre Illustré par les peintres et sculpteurs de l'école de Paris.* Geneva: A. Skira, 1946

SOTHEBY, SAMUEL L. *Principia Typographica: The block-books issued in Holland, Flanders and Germany during the 15th. century.* London: W. McDowall, 1858

STEINBERG, SAUL H. *Five Hundred Years of Printing.* London: Criterion Books, 1959

THOMAS, HENRY. *Spanish Sixteenth-Century Printing.* London: Ernest Benn Ltd., 1926

THOMPSON, E. MAUNDE. *Introduction to Greek and Latin Paleography.* Oxford: The Clarendon Press, 1932

THOMPSON, LAWRENCE S. *Printing in Colonial Spanish America.* London and Hamden, Conn.: The Shoe String Press, Inc., 1962

UPDIKE, DANIEL BERKELEY. *Printing Types, their History, Forms and Use.* Cambridge, Mass.: Harvard University Press, second edition, 1937

WEITENKAMPF, FRANK. *The Fifteenth Century. The Cradle of Modern Book-illustration.* Catalog of an exhibition at the New York Public Library, 1938

WEITZMANN, KURT. *Illustrations in Roll and Codex.* Princeton: Princeton University Press. 1947

WHEELER, MONROE. *Modern Painters and Sculptors as Illustrators.* New York: The Museum of Modern Art, 1936

WINGLER, HANS M. *Das Bauhaus — Weimar, Dessau, Berlin.* Bransche: Rasch, 1962

WINTERICH, JOHN T. *Early American Books and Printing.* Boston: Houghton Mifflin and Co., 1935

WROTH, LAWRENCE C. *A History of the Printed Book. No. 3 of The Dolphin: A Journal of the Making of Books.* New York: The Limited Editions Club, 1938

INDEX

This book was designed by Norma Levarie in Janson type,
which was brought out by the Leipzig punchcutter and typefounder
Anton Janson some time between 1660 and 1687.